To Kaley from
Mary
Christmas 1990

KB & MARY Humphrey
952 FLAME AZALEA LA
Mars Hill, NC 28754
689-3637

The Sierra Club Totebooks®

A Sierra Club Totebook®

Hiker's Guide to the Smokies

by Dick Murlless
and Constance Stallings

Sierra Club Books • San Francisco

The Sierra Club, founded in 1892 by John Muir, has devoted itself to the study and protection of the nation's scenic and ecological resources – mountains, wetlands, woodlands, wild shores and rivers. All club publications are part of the nonprofit effort the club carries on as a public trust. There are more than 50 chapters coast to coast, in Canada, Hawaii, and Alaska. Participation is invited in the club's program to enjoy and preserve wilderness everywhere. Address: 730 Polk Street, San Francisco, CA 94109.

17 18 19 20

Preface

The southern Appalachian region has become too popular for its own well being. It is fast becoming a playground for the people of the eastern United States. It also represents a major source of high-quality hardwood lumber. And as the regional need for water increases, many eastern rivers with sources in the Southern Appalachians will inevitably be tapped. Thus, now and in the future, the resources of the southern mountains will be heavily used by man.

Though most of this region is being managed for timber, farming and tourism, there is one great and wild enclave: the Great Smoky Mountains National Park, set aside to preserve our natural heritage of virgin forests and fresh, unpolluted water, for all the people. What a wise move this was, for today its boundaries encompass the last large remaining mountain wilderness in the eastern United States. It is there that millions of people go to find isolation and beauty.

Unfortunately, so many people are traveling to the park nowadays that they are overloading the resources of the land and its guardian, the National Park Service. Likewise unfortunately, many of them go there to experience wilderness remotely: through a car window. All too often unprepared to cope with the problems of camping, or ignorant of the simple requirements of the out-of-doors, they overflow the developed campgrounds and sometimes neglect to follow park regulations. The understaffed Park Service personnel consequently spend most of their time and energy coping with traffic jams, people problems, people-caused bear-problems, garbage and sewage. Well-trained rangers are going to waste, tied up collecting fees at the campgrounds.

With so much emphasis on the millions straining the park at the developed areas, the back country—the source of the true wilderness experience—has been severely neglected. During the last few years trail patrol has been almost nonexistent. As just one example of the bad situation, most park rangers (and officials) cannot find the time to visit back-country campsites.

This is not an indictment of the National Park Service or its dedicated local personnel. They realize the severity of their problems and are making a serious attempt to find some way to manage the back country better. In 1972, during the writing of this guidebook, the Park Service began a new policy of rationing back country use in the more popular areas of the park. The number of back-country campsites almost doubled this past summer. The Park Service also has intentions of opening several major new trails. These and other changes presented problems to the writers and editors of this guide. While we have done our best to present accurate, current information, the user of this guide should be aware of the possibility of further changes in Park Service policies. You are invited to submit any inaccuracies or oversights you may discover in the trail descriptions, plus appropriate corrections, to either Sierra Club Books, 730 Polk Street, San Francisco, CA 94109, or to Dick Murlless, Wilderness Southeast, Inc., Rt. 3, Box 619, Savannah, GA 31406.

We hope, as do all wilderness enthusiasts, that the Park Service is able to develop a management program which will really preserve the high quality of a wilderness experience. But they need more staff and more money. We should all try to help them by letting them know about relevant wilderness failures and successes we may hear about elsewhere, and by pushing for additional federal funding earmarked specifically for improved wilderness management.

Meanwhile, this guidebook has been written to help all the visitors who wish to experience wilderness under their own locomotion. Some are veteran hikers who no longer enjoy the increasingly crowded Appalachian Trail. (It, too, suffers from its own popularity.) This book will guide them along the park's other 580 miles of trails. Other readers may be novice hikers who will use this book to discover what the park and wilderness are really all about.

Let us hope that happy, nonlittering, interested and responsible hikers are the wave of the future.

— *The editors*
May, 1973

About the Editors

Dick Murlless, author-editor of *Hiker's Guide to the Smokies*, walked countless miles of trail, interviewed a score of other hikers, pored over maps and delved into local archives before sitting down at his typewriter to provide the detailed introductory sections and trail descriptions contained in this volume. A native of New Jersey, Mr. Murlless developed a special affinity for mountains while attending Duke University, where he was president of the Mountain Club. Later, he moved to Georgia and was active in organizing outings for the Chattahoochee Chapter of the Sierra Club. He is currently pursuing a Ph.D. degree in Zoology at the University of Georgia, and from a base at the Science Museum of Savannah conducts an ecology workshop for high school students of the Chatham County School System.

Constance L. Stallings, associate editor of this guidebook, furnished historical information, researched geographical details, cross-checked statistics, and edited Mr. Murlless's text. Previously she was assistant editor of Sierra Club Books where she was responsible for the development of the Totebook series. Raised in New Jersey, Ms. Stallings acquired a bachelor's degree in English from Oberlin College, traveled extensively overseas for the Foreign Service, and then worked for 3½ years in the office of correspondents covering New York City news for *Time* magazine. She was able to combine conservation, her major interest, with journalism when she later became associate editor of *Open Space Action* magazine. She has contributed to two anthologies—*Space for Survival: Blocking the Bulldozer in Urban America*, and *Ecotactics: the Sierra Club Handbook for Environment Activists*. Her work has appeared also in *Commonweal*, *Reader's Digest*, and *Audubon* magazine.

Contents

APPENDICES

Things to Know Before You Go

A Word to the Wise

1. The weather in the Smokies can be severe, especially during the winter. Visitors from the Gulf Coast, who may have worn shorts the day before back home, are frequently surprised at the blizzard conditions. Pack warm clothes.
2. It rains a lot, so go prepared with rain gear and a stove.
3. The vegetation is incredibly thick and sometimes confusing. Visitors from the West have probably never seen such dense vegetation. A compass is a good idea—just in case.
4. Never leave an established trail unless you are prepared for off-trail conditions.
5. If you can carry it in full, you can carry it out empty. Pack out all of your trash.
6. Bears are dangerous animals. Read the section of this guidebook on the Backpacker and Bears.
7. The park is a living museum where all living and nonliving things are protected by law.
8. The Appalachian Trail is extremely overcrowded. Travel instead on the other trails.
9. Boil or treat *all* your drinking water.

History of the Park

The Great Smoky Mountains are the most massive and lofty mountain range in the eastern United States. They are part of a larger mountain system, known as the Southern Appalachian Mountains, which generally runs northeast to southwest. That system can be thought of as a giant oval of mountain ridges with Roanoke, Virginia, at the northeastern corner and the area between Atlanta and Chattanooga at the southwestern end. The eastern side of the oval is the traditional Blue Ridge mountain system of ridges and escarpments. All of the rivers within the oval flow westward to the Mississippi River. They have cut deep gorges through the mountains which form the western rim of the oval. The river gorges create natural breaks in the western mountains, and each major segment constitutes a different range. The Smokies is one of those ranges.

The Great Smokies Range runs for about 70 miles on almost an east-west line between the states of North Carolina and Tennessee. The Pigeon River flows along the eastern side, and the Little Tennessee River flows along the western side.

In the eastern part of the Smokies, there are 16 peaks over 6,000 feet high. The crest does not dip below 5,000 feet in elevation for almost 34 miles. To the west, the crest is generally lower. This is "bald" country, where grassy meadows sometimes cover the mountaintops and allow panoramic views in all directions. But lofty as the Smokies are, the highest peak in the East is Mount Mitchell, in the

Black Mountains, a small cross range to the east. At 6,684 feet, it is 42 feet higher than the Smokies' highest peak, Clingmans Dome. Another cross range, the Balsam Mountain Range, extends south and east from the Smokies. Today the Blue Ridge Parkway uses the Balsams to connect the Blue Ridge Mountains with the Great Smoky Mountains.

This is an old, old region—both in terms of geology and human habitation. The Smokies were "built" 125 million years before the Rockies. And for untold years before the arrival of the white man, the region now occupied by Great Smoky Mountains National Park was part of the Cherokee Indian Nation. Several small Cherokee villages were scattered in the low country along the Oconaluftee River and Raven Fork. The story of the appropriation of the Cherokee land by the whites is a shameful one. It is briefly covered elsewhere in this guidebook, in the introduction to the Raven Fork section.

In 1775 botanist William Bartram of Philadelphia visited the general region immediately south of the Smokies and later published a journal of his observations. His accounts of the flora and fauna and of his friendly encounters with the Cherokees make very interesting reading.

During the late 1790s and early 1800s, the first white settlers arrived in the Smokies and established simple farms in the coves and valleys. At that time this region was the western frontier, so hardy independent pioneers moved in looking for new opportunities. Soon the frontier moved west into central Tennessee and Kentucky, and the Smokies became a backwater. The settlers who remained nevertheless increased in number and began to put a strain on the available resources. Although the first generation had lived well on the rich soil of the bottomlands, the second and third generations were forced to move farther up the valleys to poorer soil and marginal farming. Fortunately, the

mountaineers were very resourceful and fulfilled their basic
needs by constructing tools and implements from native
materials, especially wood. Corn was the principal crop.
They ate it themselves, fed it to their animals and from it
made whiskey, their only saleable product. But the living
was hard, and disease was plentiful because there were no
sanitation facilities or doctors, and the home remedies they
concocted from the great variety of plants growing roundabout just were not good enough.

As the years passed, the people grew more and more
isolated. The outside world changed, while the mountaineers basically retained their original culture. The Smokies
became a forgotten land, one almost unknown to the outside world. In 1904 when writer Horace Kephart journeyed
to the Smokies he remarked that he had not been able to
locate a single current magazine article or book describing
the Smokies or the people who lived there.

Loggers arrived in the Smokies just after the turn of the
century. Their record of depredations to the land was
shameful. They clearcut entire watersheds of venerable
hardwoods, and devastating fires resulted from their logging
operations. Fortunately, some of the lumber companies
went bankrupt before they could finish the job, and moved
on to areas more easily accessible and thus more remuner-
ative. In the end, about 65 percent of the park was logged
by the lumbermen, and probably many portions of the remaining 35 percent were selectively cut for choice specimens.

At about the same time the loggers arrived, the national
park movement was gaining momentum throughout the
United States. There was no national park east of the
Mississippi, but there was a great demand for one. Before
World War I, Stephen T. Mather, first director of the
National Park Service, and his assistant, Horace M. Albright,
were on the lookout for an appropriate site. They were

deluged with suggestions; every community seemed to have its own idea of where the best place might be. Mather and Albright examined proposals for national parks everywhere from the Indiana Dunes to Niagara Falls. After the war the secretary of the interior appointed a special committee—the Southern Appalachian National Park Committee (later Commission)—to study all possibilities and make a recommendation. For the better part of a year, committee members traveled about the East and finally recommended national parks at both the Great Smokies and the Blue Ridge. Thereafter, the movement for a Smokies park was combined with the movement for a Shenandoah park. In 1926 Congress authorized the secretary of the interior to determine both parks' general boundaries—but refused to appropriate federal money for land purchase.

The drive for funds was on. Interest in the park ran high in both North Carolina and Tennessee. Local fund-raising projects were begun by enthusiastic communities. School children wrote essays on why they wanted the park and donated nickels and dimes. The legislatures of both states appropriated several million dollars each. In 1926 the first tract was purchased, from the Little River Lumber Company, which owned the Elkmont and Tremont areas.

As could be expected the 18 timber companies that owned 85 percent of the park land were generally not cooperative. They had always favored a national forest. (They could continue logging a national forest.) Unfortunately, several companies demanded such high prices for their property that they threatened the whole park project. Some litigation with timber companies went to the Supreme Court before they would agree to sell. The Champion Fibre Company owned the largest tract—92,800 acres of the best high country, including the crest from Mount Guyot to Clingmans Dome. It was the heart of the uncut virgin timber and its loss could have destroyed the park.

After much negotiation the owners agreed to sell for about one-fourth the price they first demanded.

In any case, acquisition was a gigantic job. The Park Commission had to cope with the purchase of more than 6,500 separate tracts, and meet the demands of thousands of land holders.

The necessary money was proving hard to come by. The states of North Carolina and Tennessee were not prosperous and had already donated more than their share. Acquisition slowed down; the situation became critical. The solution to the problem finally arrived in 1928 when John D. Rockefeller, Jr., donated more than $5 million toward the park as a memorial to his mother. The Rockefeller gift essentially doubled the available funds and made it possible for acquisition to continue. Later on, about $3.5 million of federal funds were appropriated to aid the final stages of purchase. By 1935 there was enough land to achieve full national park status.

Some problems of inholdings still remain in the Smokies. For instance, the North Carolina Exploration Company owns 1,920 acres in the Eagle Creek watershed, where copper was once mined. This tract is isolated now but would become accessible if a road were built along the north shore of Fontana Lake. Indeed, the Park Service agreed to build one, in 1943, after the creation of Fontana Lake flooded a narrow road connecting Bryson City with Fontana Dam.

The intention was to compensate Swain County for its losses. The original route was planned along the north shore of the lake, cutting across several major watersheds. After much opposition to that route, a disastrous alternative was chosen that would have crossed the high mountains and cut up the largest mountain wilderness area in the eastern United States. Then, in 1966, wilderness hearings were held for the Smokies. Public outrage at the transmountain road was so great that Interior Secretary Stewart Udall withdrew the plans. Today, the new road from Bryson City to Noland Creek exists as the only tangible evidence of these abandoned highway projects.

In 1971 the Park Service proposed replacing the trans-mountain road with a parkway to encircle the entire perimeter of the park. Although this plan has a few flaws as to exact location, the general idea is the same as one conservationists had proposed in 1968. Certainly there is no doubt that the present road system around the park (especially in North Carolina) is inadequate and that Swain County deserves compensation for its losses of property. Nevertheless, some people still want more roads through the park itself, so until the wild portions of the Smokies are fully protected under the National Wilderness System, the preservation of the back country of the park will remain uncertain.

In the 1930s and early 1940s, when the United States government operated 16 Civilian Conservation Corps camps in the Smokies, young men between the ages of 17 and 23 worked to improve the park's trails and roads, some of which followed old railroad grades from the logging days. During this time many of the older trails were rerouted and graded to a slope of less than 10 percent. Most of the graded trails now in use are the result of the CCC program.

Yet today's network of more than 600 miles of usable trails is only a small part of the vast network originally used by the early mountaineers. Most of the original trails, including some that were improved by the CCC, are now grown over and impassable because of lack of funds for proper maintenance. With a tremendous influx of car campers into the park, the Park Service has felt obligated to place a higher priority on developed campgrounds than on trail maintenance. The trail system has suffered accordingly.

Weather

The weather in the Great Smokies is an important consideration for any hiking trip. Since the southern Appalachians are the largest and tallest mountain mass in eastern North America, they generate a weather pattern which is much wetter and colder than that of the surrounding region. Become aware of the seasonal and altitudinal weather patterns, for they can affect your comfort and safety.

Air temperature in the Smokies declines as the elevation increases. There is a 10 to 15°F. difference between the low valleys and the high country, or almost 3°F. per 1,000 feet in elevation. This means colder nights on the ridge tops; it also means a later spring and an earlier fall. Spring takes about six weeks to climb the mountains, so a hike down a mountainside in late spring will usually offer an interesting variety of early, mid and late spring flowers.

The park's nearest weather station is located in Gatlinburg, where the elevation is only 1,454 feet. Therefore, it is usually 10 to 15°F. colder on the mountaintops than the Gatlinburg temperatures provided here in Table I. Even so, the nightly lows in Gatlinburg are usually well below freezing from December through February. In spring the temperatures rise rapidly, but there is still a 90 percent chance of freezing temperatures after April 13, and a 10 percent chance after May 16. The summer months are warm but usually not very hot except at low elevations. In the high country it can still be a bit chilly at night, so carry adequate sleeping gear. Warm weather lingers into fall but drops rapidly in late October and November. Thanksgiving hikers should be prepared for temperatures down into the mid-20s. After November 3 there is a 90 percent chance of freezing temperatures. November 23 is the average date for the first fall night when the temperature drops below 20°F.

"Rain, rain, Smoky Mountains is thy name," wrote Michael Frome. Rain increases there as elevation increases; thus the mountaintops are essentially temperate rain forests. At elevations over 6,000 feet, the average annual rainfall may exceed 90 inches per year—the heaviest rainfall in the United States except in the Pacific Northwest. While you may not appreciate hiking for days in the rain, you should keep in mind that all the water dripping around you is necessary for the fantastic beauty and lushness of the mountains. It is all part of a Smokies trip.

The greatest number of cloudy days occurs in winter, the fewest in fall. September is the driest month. The greatest rainfall occurs in summer, usually as thundershowers, when the steep mountains cause uplifting of moist air masses which cool until precipitation takes place. But winter and early spring also show an increase in rainfall, mainly because of large frontal storms moving over the southeastern region. Snow is highly variable but is not at all unusual at high elevations during the winter. Surprisingly, the month of March has the maximum amount of snow and sleet. This fact was corroborated by one editor's personal experience of trudging through three feet of fresh snow to reach Ice Water Spring Shelter—on March 10.

There is no data readily available on wind in the Smokies, but wind is an extremely important safety factor in chilly weather because it removes heat from the body *very* efficiently. With an air temperature of 40°F., a wind speed of 20 mph will create an effective temperature of 18°F., i.e., of still air at 18°F. Additionally, wind combines with wetness to create a dangerous condition which can lead to

excessive body chill. Clothes lose about 90 percent of their
insulating value when wet. Even at 50°F., a wet person in a
slight breeze can suffer from exposure. Excessive exposure
is probably the number one killer of outdoor recreationists.
Do not underestimate the effects of being cold and wet.
Keep dry and seek shelter from the wind. Make an emergency camp if persistent shivering occurs. Avoid pushing
yourself to exhaustion.

TABLE I
GATLINBURG TEMPERATURE SUMMARY

Mo.	Typical 24 hr.-Day			35-Yr. Extremes		Usual Number of Days	
	High	Low	Avg. Temp.	High	Low	Over 90°	Under 32°
Jan.	50.7	27.8	39.3	81	-10	0	21
Feb.	54.3	29.4	41.9	80	-13	0	18
Mar.	61.2	34.3	47.8	85	-3	0	18
Apr.	71.4	42.3	56.8	93	19	0	6
May	79.4	50.1	64.8	98	28	2	1
June	86.0	58.0	72.0	106	36	8	0
July	87.8	59.3	73.6	105	43	12	0
Aug.	87.1	60.2	73.7	100	40	9	0
Sept.	83.1	54.6	68.9	102	27	5	0
Oct.	72.7	43.0	57.9	94	15	0	5
Nov.	60.5	32.9	46.7	85	2	0	16
Dec.	52.2	28.2	40.2	80	-12	0	20

Geologic History
of the Smokies

About 800 million years ago, large amounts of sediments were being deposited on a sea floor in deep water along an ancient Precambrian coastline. The sediments were derived from a rapidly decaying coastal mountain range that had been uplifted earlier. They were a heterogeneous mixture of quartz, feldspar, clays and rock fragments. Turbidity flows wooshed tongues of sediment into deeper water where the heavier particles settled first, then successively finer grains, to produce graded layers. Between turbidity flows finer sediment accumulated on the sea floor in larger amounts. In some areas the fine sediment was rich in organic matter and the basin was so oxygen-starved that black muds accumulated. The organic matter was produced by organisms lacking hard parts, so the sediments were barren of fossil remains. As the old mountain chain was worn down and the adjacent continental margin became covered with sediments, the sea became shallower. That original mass of sediments, in places as much as 40,000 feet thick, is now called the Ocoee Series.

Later, the Ocoee Series, and a few life forms with hard parts which by then inhabited the sea floor, were covered by cleaner, more traveled sands and muds, which now make up the shales and sandstones called the Chilhowee Group. The older rocks beneath became pressed and cemented into black and gray shales and impure graded bedded sandstones (graywackes). Still more, younger, shallow-water fossil-bearing sediments were laid down about 500 million years ago. These were calcareous muds and sands which formed thick beds of limestone.

While the earliest sediments had been accumulating along the edge of the continent, an oceanic trench had developed to the east. It was the result of westward-moving oceanic crust passing down and beneath the ancient North American continent—a kind of swallowing of the ocean floor. These movements created friction, which generated considerable heat, while increased pressures caused the sedimentary rocks to fold and crumple. By about 500 to 400 million years ago, during the Early to Mid Paleozoic, these rocks were altered by the intense heat and pressure to become metamorphic rock. Additionally, this swallowing of ocean floor diminished the distance between Africa and North America and caused them to collide about 300 to 250 million years ago. The collision culminated in the formation, from the sediments, of the original Appalachian mountain system, a majestic chain which extended from Alabama to Scandinavia and was as broad and lofty as the present Andes. During collision, the Ocoee Series rocks were pushed perhaps 75 miles northwestward on a great thrust sheet over the much younger Ordovician rocks. Those overthrust Ocoee Series rocks made up most of today's Smoky Mountains. Chilhowee Mountain to the west of the park was part of the leading edge of the overthrust and contains shale and sandstone from the Chilhowee Group.

Near the end of the long, gradual period of mountain building, a series of faults formed which remain expressed in today's topography. The Oconaluftee Fault begins near the present site of Smokemont and extends northwest, forming the main trend for the upper Oconaluftee Valley, where the Newfound Gap Road now runs. The fault crosses the crest at Indian Gap, and then follows along the Road Prong Trail and stream for about 1.5 miles. The surface trace of the fault then goes over Sugarland Mountain and drops into the Little River Valley, where the Cucumber Gap Trail follows it at the base of Bent Arm Mountain. It continues westward around the northern base of Meigs Mountain, following an abrupt increase in slope and paralleling the Meigs Mountain Trail. To the west, the Finley Cove Trail also follows the Oconaluftee Fault, again along the break in the topographic slope.

About 180 million years ago the mountain-building process was finally completed, resulting in a majestic mountain chain. From that time until the present, except for minor upward readjustments, the mountain chain has been subjected to erosion and decay. Today the highest points of the Smokies and the Kilmer-Slickrock area, though inspiring, are mere remnants of a great range of another age. One distinctive result of the erosion appears in the northwestern section of the park in the valley of Cades Cove, and north of the park at Wear Cove and Tuckaleechee Cove. There erosion has worn through the older, overlying rocks to expose the younger limestone below. Each cove has a floor of limestone which appears like a "window" through the older, overthrust rock. The rocks of the valley floor of Cades Cove are about 300 million years younger than the Ocoee Series rocks of the surrounding mountains.

Long and extensive decay and erosion are the major processes which have shaped the Smokies and the Kilmer-Slickrock landscape. An additional factor has been the sporadic cold climate of the past million years. Although no glaciation ever extended south of the Ohio River, the proximity of the ice did make the southern Appalachian region much colder than it is today. The tops of the mountains had a timber line like that in today's New England. Extensive frost action produced many large boulders of metagraywacke that cover the upper slopes of the high ridges, as on Clingmans Dome. Some rolled or crept downhill to clog streams and thereby created a moss-covered wonderland of waterfalls and cascades. An excellent example of such a boulder field can be seen on the Buckeye Nature Trail on the Tennessee side of the Newfound Gap Road.

Erosive processes continue today but they are inhibited by a lush vegetative mantle. Any disturbance of this cover by roads, logging, campgrounds, or even poorly maintained foot trails, results in an acceleration of erosion and eventual destruction of some of the beauty of the area.

Our existence on this planet is dependent upon our ability to tamper with and control natural systems. We exist, however, only by the consent of geologic and other natural processes, so we should be careful where, and how much we tamper, lest we cause our own destruction. There are some parts of our planet that should be left untouched. The Smokies and Kilmer-Slickrock areas are two such places.

−by Dr. Robert D. Hatcher, Jr.
Associate Professor of Geology
Clemson University

Flora and Fauna

Great Smoky Mountains National Park guards the last large remnant of the original southern Appalachian forest which once covered over four million acres. The park's wide range of elevation and subsequent varied climatic conditions provide an unparalleled diversity of habitats. The flora and fauna of a New England coniferous forest is well represented on the mountaintops; the coves contain magnificent stands of virgin hardwoods. This lush vegetation is the primary reason the park was established. More than 100 species of native trees, almost as many as in the entire continent of Europe, grow inside the park. The conditions for growth are so nearly optimal that between 15 and 20 tree species reach their world-record size there. Not less important, but less obvious at certain times of year, are the 1,300 kinds of flowering plants. Visitors arrive from all over the country to see the Smokies wildflowers, especially during the spring when the variety of blossoms is often spectacular.

During the last glaciation, about one million years ago, a more northern flora and fauna lived in the Southeast. The Smokies were not covered with glacial ice, but a tree line probably existed at the high elevations. As the climate became warmer and the glaciers eventually receded, the cold weather biota migrated to the north, but some of those plants and animals took up residence on the southern mountain peaks where the climate was still cool. They live on today to delight the hiker with a pleasant change of scenery. Climbing from a cove to some mountaintops, the hiker views a flora he would otherwise see only by traveling 1,000 miles to the north.

The Fraser fir, often called the balsam fir, is the dominant tree above 6,000 feet. The red spruce often grows associated with the fir; together they form the coniferous forest. The Fraser fir can be identified by its upright cones and blunt needles, which have gray-white stripes on the underside. The red spruce has pendant cones and sharp needles, which are the same color green on both sides.

The forests of the Smokies are generally described as being composed of six major types. For a description of these forests and some of the wildflowers, we have borrowed the following passage by Arthur Stupka, the foremost authority on the natural history of the Smokies, from *Great Smoky Mountains National Park Natural History Handbook, Series No. 5*, published by the U.S. Government Printing Office (see Recommended Reading):

Cove Hardwood Forests

These forests occur in sheltered situations, at low and middle altitudes (below 4,500 ft.) where there is a considerable depth of soil. Dominant trees are yellow buckeye, basswood, yellow-poplar, mountain silverbell, eastern hemlock, white ash, sugar maple, yellow birch, American beech, black cherry, northern red oak, cucumber-tree, and, in former years, American chestnut. All these grow to record or near-record proportions in the park. Wherever a number of these are found together, and where the ropelike strands of the common Dutchmanspipe make good growth, we find ourselves in the splendid big-tree groves of the Great Smokies. It is largely due to the occurrence of various unspoiled stands of these cove hardwood forests, along with the stands of Canadian-zone spruce and fir at the higher elevations, that Great Smoky Mountains National Park deserves its reputation as an outstanding wilderness stronghold.

It may be difficult for some of us to realize that the cucumber-tree grows to be greater than 18 feet in circumference, yet such a tree stands in the Greenbrier area of the park. A yellow buckeye is almost 16 feet in circumference, a yellow birch over 14 feet, a mountain silverbell almost 12 feet, a sugar maple over 13 feet, and a yellow-poplar over 24 feet—these are circumference measurements taken at 4½ feet from the ground. All are cove hardwood species in the park.

Fraser magnolia, one of the many smaller trees in these forests, also reaches record proportions here; specimens are known to attain a height of over 75 feet and a trunk diameter of more than 2 feet. A number of shrubs, one of the most prevalent of which is the rosebay rhododendron, and a long list of spring-blooming herbs are to be found in the cove hardwood forests.

Hemlock Forests

The eastern hemlock is a common tree along streams and lower slopes up to an altitude of 3,500 to 4,000 feet. It also occurs on exposed slopes and ridges at middle altitudes and up to almost 5,000 feet, where it stops rather abruptly, there being practically no hemlocks above 5,500 feet. Associated with the hemlock are such trees as the red and sugar maples, American beech, yellow and sweet birches, black and pin cherries, American holly, yellow-poplar, and mountain silverbell. Both the rosebay and catawba rhododendrons are common shrubs in hemlock forests, the former being an abundant streamside understory while the latter occurs in heath "balds" on the higher exposed ridges. Drooping leucothoe, smooth hydrangea, scarlet elder, thornless blackberry, mountain-laurel, and hobblebush are the other shrubs one might expect here. The variety of spring-blooming herbs is not nearly as extensive as in the cove hardwood forests.

Northern Hardwood Forests

These forests, largely dominated by yellow birch and American beech, occur mostly above 4,500 feet. Often they are almost surrounded by red spruce and Fraser fir. Such trees as sugar maple, black cherry, and eastern hemlock—all a part of the northern hardwood forests—reach their uppermost limits at, or near, the 5,000-foot elevation. Red maple, striped maple, American beech, yellow buckeye, and Allegheny serviceberry drop out before, or at, the 6,000-foot elevation. Yellow birch, pin cherry, and mountain maple may reach the summits of the higher mountains where, normally, spruce and fir are dominant. The variety of shrubs in these forests is limited mostly to smooth hydrangea, drooping leucothoe, catawba and rosebay rhododendrons, thornless blackberry, and hobblebush. Herbaceous plants, especially those which bloom in the spring, are of considerable variety; some of the most abundant of these include the Virginia springbeauty, common fawnlily, creeping bluet, American woodsorrel, fringed phacelia, great starwort, trilliums, violets, crinkleroot, and yellow beadlily.

Spruce-Fir Forests

Along the high State-line ridge which runs the length of the park, a forest of spruce and fir extends in an almost unbroken stand from the western slope of Clingmans Dome to near Cosby Knob, close to the park's northeastern corner—an air-line distance of approximately 25 miles. Only in the vicinity of Charlies Bunion, swept by the great fire of 1925, is there an appreciable break in the evergreen chain. On the Tennessee side of the park, the finest growth is on Mount Le Conte, third-highest peak in the Smokies; on the North Carolina side, the area southward from Mount Guyot (second-highest peak), between Hughes Ridge and Balsam Mountain, contains the most extensive spruce-fir stand. Above the 6,000-foot altitude, the only trees occasionally associated with the red spruce and Fraser fir are yellow birch, pin cherry, American mountain-ash, and mountain maple.

So dense does the growth of trees become that shrubs and other plants may be practically absent over wide areas. However, in places the following shrubs may be found: catawba and Carolina rhododendrons, southern bush-honeysuckle, Allegheny menziesia, scarlet elder, dingleberry, thornless blackberry, roundleaf gooseberry, hobblebush, witherod, and Blueridge blueberry. Ferns prevailing at these high altitudes include the toothed woodfern and hay-scented, lady, and common polypody ferns. Most conspicuous of the spring-blooming herbs include creeping bluet, Virginia springbeauty, American woodsorrel, pallid violet, painted trillium, erect trillium (white and purple forms) and yellow beadlily; the summer-blooming herbs that you are most likely to see include acuminate aster, white wood aster, cluster goldenrod, pink turtlehead, Indianpipe, and Rugel's groundsel.

Closed Oak Forests

On intermediate to dry slopes, at low and middle altitudes, the forests are dominated by four kinds of oaks (white, chestnut, northern red, and black), three hickories (pignut, red, and mockernut), and by red maple, sweet birch, sourwood, yellow-poplar, black-gum, black locust, and mountain silverbell. Formerly, the ill-fated American chestnut was a very important component of this forest. Small trees, especially flow-ering dogwood and witch hazel, and such shrubs as mountain-laurel, rosebay rhododendron, smooth hydrangea, flame azalea, oil-nut, buckberry, and pale sweet shrub are often present. Vines include the com-mon greenbrier and Virginia creeper, while common herbs and herblike plants include galax, trailing-arbutus, white wood aster, halberdleaf yellow violet, false foxglove, early pedicularis, and goldenrods.

Open Oak and Pine Stands

Four kinds of oaks and an equal number of pines dominate these forests which occur on dry exposed slopes and ridges. The terrain is usually rocky. Where-as the trees normally do not form a closed canopy, the shrub layer may be quite dense and is often dominated by the evergreen mountain-laurel. The northern red oak of the closed oak forests is replaced by the scarlet oak in these drier stands; otherwise the same species of oak are dominant. Pines (Table-Moun-tain, pitch, and Virginia) are most plentiful on the driest sites; eastern white and shortleaf pines may occur along with red maple, sourwood, blackgum, sassafras, Allegheny serviceberry, and black locust. American chestnut persists as basal sprouts. The majority of the tall-growing shrubs of the closed oak forest are also to be found here. In addition, huckle-berries and blueberries may become abundant. Check-erberry wintergreen, trailing-arbutus, eastern bracken, galax, various asters, and pussytoes are common lower plants. (End of Stupka passage.)

The park also has some outstanding examples of a vegetational enigma, the southern Appalachian balds. These areas, located on high ridges and mountaintops, are so named because they lack trees. They are of two types: the heath bald (dominated by shrubs such as mountain laurel, blueberry and rhododendron) and the grass bald (primarily covered by grasses and sedges). The heath balds are sometimes called "slicks" because they may appear to be smooth from a distance. In reality they are incredible entanglements, sometimes head-high, which are almost impenetrable. Hence their other name—"hells." These balds offer a floral display in mid-June which is world famous for its luxuriant beauty.

The grass balds, such as Gregory Bald, are open areas which invite a pleasant stroll through high fields, with fantastic panoramic views. The wild flame azalea is often found growing in the grassy balds and adds to their beauty in late June. In prepark days these high pastures were grazed by the settlers' cattle, and small huts were established there for the herders.

The origin of the balds is unclear, but it is believed that, at least in the grass balds, fire has been a major factor, along with grazing. Several of them are now filling in with shrubs and trees, so it seems reasonable to assume that some activity of man has helped maintain them in the past. The balds are definitely not a form of tree line caused by altitude—many higher peaks adjacent to a bald are completely forested. Whatever explanation is proposed in the future must take into account the fact that several balds are part of Indian tradition and thus have existed for a very long time.

One major tree is no longer king of the forest. That is the American chestnut (*Castanea dentata*), which formerly reached a diameter of 9 to 10 feet in the Smokies. A similar species still grows in Asia, where a parasitic fungus lives in harmony with its host. In 1904 near New York City, that fungus was accidentally introduced to North America. But the American chestnut did not have any resistance to the fungus, and our most valuable forest tree was literally destroyed. The blight arrived in the Smokies around 1925, and by 1938 more than 85 percent of the chestnuts were dead or dying. Today the tree still lives, in a manner of speaking, because its roots seem to be resistant to the disease. Sprouts grow up from the root system and last several years until the disease strikes once again. The greatest legacy of the chestnut is its ash-gray trunk which is often seen standing or lying on the forest floor. It is a ghost of a past forest. Now it has been replaced mainly by various oaks.

The most famous park animal is the black bear, which is described in a later chapter of this guide. In years past the Smokies sheltered bison, elk, wolf, otter, fisher and mountain lion, but these are now gone. While reports of mountain lions persist throughout the southern Appalachians, it is doubtful that these animals exist in the park.

More than 50 kinds of mammals do live in the park. In the high country the red squirrel or "boomer" is often heard or seen because of its big voice and vigorous actions. Woodchucks are found in grassy areas along roads or in the open coves. White-tailed deer are plentiful in Cades Cove, where early morning visitors will usually see them in the fields. With luck, an occasional wild turkey may also be seen. Skunks and opossums may visit back-country campsites, foraging for food. At night the more secretive flying squirrel, raccoon, fox and bobcat will roam the forest.

The European wild boar (*Sus scrofa*) has found its way across the Little Tennessee River into the southwestern part of the park. This animal is formidable. It is not likely to charge, however, unless cornered, so avoid that situation, and give it the right of way.

More than 200 birds have been seen inside the park—too

many for detailed discussion here. The most likely to be seen by a hiker in the high country is the Carolina junco. It nests on the ground, frequently in a depression on the trail bank. Don't be surprised if a small slate-gray bird very suddenly flies away from your side along the trail. Notice the flash of white tail feathers. Back off a few feet and wait for the junco to return to its nest. Instead of migrating a long distance, the junco merely flies down the mountainside to the warmer foothills when winter comes.

The raven is also sometimes seen in the high country. This bird resembles a crow but has a deeper, throaty call and is not found at low elevations. The ruffed grouse is fairly common at all elevations. In April or October the male performs his drumming—a sound symbolic of wildness. He perches on a log and beats his wings to create a muffled crescendo, which is easily identified.

There are 23 different snakes in the park but only 2 of them are poisonous. The timber rattlesnake is not uncommon up to 5,000 feet of elevation and is most likely encountered when hiking off-trail in an area of rocky outcrops. Also, it prefers warm, sunny southfacing slopes of mountains. The smaller copperhead is found at middle and low elevations, often in the same habitat as the rattler. Though less poisonous, this snake does not offer the courtesy of an audible warning. Copperheads are secretive and are often found in the vicinity of old sawdust piles. Although you should be prepared for poisonous snakes, you are unlikely to encounter one on the trail. It is possible to hike hundreds of miles in the Appalachians without seeing a single poisonous snake.

The Smokies, with a wealth of moisture, offer an ideal habitat for amphibians. The park has the most varied and abundant salamander fauna in the United States. The red-cheeked salamander is noteworthy because it is found only within this park. This blue-gray-black creature has bright red cheeks and lives under logs and rocks at high elevations.

The Backpacker and Bears

The protected status of the black bear in Great Smoky Mountains National Park, its evident preference for the food and garbage of visitors, and its relative loss of fear of man result in problems for the National Park Service. The ready availability of food in areas frequently used by man encourages some bears to concentrate there. Although man's food and garbage make up only a very small percentage of the bear's diet (more than 90 percent of the food it eats in the park is natural vegetation), it apparently is attracted to man's type of food. The more frequent the contact between an individual bear and the visitor with his food or garbage, the more bold and aggressive the bear may become. Therefore, the places with the greatest number of picnickers and campers are also the places having the most confrontations.

Some of the bears that have adapted to man's presence within the park appear quite docile. Nevertheless, visitors should remember that these animals, which seem so tame, are capable of inflicting serious injuries. Their prowess in terms of strength, agility and speed far exceeds that of man. The more bold individuals occasionally will "charge" at a visitor. This charge may be accompanied by snapping of teeth, a subtle groan and "woofing" (exhaling air rapidly through nose and mouth). It is generally a bluff. Some black bears are extremely shy and secretive and may never be seen; others will not leave a campsite or picnic area until a ranger applies force. This variability in behavior emphasizes the danger of assuming that the behavior of one "tame" or panhandler bear will be the same as another's. Most aggressive and potentially dangerous bears in the park are solitary males. This is no guarantee, however, that a sow (female) and her cubs or yearlings will not cause problems. Additionally, in any population of animals there is always the possibility that one individual may not fit the typical behavior pattern. Placing confidence in how a bear will react to a given situation is dangerous. The sensible visitor will always keep his distance.

"Problem" bears represent only a very small portion of the total bear population in the park—typically fewer than 10 in a given season. Estimates of the total number of bears have ranged from 100 to 500 but average about 300. The number fluctuates widely depending largely on the abundance and availability of fall food (acorns, hickory nuts, beech nuts and black cherries). During periods of food scarcity, bears travel considerable distances. Many move to the perimeter of the park and even outside its boundaries where they are not protected. Heavy hunting pressure, both legal and illegal, takes a heavy toll. Apparently, the availability of fall food and concomitant hunting pressure are the chief influences on the number of bears in the park the following summer.

There is little likelihood of a hiker or camper coming in contact with a bear between October 15 and June 1. In fact the backpacker will seldom see a bear in back country at any time, except at shelters, because of the thickness of vegetation, the bear's keen sensory abilities and its usual purposeful avoidance of people. Bears are attracted, however, to shelters on the Appalachian Trail, developed campgrounds and picnic areas, and are commonly seen by visitors between June 15 and Labor Day. The peak of bear observations and "incidents" (injuries and property damage) occurs at the peak of visitor use of the park during

July and August. August, incidentally, is the time when the bears are most actively foraging for food. But bears move about. They usually have a home range covering several square miles. Probably there is a major artificial food source (shelter, campground or picnic area) within the home range of most of the park bears. Therefore, a confrontation is possible anywhere inside the park.

Whether a backpacker plans on spending his nights at shelters or in back-country campsites, he should take certain precautionary measures. These will decrease the likelihood of bear incidents, and, just as important, help maintain the bears as a truly wild population. Here are some basic procedures:

Regardless of the location, length of trip, or type of food or refuse, *all* unburnable garbage (cans, plastics, etc.) should be carried out of the park. If you can pack it in full, you can pack it out empty.

While camping, keep food and garbage in airtight containers as much as possible. A good deodorizer may also help. Store food containers in any caches provided by the Park Service, or hang them inside enclosed trail shelters. The fronts of most shelters are covered with chainlink fencing and are referred to as being "bear-proof." Unfortunately, some individual bears may have learned to associate backpacks with food. Therefore, the food and equipment of all campers at a shelter site should be kept inside the shelter for the night, even if there is no room for the campers themselves. At primitive sites the best technique for protecting food is to suspend it between two trees on a strong rope (higher than a bear can reach—over eight feet). Placing food in a tree is not recommended because the black bear is extremely adept at climbing. Almost anywhere you can put food in a tree can also be reached by a persistent bear. Above all, you should never take food to bed with you or even eat food over your bedding gear; nor should you pack food and bedding gear together.

Limit the size of your hiking group. Most shelters will accommodate only 12 people comfortably. A large number of people anywhere means a greater concentration of food and a greater likelihood of attracting bears.

If you are visiting the park between June 1 and Labor Day, it would pay to check with the local subdistrict park ranger about the current bear situation. (He can also issue you your camping permit; see Park Service Regulations.)

If you meet a bear:

1. Never feed or harass it.
2. Do not approach a feeding bear or a female with young.
3. In case of a close confrontation, give the bear a wide berth and the benefit of the doubt.
4. Report any incidents of feeding or harassment to a park ranger as soon as possible.

Remember, *you*, not the bear, are the visitor to this outdoor museum. The park flora and fauna should be respected as highly as any works of art in an indoor museum.

—by Michael R. Pelton
Assistant Professor of Forestry (Wildlife Biology),
Department of Forestry
University of Tennessee

Author's note: In recent years, problems with bears in the backcountry have become worse. Campers must hang all food 10 feet off the ground and 4 feet from any nearby tree trunk or limb. Never bury or burn garbage; pack it out. Never leave packs unattended on the ground. Try to eat dinner and clean up before dusk, when bears are most active.

Maps

The best single map for trail hiking in Great Smoky Mountains National Park is the Sierra Club map (first published 1972, revised 1977) which accompanies this guidebook. On the scale of 1:125,000 (1 inch = 2 miles), it was made by combining several overlays of the 1961 U.S. Geological Survey map, described below, with a new overlay giving up-to-date trail information. The maintained trails are overprinted to indicate current conditions and locations. Eighty back-country campsites, several new shelters and ten new access roads have been added. Incorrect statements pertaining to the park have been corrected. The trails are numbered consecutively from east to west within each state for easy reference. Caution: do not try to use the map while it is still attached to the book. Carefully cut the map loose for ease of reference on the trail.

The most detailed maps of the park are the USGS-Tennessee Valley Authority quadrangles. These are contoured maps in the 7½ minute series, on a scale of approximately 0.4 mile to one inch. They give a very accurate representation of the topography. Each trail description in this guide includes a list of the quadrangles which cover that trail's route. Unfortunately, several maintained trails are not shown on these maps, and some recent road additions are missing. But when attempting off-trail hiking, these quadrangles are absolutely essential. They allow the hiker to become familiar with the landscape in advance of the trip and help him to avoid possible difficult terrain features.

MAPS   41

Some serious hikers may wish to purchase quadrangles
for the entire park. This set would include the following
quadrangles: Tapoco, Fontana Dam, Tuskeegee, Noland
Creek, Bryson City, Smokemont, Bunches Bald and Cove
Creek, North Carolina; Calderwood, Cades Cove, Thunder-
head Mountain, Silers Bald, Clingmans Dome, Dellwood,
Mount Le Conte, Mount Guyot, Luftee Knob, Hartford and
Waterville, Tennessee-North Carolina; Kinzel Springs, Wear
Cove, Gatlinburg, Blockhouse and Jones Cove, Tennessee.

The price of each quadrangle is 75 cents. They can be
obtained from the U.S. Geological Survey, 1200 S. Eads
Street, Arlington, Virginia 22202. These maps are also available at the Tennessee Valley Authority, 416 Union Avenue,
Knoxville, Tennessee 37902.

The government has issued two other kinds of maps for
Great Smoky Mountains National Park.

The entire park is covered on the 1961 USGS map titled
"Great Smoky Mountains National Park and Vicinity." This is
a useful map because it gives a comprehensive topographic
view of the entire trail system—with some exceptions. The
maintenance status of many of the trails has changed, so
hikers relying completely on this map could be easily con-
fused or become lost. It contains at least 45 errors or
omissions concerning the trails. Additionally, eight roads
indicated as being restricted are now open to the public,
and ten new roads built since 1961 of course do not appear
at all. This map is available in two versions—with the usual
contours, or with shaded relief plus contour lines. It is sold
by the USGS for $1.00. It has a scale of 1:125,000 (1
inch=2 miles) and a contour interval of 100 feet. It is large
(28 x 36 inches) but can be folded to fit into a pack.

In 1931 the USGS issued the East Half and West Half
maps for the park. These were reprinted in 1965 to show
more recent road information, but the trails are the same as
in the older version—trails once used, prior to the park, by
local hunters, fishermen and mountaineers. Because most of

those trails are now completely overgrown, these two maps are generally of interest only to the off-trail or historically inclined hiker. They are available from the USGS for $1.00 per set of the two maps. The scale is 1:62,500 (approximately 1 inch=1 mile) and the contour interval is 50 feet.

Roads

Some familiarity with the roads of Great Smoky Mountains National Park will ease the problems of locating remote trailheads and save precious time for more enjoyable activities.

An extensive road system encircles the park in the general pattern of a long oval. Through the middle of the oval is a diagonal slash, which is the Newfound Gap Road. (Its name was changed from U.S. 441 after the road was closed to commercial vehicles.) The perimeter road system is composed of many separate park, state and federal roads. The following directions will lead you on a tour around the park, starting from park headquarters near Gatlinburg and driving counterclockwise. The side roads mentioned along the perimeter are more carefully described in the various introductions to the park sections.

Drive west on old Tenn. 73, now called the Little River Road when inside the park. This paved road follows an old rail bed alongside the Little River and is subject to flooding during periods of heavy rainfall. After passing the side road to Elkmont on the left, the road curves for many miles through the Little River Gorge.

The next major intersection is the Townsend "Y," where Cades Cove Road goes straight while the Little River Road bears right. It soon leaves the park and becomes Tenn. 73. On it pass through Tuckaleechee Cove and the towns of Townsend and Kinzel Springs, then turn left onto the Foothills Parkway. Drive southwest along Chilhowee Mountain, passing Look Rock Developed Campground after about 10 miles. The parkway is a scenic drive recommended for its views of the Smoky Mountains. Continue to the Little Tennessee River and turn left on U.S. 129. Soon a side road leads left to the Abrams Creek Ranger Station and Primitive Campground. Follow U.S. 129 along the river and then through the mountains for many long miles. After crossing the state line into North Carolina, turn left at the next major intersection onto N.C. 28. Pass the Twentymile Creek Ranger Station side road on the left and continue to Fontana Village. Not far past the resort, note County Road 1245, which leads left to Fontana Dock, Fontana Dam and the Appalachian Trail within the park. N.C. 28 winds for many miles through the mountain area south of Fontana Lake, passing through the villages of Stecoah and Almond. The Tsali and Cable Cove Forest Service Campgrounds are located to the north of this route on the shores of Fontana Lake.

Turn left on U.S. 19 and go to Bryson City, where roads lead north to Deep Creek and Noland Creek. Continue on U.S. 19 to Cherokee, where U.S. 441 goes left (north) to cross the park as the Newfound Gap Road. Continuing east on U.S. 19, cross the Blue Ridge Parkway at Soco Gap. From there, the Blue Ridge Parkway leads to near Cherokee, and has a spur road which runs north (right) to the Balsam Mountain Campground and one-way road. Descend on U.S. 19 through Maggie Valley and at the stoplights go left on U.S. 276. Follow U.S. 276 to Interstate 40 near Cove Creek, where N.C. 284 leads northwest to Cataloochee. Follow I-40 north through the mountains. The Mount Sterling exit provides access to Mount Sterling Village, Big Creek and the Appalachian Trail at Davenport Gap. Continue on I-40 to the Foothills Parkway exit and proceed west on the parkway to Tenn. 32 near the town of Cosby. Turn left on Tenn. 32 and after a few miles go right on

Tenn. 73. (Tenn. 32 continues east, passing the Cosby entrance to the park.) Tenn. 73 runs west to Gatlinburg. On the way it passes the Greenbrier Road, which leads left (south) into the park.

The Smokies portion of the Blue Ridge Parkway is closed during the winter because of small rockslides which obstruct the roadway. The gravel roads that penetrate toward the interior of the park are all closed to winter traffic because they are not cleared The eastern section of the Foothills Parkway is also closed all winter, but the western section remains open except after snow. The following roads can usually be expected to be open: Cades Cove Road, Cades Cove Loop Road, Little River Road, New Cataloochee Road, Clingmans Dome Road, Elkmont Road and Cherokee Orchard Road. But heavy snow can temporarily close any road and will most likely affect the Cades Cove Loop Road, Clingmans Dome Road and access to Cataloochee via old N.C. 284. Newfound Gap Road has the highest priority for snow clearance and is usually open.

A word of caution to all drivers: traffic on the Newfound Gap Road can be very heavy, especially during holiday weekends and the peak season for fall color—about mid-October. The situation is worsened when drivers stop to observe roadside bears, causing "bear jams." This can block traffic, sometimes for many miles.

Camping Facilities

You can camp in the Smokies park at campgrounds accessible by car, at designated back-country campsites, off-trail in the back country or in shelters.

In the auto campgrounds there are no sleeping shelters, showers or utility hook-ups for trailers. Each camper must supply his own equipment. Firewood is usually scarce, and usually there is no place to buy supplies. Most campgrounds are closed from November to mid-April.

Campgrounds accessible by auto are of two general types—developed and primitive. Developed campgrounds provide water, picnic tables, fireplaces, comfort stations, and tent and trailer-parking spaces. They have a resident ranger and generally provide some interpretive services such as evening programs. At the Cades Cove and Smokemont areas, a small campground store is operated from May 15 to September 15. The Cades Cove, Elkmont and Smokemont campgrounds operate on a reduced scale during the winter season. All others are closed.

Primitive campgrounds are usually located in more remote areas of the park. Facilities include a water source, picnic tables, fireplaces and pit toilets. Instead of having a ranger in residence, a ranger station is located nearby.

A word of caution about bears in the campgrounds: they will try to steal food. You should not store food in tents but lock it in your car or suspend it out of reach between trees by means of ropes. If your car is a convertible, you should lock your food in the trunk. Portable ice chests are not safe places since bears will often roll and smash them to get at the food inside.

TABLE II
CAMPGROUNDS ACCESSIBLE BY CAR

	Elev.	Number of Campsites	Extra Facilities	Location	Comments
Developed Campgrounds					
Balsam Mtn.	5,310	47	Wood for sale.	10 mi. N of Soco Gap, N.C., on Blue Ridge Pkwy spur road.	Only campground in spruce-fir.
Cades Cove	1,807	224	Wood for sale. Limited supplies at camp store.	10 mi. W from Townsend, Tenn., park entrance.	Crowded.
Cosby	2,459	230		Cosby entrance off Tenn. 32, 20 mi. E of Gatlinburg.	Space usually available.
Deep Creek	1,800	128	Group camping.	2 mi. N of Bryson City, N.C.	Crowded.
Elkmont	2,150	340	Wood for sale. Group camping.	9 mi. W of Gatlinburg, Tenn. on Little River Rd.	Crowded.
Look Rock	2,500	92		11 mi. from Walland, Tenn. on Foothills Pkwy.	
Smokemont	2,198	180	Wood for sale. Limited supplies at camp store. Group camping.	7 mi. N of Cherokee, N.C. on Newfound Gap Road.	Extremely crowded.
Primitive Campgrounds					
Abrams Creek	1,125	20		Extreme W part of park, 0.5 mi. past the Abrams Creek Rngr. Sta., Tenn.	Boil water from the creek.
Big Creek	1,700	9	Tents only.	Extreme E part of Park, 0.5 mi. past Big Creek Rngr. Sta.	Crowded.
Cataloochee	2,610	28		E part of park, on Cataloochee Road.	Open during winter.
Greenbrier	1,630	12	*Area closed to camping*		

A list of backcountry campsites and shelters follows. Capacities for campers are shown as (12); horse hitch racks shown as (H-12). The facilities at these campsites are usually limited but have, at least, a water source and level clear ground.

Greenbriar–Cosby–Big Creek–Cataloochee Areas

Porters Flat (15)
Big Creek (20) (H-20)
Snake Den Mtn. (10)
Sugar Cove (15)
Gilliland Creek (15)
Cataloochee (20) (H-20)
Walnut Bottoms (20) (H-20)
Mt. Sterling (20) (H-20)
Pretty Hollow (20)
Big Hemlock (10)
Caldwell Fork (10)
Spruce Mtn. (10)

Oconaluftee Area

Mt. Chapman (10)
McGhee Springs (12)
Straight Fork (20) (H-20)
Enloe Creek (8)
Upper Chasteen (8)
Cabin Flats (20) (H-20)
Lower Chasteen Creek (15)
Towstring (20) (H-20)

Deep Creek Area

Newton Bald (8) *No water*
Poke Patch (12)
Nettle Creek (8)
Pole Road (15)
Burnt Spruce (10)
Bryson Place (20) (H-12)
Nicks Nest Branch (6)
McCraken Branch (6)
Bumgardner Branch (10)

Noland Creek Area

Bald Creek (12) (H-6)
Upper Ripskin (12) (H-6)

Jerry Flat (10) (H-6)
Mill Creek (20) (H-12)
Bear Pen Branch (8)
Lower Noland Creek (10)
Goldmine Branch (10)

Forney Creek Area

Steel Trap (8)
Huggins (12)
Jonas Creek (12) (H-6)
CCC (12) (H)
Whiteoak Branch (8)
Bear Creek (15)(H-6)
Lower Forney (12)
Hicks Branch (6)
Kirkland Creek (12)

Hazel Creek Area

Hazel Creek Cascades (12)
Proctor Creek (15)
Calhoun (15) (H-10)
Bone Valley (20) (H-10)
Sugar Fork (8)
Sawdust Pile (20) (H-10)
Proctor (20) (H-12)

Twentymile Area

Haw Gap (8)
Pinnacle Creek (8)
Lower Ekaneetlee (8)
Lost Cove (12)
Upper Lost Cove (10)
Upper Flats (14)
Twentymile Creek (14)
Long Hungry Ridge (8)
Wolfe Ridge (8)
Eagle Creek Island (10)
Big Walnut (10)
Chambers Creek (10)

Elkmont–Tremont Area

West Prong (8)
Upper Henderson (8)
King Branch (10)
Medicine Branch Bluff (8)
Old Sugarlands Road (12)
Camp Rock (8)
Rough Creek (14)
Lower Buckeye Gap (8)
Dripping Springs Mtn. (8)
Lower Jakes Gap (8)
Marks Cove (20)
Otter Creek (10)
Three Forks (12)

SHELTERS

Davenport Gap (12)
Cosby Knob (12)
Tricorner Knob (12)
Pecks Corner (12)
Ice Water Springs (12)
Mt. Collins (12)
Double Springs (12)
Silers Bald (12)
Derrick Knob (12)
Spence Field (12)
Russell Field (14)
Mollies Ridge (12)
Birch Springs (12)
Mt. LeConte (12)
Kephart (14)
Laurel Gap (14)
Rich Mtn. (8)
Scott Gap (8)

Trail Use Patterns

During each summer month, more than 1 million visitors enter the park and share the roads, rangers and general facilities. To leave all that behind, 350,000 people a year escape on the trails. About 13 percent of them go on horseback, mostly on the trails near the horse concessions, many of which are not described in this guidebook. But the majority of the trail users, 87 percent, travel on foot. Most are day hikers (75 to 80 percent), but about 20 to 25 percent are backpackers who plan to camp out if they can find a place. Each year there are about 60,000 overnight visits to the back country, and the number seems to be increasing.

More than half the backpackers go to the park during the months of June, July and August. Since the weather is great in September, that month is also popular, and of course the fall color in October draws a few people as well. The graph on p. 52 shows the number of overnight visits recorded in the back country throughout 1970.

Although the park has more than 650 miles of trail, most backpackers seem to prefer the 70 miles of the Appalachian Trail. A survey of park camping permits by a University of Tennessee student shows that about 80 percent of the backpacking trail use for the entire park during May and June of 1970 was on the Appalachian Trail. The results of such heavy usage have been extreme overcrowding, massive litter problems, and a significant decline in the quality of the wilderness experience. At the shelters the

Kon
M. Stipes
+
Allen de Hart
peppermints
card Brooks
get poetry back

surrounding landscape has suffered from erosion and the cutting of all dead and some green trees for firewood.

The most heavily used sections of the Appalachian Trail are those adjacent to the central highways: Newfound Gap to Icewater Spring (3.5 miles long) and Clingmans Dome to Double Springs. These two sections of trail receive roughly 15 to 20 percent of the trail use for the whole park. During major summer holidays, the overcrowding problem is increased. For instance, on Labor Day weekend in 1971 during a six-hour period, there were 1,167 people hiking on the Newfound Gap-Icewater Spring section.

Throughout the park the most severe crowding occurs at the camping areas. About 30 percent of the backpackers camp at one of the back-country campsites distributed throughout the hinterland. But 70 percent spend the night at the 25 shelters, most of which are located on the Appalachian Trail. Traditionally, there have never been any restrictions on use of the Appalachian Trail. But recently, the problems have come to resemble those of a ghetto. Imagine 132 backpackers spending the night around the 12-man shelter on Mount Le Conte; that happened on September 25, 1971. It is not uncommon for 50 to 100 people to have used the same shelter area for the night. The problem has been particularly bad at Mount Le Conte, Icewater Spring, Double Springs and Spence Field.

The Park Service is painfully aware of the crowding problem and has investigated various management alternatives. In June of 1972 the Service adopted a new policy to ration the use of overpopular back-country areas. Camping permits will be issued only up to the bunk capacity of any shelter (see the end of the Regulations chapter).

Many people hike to find peace and solitude. In the Smokies this is possible by avoiding the Appalachian Trail and Mt. Le Conte and using instead the park's other 580 miles of trails. This guidebook will lead you on new safe routes along trails often as well maintained as the Appalachian Trail. Although the shelters are scarce, the backcountry campsites usually provide the necessary facilities. As for views, the vistas from High Rocks, Mount Sterling, Rich Mountain, Maddron Bald, Cove Mountain, Greenbrier Pinnacle, Blanket Mountain, Andrews Bald, Spruce Mountain and Gregory Bald are all outstanding and they are off the Appalachian Trail.

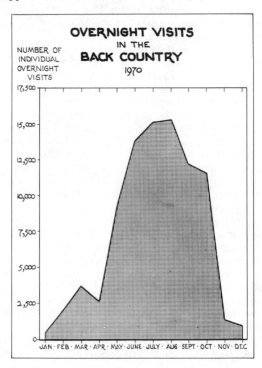

Off-Trail Hiking

Trails help you to enjoy any area and lead you to many scenic features. Therefore, this guidebook leans heavily on the existing trail system in Great Smoky Mountains National Park. But there are many other beautiful features located far away from the trails. What about off-trail cross-country hiking? Is it permissible, and safe? Is it rewarding?

There are no general restrictions on hiking anywhere in the national parks or national forests. There are, however, infrequent occasions when extreme danger of fire or other hazards may cause temporary restrictions on (or discouragement against using) certain trails. Additionally, during hunting season it may be unwise to hike at all in some of the national forests and game management areas.

Safety is a relative quality. It is deceptive to say that you will always be safe on trails. You may be safer off trail in an open wood than on a trail that traverses a steep rocky slope. Nevertheless, if you lack physical strength or have no experience or confidence in your hiking ability on trails, you should not attempt off-trail hiking.

Some of the most rewarding outdoor experiences in the mountains come from off-trail hiking. A well-planned leisurely trip into high, wild country where the only trails are tumbling streams or wooded ridges can bring memorable rewards. Although you must put more thought, physical effort and proper equipment into an off-trail trip, when it is finished you will have the satisfaction of knowing you will never again *need* a trail. Of course you may willingly use

trails again, but deep inside you know you have achieved a
rare freedom—the freedom to roam where you will in
rugged mountains, perhaps even to step where no man has
stepped before.

Here are some basic procedures you should observe
when traveling off trail.

Know the terrain. Carry the necessary maps and compass
with you but also memorize the general features you expect
to encounter so that even if you lose map, compass or your
companions you will still know an "escape" or way out to a
trail or road.

Avoid traveling alone. No matter how adept you may
become in scrambling along rocky streams or at wriggling
through thick vegetation, you could get hurt or become ill.
If there is no one to help you, even a twisted knee or an
upset stomach could plunge you into a disastrous situation.
A temporary panic could lead to further mishap. If adverse
weather arrives, you could very soon be struggling for your
life—and lose the battle.

Travel during daylight hours and only in reasonably
good weather. You and your companions are already taking
some risks in being off trail. Do not add unnecessary ones
by traveling in the dark, or in cold weather when icy rain
could coat the rocks, or in heavy snow, which makes
footing treacherous and travel slow and exhausting.

Stay with your companions. Even if you know where
you are and where you are going, if you do not stay in
touch with them, they might decide you are lost. They
would then needlessly lose valuable time and expend much
effort in your behalf. Be considerate, and keep in touch—
besides, they may need you.

Let some responsible person in a "safe" area know your
itinerary and then stick to it. Except in the unlikely case of
your doing random, unlimited roaming, you will have a
travel objective and the length of your trip will be limited

by either the time you have or problems of supply. Tell a friend or relative where you are going and when you expect to return, or give the information in note-form to Park Service or Forest Service personnel. Then try to stick to your route and time schedule.

Get into good physical condition. Off-trail hiking is much more strenuous than trail hiking, which in the Smokies seldom has grades over 15 percent. On trails you can average about 2 miles per hour. In contrast, off-trail hiking often involves working around boulders and cliffs or through heavy growths of briers, rhododendron and laurel. (Extensive patches of such vegetation are locally called "hells"—an apt name.) In such terrain your energy, determination and judgment run down rapidly; even strong, experienced travelers may progress at a rate of less than a half-mile an hour. It takes stamina to lift (not swing) the legs up and over logs and rocks, repeatedly, and to climb three feet up a steep slope, only to slide back two feet. Try to anticipate such conditions. It is wise to consult local trail clubs or Park Service or Forest Service rangers when planning an off-trail venture. Above all, do not be deceived into thinking that your ability to hike 20 miles a day on trail will prevent aching muscles after a 5-mile trip off trail. The beginner often discovers unknown muscles. The best training for off-trail hiking is to take it in small doses until your capabilities improve. But no one should expect to make any more than 5 or 6 miles per day in off-trail hiking in the Smokies.

Have clothing and equipment in top condition. Clothing should be tough enough to resist abrasion by sharp rocks and logs, and it should not be so loose that it snags easily on shrubs. Boots, 6 to 10 inches high, should be able to stand up to much abuse, including being wet all day. Packs should be as small and smoothly contoured as possible to minimize getting tangled in vegetation; many of the modern metal frames stick out too much. Pack straps and flap closures should be strong enough not to tear under strain and let your food or other essentials spill out. Valuables should be removed from loose or open pockets, wrapped up and tucked securely in a deep, closed pocket or in the pack. If you wear glasses, secure them in place with a strong cord or a head band.

Relax and enjoy being off trail and on the loose. It is neither as difficult nor as dangerous as it may seem—if you are prepared.

—by Leroy G. Fox
Knoxville, Tennessee

National Park
Service Regulations

It is essential that the millions of people visiting Great Smoky Mountains National Park follow park regulations. Here is an outline of the current ones. They are subject to change, so hikers should check with a ranger before starting out. It is anticipated that the rules for back-country use will be altered significantly in the future as the Park Service develops new management policies. For the most up-to-date information, write to the Superintendent, Great Smoky Mountains National Park, Gatlinburg, Tennessee.

Developed and Primitive Campgrounds. Camping regulations are posted in each campground. A user fee of $3.00 per site is charged.

Reservations. No individual camping spaces may be reserved at any of the park's regular camping facilities. Special camping areas may be reserved for groups such as scouts, YMCA, or church outings.

Backcountry Use. The popularity of backcountry camping has resulted in overuse of campsites and decreasing opportunity to find solitude. In an effort to restore and preserve the wilderness values of the park, some use limitations and regulations have become necessary. Only through user cooperation and compliance with park regulations and adherence to good backcountry practices can the wilderness character be preserved and the park continue to provide for the enjoyment of present and future visitors.

All persons camping overnight in the backcountry must have a camping permit. Backcountry permits may be obtained at any Visitor Center or Ranger Station within the park during the hours that the facilities are open. It is preferable that permits be obtained at stations serving the areas in which the trip is planned. Permits will not be issued more than 30 days in advance of any trip, and not more than 24 hours in advance of trips involving the use of any shelter area. Camping party size should be limited to no more than 8 persons, and backcountry overnight use is limited to 14 consecutive days.

Shelters. Shelters are located on the Appalachian Trail, Mt. LeConte, Kephart Prong, Scott Gap, Rich Mountain, and Laurel Gap. Use will be limited to the number of bunk spaces in each shelter. Camping outside shelters is not permitted, except to holders of "Through" permits issued by the Chief Ranger's Office or by the rangers stationed at Twentymile and Big Creeks (when bunk space is available they are expected to stay inside shelters). "Through" permits are issued to persons hiking the length of the Appalachian Trail, or when the hike originates and terminates more than 50 miles outside the park.

Except for "Through" hikers, shelter permits will not be issued more than 24 hours in advance of departure on trail, and the applicant must obtain permits in person. Telephone or mail requests will not be honored for other than "Through" permits.

No individual shelter may be used by the same person on consecutive nights. When shelters are filled to capacity, hikers will be re-routed to backcountry campsites.

Backcountry Campsites. To maintain wilderness character and minimize impact, maximum capacities have been assigned for each backcountry campsite (see pp. 48–49 for a list of campsites and capacities). Occupancy of these sites is limited to 3 consecutive nights per site. Permits may be issued by any Visitor Center, ranger, or by mail 30 days or less in advance.

Backcountry Regulations.

1. Pets, bicycles, and motorized equipment are prohibited on trails and cross-country hikes.
2. Firearms and fireworks are prohibited in the park.
3. Plants, wildlife, and all natural features are protected. Hunting is not permitted. Feeding wildlife is prohibited.
4. Build fires at designated sites only. Use dead and down wood only. Cutting live trees is prohibited. Keep fire small and never leave it unattended. The use of backpack stoves whenever possible minimizes impact upon the backcountry environment.
5. All non-burnable trash packed in must be packed out. Do not pack in glass containers.
6. Camping within 25 feet of any stream, spring, or other water source is prohibited. Do not wash dishes or use detergents in water sources.
7. For proper sanitation, make toilets in a shallow hole 100 feet or more from camp or water source and cover with dirt after use.
8. Do not shortcut on trail switchbacks.
9. Be considerate of others. Keep noise low.

Regulations for Cross-Country Use.

The Backcountry management plan makes concession for cross-country hikers, in that they are not required to use established campsites. Cross-country use is defined as backcountry use of an area when maintained roads or trails are not utilized for travel. The hiker may enter or exit near or at a trailhead, but the entire trip must be off-trail to qualify as a cross-country hike. Hikers are required to:

1. Pinpoint as closely as possible on a map where they intend to spend each night, and the area is to be specified on the permit.
2. Camp at least 1 mile from any road, developed area, or designated campsite, and ½ mile from any trail.
3. Group size for these hikes is limited to 6 persons.

4. Requests for such permits should normally be referred to sub-district personnel, if the request involves only one sub-district. If the use crosses sub-district boundaries, or if sending the visitor to a sub-district station imposes an inconvenience on them, the permit may be issued by any ranger, Visitor Center, or other personnel normally issuing permits.

5. Campsite occupancy is limited to 3 nights.

   Bears. Park bears are wild! Remember, the wilderness is their home. Bears are usually shy; however, do not attempt to get close, feed, tease, or otherwise molest them in any way. They have an excellent sense of smell, so keep food and food odors away from clothing, packs, and sleeping gear. Food must be suspended on a line between stout trees so that it is at least 10 feet above the ground and 4 feet from any tree. Sanitize all empty food containers by washing or burning. Cook away from sleeping site. Keep camp free of food residue and refuse. Never bury refuse or throw it in pit toilets.

How to Use
This Guidebook

This guidebook presents information on the entire trail system of Great Smoky Mountains National Park and the Joyce Kilmer Memorial Forest and Slickrock Creek. With that information you can plan almost any type of trip, short or long, easy or difficult.

The trails are grouped in sections which usually correspond to the major watersheds of the park. The sections are presented as a linear sequence from east to west—first within North Carolina, then within Tennessee—so that the physical integrity of the terrain is maintained in most cases. A hiker traveling westward in the park should find the next trails he comes to described in the next few pages of the book. A hiker traveling north or south over the main crest of the Smokies will be interrupting the east-west sequence and will have to look for the next trails in another part of the guide.

Within each section the trails are generally presented in the order that the hiker would encounter the trailheads as he enters the area by car. Wherever possible, they also are described in sequence from east to west. The point of view is that of a hiker starting from the periphery and moving toward the remote interior regions of the park.

Each trail description begins with a standard summary which looks like this:

$\left(\, 25 \,\right)$ **HYATT BALD** (Beech Gap) 2.9 mi.

Horse trail / Max. elev. gain 1,840
Start: Round Bottom, 3,060 ft.
End: Hyatt Ridge, 4,940 ft.
USGS quads: Luftee Knob, N.C.
Trail connections: Hyatt Ridge

Following are explanations of the components of the summary:

$\left(\, 25 \,\right)$ —*Trail number on the guide map.* It appears on the map at both the trailhead and terminus. The trails are numbered consecutively as they are described in the text, approximately east to west.

HYATT BALD—*Trail name used in this guidebook.*

(Beech Gap)—*Synonym for the trail name.* Synonyms are supplied because there is no standardized nomenclature for the park trails. Often the Park Service has assigned names based on the USGS maps, which sometimes do not match the names used locally. Additionally, the *Guide to the Appalachian Trail* uses somewhat different names for the side trails connecting with the Appalachian Trail. This confusing business was resolved by assigning each trail with the name that makes the most sense to a hiker starting at the bottom, and by mentioning all others within parentheses. Finally, in a few cases several short trails have been combined into one. The name for the dominant trail is used and the other is mentioned within parentheses.

2.9 mi.—*One-way trail distance.* The distance from the trailhead to the terminus. Each trail in Deep Creek, Forney and Noland creeks, Hazel Creek and Kilmer-Slickrock was measured by rolling a counting wheel along it. The other trail distances were very carefully determined by using a map measurer on the USGS quadrangles. (This technique was tested against the wheel and proved to be accurate to within 0.1 mile in most cases.)

Horse trail—*Maintenance condition.* The maintenance condition of each trail falls into one of the following categories:

Gated road: a gravel road used often by Park Service for maintenance but closed to private vehicles.

Gated jeep trail: a rough jeep track used by the Park Service for back-country maintenance. It receives variable usage and is closed to private vehicles.

Horse trail: the trail is usually graded and about four feet wide. It receives good maintenance but is sometimes muddy because of heavy horse traffic.

Foot trail: the trail is two feet wide, and may or may not be graded. It is usually adequately maintained.

Manway: the trail receives little maintenance and is usually not graded. It may be extremely rough or overgrown, or it may be quite passable.

Unmaintained: this trail receives no Park Service maintenance. Surprisingly, it may be passable because of use by local fishermen, but in most cases it does not exist at all. The gated roads, gated jeep trails, horse trails and foot trails are all acceptable for normal hiking except where noted in the guide. Only experienced hikers should attempt the manways or unmaintained trails.

Max. elev. gain 1,840—*The maximum gain in elevation when traveling in the direction described.* This is the greatest change in elevation which the hiker will realize as he travels from the lowest to the highest point along the trail, hiking in the direction described. In most cases the trail runs from a low to a high elevation so the hiker will be ascending approximately the maximum elevation gain. But in cases where the trail goes up and down over peaks, the hiker will climb a greater distance than the maximum elevation gain. And in the Slickrock area several trails run *down-hill*, so the gain will be realized only if the trail is hiked in the opposite direction.

Start: Round Bottom, 3,060 ft.—*Starting point and elevation.* Locating the trailhead is sometimes the most difficult part of a trip, especially if the hiker is unfamiliar with local roads. The main roads are described under Roads. Each section introduction provides a more detailed description of the roads and trailheads in that area. Each trail description devotes a paragraph to the specifics of the trailhead, including the road mileage from some landmark. In general the hiker should use the section introduction to get to the vicinity of the trailhead and then refer to the specific trail to finish his journey.

End: Hyatt Ridge, 4,940 ft.—*Trail terminus and elevation.*

USGS quads: Luftee Knob, N.C.—*The U.S. Geological Survey 7½ minute quadrangle maps which cover the trail route.* In some cases the trail does not appear on the map and the guide will so indicate.

Trail connections: Hyatt Ridge—*A trail that connects with the main trail* (Hyatt Bald). The connections are listed so that the reader may quickly scan all possibilities if he wishes to link several trails together for his hike. They are furnished in the order in which they are encountered on the main trail. Also included as a connecting trail is any side trail which is directly accessible within 0.5 mi. from the main trail. For example, as you hike along the main tràil described, you encounter a connecting trail. Within 0.5 mi. down that connecting trail another side trail begins. The latter trail is listed as connected to the main trail.

Trail Descriptions

Big Creek Section
(North Carolina)

Introduction

Big Creek watershed has been under consideration for inclusion in the National Wilderness System.

The Big Creek section lies in a primitive part of the park. Big Creek itself is a beautiful mountain stream with excellent trout fishing. The area was logged from 1909 to 1918 by the Crestmont Lumber Company. Although the lower section was then developed with homes, a school and a large band mill, the entire area was nearly abandoned soon after the timber was depleted. During the 1930s the CCC had a large camp at Crestmont. At that time they improved the road up to Walnut Bottoms and graded the trails in the watershed. Nowadays, the Park Service, having made no attempt to develop Big Creek, is considering permanent closure and seeding of the road beyond the Big Creek Primitive Campground. The watershed should then qualify for inclusion in the National Wilderness Preservation System. Without such protection, tremendous pressure for development of recreational facilities will be likely to occur.

The Big Creek watershed is bounded on the north by Mount Cammerer and the main crest of the Smokies, on the south by Mount Sterling Ridge and on the west by Mount Guyot (6,621 feet) and Balsam Mountain.

The largest tree ever cut in Haywood County was felled in the Big Creek area by loggers during the early 1920s. Mack Caldwell of Big Creek described it: "We measured the stump, a little above the ground, with a 10-foot rail, measuring straight across the center. The 10-foot rail wouldn't reach across the center of the stump." Caldwell said the tree had measured nearly 12 feet in diameter.

Hiking in this once remote area is definitely on the increase. The backbone of the trail system is the Big Creek Trail, which follows a gated road up the valley. The five other trails in the basin are side trails off the Big Creek Road, and lead to the surrounding ridge systems. Hiking must begin near the ranger station or campground at low elevation—about 1,700 feet. Therefore considerable climbing is necessary to reach any ridge top or mountain peak. The least climb is 2,500 feet, to Low Gap; the greatest is 4,100 feet, to Mount Sterling.

Car camping, with tents only, is possible at Big Creek Primitive Campground near the ranger station. The campground is nearly always full in summer but has been closed after Labor Day for lack of operating funds. The opening date in the spring is uncertain but is usually in mid-April or May. An alternative base camp can be established at a stream-side primitive site below the stone schoolhouse nearby in Pisgah National Forest. Many Appalachian Trail hikers now go to Walnut Bottoms back-country camp one day and climb to Low Gap on the Appalachian Trail the next. Walnut Bottoms backcountry campsite is used by both hikers and horse parties, and in 1977 was the most heavily used site in the park. Space may be at a premium.

It is possible to buy some provisions at the old general store in Mount Sterling Village. *Warning*: recently there has been considerable danger of car theft in this general area. Do not leave your car alongside the road, even when it is locked. When you are getting your camping permit from the helpful ranger at Big Creek, check with him about where to leave your vehicle. For car shuttling service, write Mr. W. Hocksteller, Waterville Star Route, Newport, Tennessee 37821.

To reach Big Creek, take the I-40 Waterville Exit No. 451 toward Waterville. Cross the bridge over the Pigeon River (badly polluted), turn left down to the road beside the stream and drive 1 mile to the Carolina Power and Light plant at Waterville. This plant, incidentally, is the company's largest hydroelectric power plant. When it went into operation in 1930 it was the highest-head plant east of the Rockies. It is also interesting because it sits astride a river that is not there: the dam is located 12 miles upstream, or 6 airline miles from the plant. A tunnel 14 feet in diameter was blasted through the solid rock of the Smokies to pipe the Pigeon River from the dam through the mountain to the plant site. The river comes boiling out of the tailrace, but above the powerhouse there is no flowing stream.

Continue on the road and pass a Forest Service primitive campground at 1.6 miles on the left beside the stream. Pass the old stone schoolhouse on the left at 1.9 miles. At 2.1 miles, at the park boundary, there is an intersection. Old N.C. 284 leads left into the village of Mount Sterling and then on to Mount Sterling Gap. To the right of the intersection old N.C. 284 leads to Davenport Gap and the A.T. The Big Creek Ranger Station is straight ahead at 0.2 mile inside the park. The primitive campground is located about a half-mile beyond the station.

(1) **BIG CREEK** 5.8 mi.

Gated roadway / Max. elev. gain 1,380
Start: Big Creek Campground, 1,700 ft.
End: Walnut Bottoms, 3,080 ft.
USGS quads: Luftee Knob, Cove Creek Gap, Water-
    ville, N.C.
Trail connections: Baxter Creek, Swallow Fork, Low
    Gap, Yellow Creek, Gunter Fork

Big Creek Trail follows the jeep road along Big Creek and
ends at the site of the back-country camp of Walnut Bottoms. This graded road ascends steadily through the valley,
passing the relics of an old logging operation, a spectacular
mountain stream and an excellent hardwood forest. It generally follows the route of the old logging railroad which
was improved by the CCC into a fairly good road. The
roadbed is solid, making for hard underfooting. Big Creek is
a large boulder-strewn creek of clear, cold mountain water
with an abundance of native trout for the fisherman. Camping is available at both ends of the trail. Water is available at
Brakeshoe Spring at 2.9 mi.

Big Creek Primitive Campground is located on the site of
the former logging village of Crestmont. Stone foundations
of the band mill can be seen at the lower end of the
campground. The campground is for tents only, with 13
sites. It is usually filled throughout the summer. It is closed
after 10:00 P.M., and no overflow camping is allowed.
Large groups should make arrangements with the ranger to
use the group camp facilities nearby. The Baxter Creek
Trail begins near the lower end of the camping area.

Trailhead: Drive beyond the gate at the ranger station for
0.5 mi. to Big Creek Primitive Campground, where parking

is available. The road may be gated at the ranger station during the night and in winter season; it is always gated adjacent to the camping area. The trail register is located beyond the second gate, at a spot overlooking the millpond of the old Crestmont logging camp.

Trail Details: The trail passes to the right above the campground. At 1.1 mi. on the right, about 200 ft. above the trail, is the Rock House—a perfectly formed room of solid rock. During logging days people lived in this natural opening until they found other shelter. At 1.4 mi. on the left of the trail is a large, deep pool of water called Midnight Hole. Mouse Creek Falls is located on the far left bank of Big Creek at 2.0 mi. Formerly a logging train passed directly in front of the falls. This area is marked by a trail sign.

At 2.2 mi. the trail crosses a bridge built by the CCC. Rainbow trout can be seen in the large pool below the bridge. Brakeshoe Spring is marked by a trail sign at 2.9 mi. The name derives from water falling over a locomotive brakeshoe that was placed there before 1918 by an engineer who enjoyed stopping his train twice a day for a drink. Look for salamanders and crayfish in the spring.

Beginning at 4.0 mi. mountain ramps (onion-like plants) grow above the trail. Mountaineers eat these wild leeks and hold an annual late-April Ramp Festival. At 4.5 mi. the trail follows a cement ford across Flint Rock Cove Branch, which is dry most of the year. Swallow Fork Trail (see p. 73) begins on the left at 5.2 mi., with a sign indicating Pretty Hollow Gap is 4.0 mi. away. (The correct distance is 3.8 mi.) One-tenth of a mile beyond the sign on Big Creek Trail is a bridge and the lower end of a back-country campsite. From there to 5.6 mi. the area is known as **Walnut Bottoms**, which was old Camp 4 during logging days. A horse hitch rack is located at this site.

There are some white walnut trees in this area. It also

has one of the park's few carpets of white fringed phacelia, which blooms from mid-April to early May, accentuated by green leaves and an occasional wild geranium. Just before sundown the flowers of the phacelia open their widest for a brilliant domination of the woodland. There are bears around; do not leave food out. Snakes are common—harmless black snakes and poisonous rattlesnakes and copperheads. Gnats may be a problem.

At the upper end of the campsite the road ends but the trail continues into the Yellow Creek Trail (see p. 78) and the Gunter Fork Trail (see p. 75). Walnut Bottoms is also the trailhead of the Low Gap Trail (see p. 74) and the Swallow Fork Trail (see p. 73).

---

(2) **BAXTER CREEK** (Craig Branch) 6.0 mi.

Foot trail / Max. elev. gain 4,142
Start: Big Creek Campground, 1,700 ft.
End: Mt. Sterling Tower, 5,842 ft.
USGS quads: Cove Creek Gap, Waterville, N.C.
Trail connections: Big Creek, Big Branch, Mt. Sterling
    Ridge

A steep climb from riverside at Big Creek Campground to the top of Mt. Sterling, Baxter Creek, is a beautiful trail which passes through a mixed forest. In the last 1.5 mi. the growth changes from hardwoods to moss-covered balsam and red spruce. The trail is not heavily used and is rewarding, but demanding, to hike. Carry water with you.

Trailhead: The trail begins at the swinging bridge near the lower end of Big Creek Campground. There is a parking lot.

Trail Details: The bridge was closed in 1971 because it was dangerously in need of repairs. The Park Service has replaced the old bridge with a permanent one, so that hikers can avoid wading or rock-hopping, which can be dangerous. On the far bank, the trail goes both up and downstream. Baxter Creek Trail goes right, as the sign indicates. Big Branch Trail, an old CCC graded trail which is no longer maintained, goes left. Big Branch is a very pleasant trail for about 1.5 mi. It immediately climbs a small cliff to give a good view of Big Creek below and then turns right to climb a ravine. This section of trail is kept open by many day hikers but the trail later becomes very overgrown. It intersects with the Baxter Creek Trail after several miles.

Baxter Creek Trail runs upstream, following Big Creek. At 0.3 mi. it crosses fields and passes old homesites. Most of these homes were built around 1910 for the people working for Crestmont Lumber Company. At 0.5 mi. the trail runs above Baxter Creek reservoir, which serves the campground below. It crosses two small streams and then climbs by switchbacks to a ridge.

The trail climbs steadily through cove hardwood forest. At 3.3 mi. water may be available. At 4.0 mi. after a sharp right turn, the trail arrives on Mt. Sterling Ridge. There, unmaintained Big Branch Trail comes in from the left. For 2.0 more miles the trail climbs Mt. Sterling Ridge through a lovely spruce-fir forest up to Mt. Sterling Fire Tower (5,842 ft.) at 6.0 mi. Excellent views are available from the tower. Mt. Cammerer to the north has a commanding position over the Pigeon River Valley. To the west, Mt. Guyot (6,621 ft.) is very imposing. A back-country campsite is located near the tower. (See p. 100 for the Mt. Sterling Ridge Trail.)

---

③ **SWALLOW FORK** 3.8 mi.

Horse trail / Max. elev. gain 2,180
Start: Walnut Bottoms, 3,000 ft.
End: Pretty Hollow Gap, 5,180 ft.
USGS quads: Luftee Knob, N.C.
Trail connections: Big Creek, Gunter Fork, Yellow
   Creek, Low Gap, Mt. Sterling Ridge, Pretty Hol-
   low Gap.

The Swallow Fork Trail connects Walnut Bottoms on Big
Creek with Mt. Sterling Ridge and the Pretty Hollow Gap
Trail into Cataloochee. It passes through a hardwood cove,
follows a trout stream and covers areas logged after the turn
of the century.

Trailhead: The trail leaves the lower end of Walnut Bottoms
campsite at 5.2 mi. on the Big Creek Trail (see p. 69) and
goes to the left. Walnut Bottoms is also the trailhead of the
Low Gap Trail, the Gunter Fork Trail (see p. 75) and the
Yellow Creek Trail (see p. 78).

Trail Details: At 0.2 mi. the trail passes through a downed
chestnut log measuring five ft. in diameter, which gives
evidence of the virgin timber that once covered this valley.
At 0.3 mi. on the left is a horse trough made of a hollowed-
out log and fed from a spring by a wooden pipe. This
spring goes dry at times, but 100 yds. on the right of the
trail is a more reliable one. The trail then climbs above Big
Creek, which can be seen on the right.
   At this point the trail is wide and follows an old railroad
bed of the Crestmont logging trains. Then it joins Swallow
Fork, crosses it at 0.8 mi. and crosses feeder streams at 1.3
and 1.9 mi. An old campsite, now closed, can be found
above the third stream crossing in a small clearing to the
right of the trail.

At 2.1 mi. immediately to the left of the trail there is a large boulder of white quartz measuring approximately four ft. long and two ft. high. At 2.5 mi. the trail crosses a small stream which flows down the mountainside over mossy rocks. This stream has speckled trout. It is also the last water on the trail.

At 3.0 mi. the trail makes a sharp switchback to the right and continues to ascend. At 3.8 mi. it reaches Pretty Hollow Gap and terminates at the Mt. Sterling Ridge Trail (see p. 100). The Mt. Sterling Fire Tower is 1.5 mi. to the left (NE), and Laurel Gap is 4.1 mi. to the right (SW) regardless of the trail sign, which is incorrect. Cataloochee Road is 5.5 mi. directly ahead on the Pretty Hollow Gap Trail (see p. 97). At the gap there is a wide clearing beneath the trees and logs for resting, but no facilities or water.

---

4 **LOW GAP** (Walnut Bottoms) 2.3 mi.

Horse trail / Max. elev. gain 1,240
Start: Walnut Bottoms, 3,000 ft.
End: Low Gap on A.T., 4,240 ft.
USGS quads: Luftee Knob, N.C.
Trail connections: Big Creek, Swallow Fork, Gunter Fork, Yellow Creek, A.T., Cosby Creek

---

Low Gap Trail connects the Big Creek Trail at Walnut Bottoms with the A.T. and provides access to Cosby and Mt. Cammerer. It runs through mixed hardwoods, and gives an excellent view of Pretty Hollow Gap and the Swallow Fork drainage. It also passes old homesites, a small old graveyard and the second-largest sassafras tree in the world. The trail gets moderate to heavy use by hikers and horsemen going to the A.T.

Trailhead: The trail starts at the lower end of Walnut

Bottoms, 5.4 mi. on the Big Creek Trail (see p. 69). It turns
right at a sign. Walnut Bottoms is also the trailhead of the
Gunter Fork Trail, the Yellow Creek Trail (see p. 78) and
the Swallow Fork Trail.

Trail Details: The first 0.7 mi. goes back down Big Creek.
At 0.4 mi. the trail runs below a knoll where there is an old
cemetery of nine graves on the left. (An arrow on a tree
points out the cemetery.) The world's second-largest sassafras tree grows below the trail near Walnut Bottoms. At 0.8
mi. the trail turns left to climb parallel to Low Gap Branch;
on the way there is a large spring nearby at the homesite of
Dan Gunter. The trail continues to follow the drainage of
Low Gap Branch. At 1.2 mi. you can look back at Pretty
Hollow Gap and the Swallow Fork drainage. At 1.8 mi. the
trail crosses Low Gap Branch, which provides the last reliable water. Then it climbs until it reaches the A.T. at Low
Gap. To the right (E) Davenport Gap is 7.1 mi. and Mt.
Cammerer 2.5 mi. The Cosby Shelter is 0.8 mi. to the left
(W). Straight ahead is the terminus of the Cosby Creek Trail
(see p. 216).

---

(5) **GUNTER FORK** 4.5 mi.

Foot trail / Max. elev. gain 2,440
Start: Walnut Bottoms, upper end, 3,080 ft.
End: Balsam Mtn., 5,520 ft.
USGS quads: Luftee Knob, N.C.
Trail connections: Big Creek, Low Gap, Swallow
    Fork, Yellow Creek, Balsam Mtn.

This is one of the park's prettier trails because of its
waterfalls, cascades and rich, diverse environment. At first
the trail follows a mountain stream but it soon leads out of
the rich cove hardwood forest, ascends a dry ridge and

finally ends in the moist spruce and fir forest at a high elevation. Excellent views of Big Creek Valley are available. The trail is adequately maintained, infrequently used and very comfortable to hike. Along the lower half, creeks supply abundant water. There are no camping sites on this trail, but there are good accommodations near either end—at Walnut Bottoms and Laurel Gap. This trail is the only direct connection between Big Creek and the Balsam Mtn. trail system.

Trailhead: The trail starts at the upper end of Walnut Bottoms camp at 5.8 mi. on the Big Creek Trail (see p. 69) where a sign reads "Camel Gap A.T., 5 mi. (Yellow Creek Trail), Gunter Fork to Balsam Mtn., 4½ mi., old N.C. 284, 6½ mi." Walnut Bottoms is also the trailhead of the Low Gap Trail and the Swallow Fork Trail (see p. 73).

Trail Details: The trail follows the right side of Big Creek, running concurrently with the Yellow Creek Trail (note the hairy alumroot growing on the rocks) until the trails separate at 0.5 mi.: Yellow Creek Trail straight ahead, Gunter Fork Trail to the left. Gunter Fork Trail soon crosses Big Creek on a slippery foot log; use caution. Beautiful moss grows on the rocks along the stream.

The trail continues through a flat cove, crossing four smaller creeks and passing stands of Fraser's sedge and the orchid called rattlesnake plantain. At 1.3 mi. the cascades of Gunter Fork can be seen through the laurel on the right of the trail. At about 2.1 mi., where the trail runs along the left side of a small ravine, a large white rock on the right marks the location of a small waterfall you cannot see from the trail. Scramble about 40 ft. down to see the beautiful 9-ft. falls crash through a cleft and into a deep plunge pool. The trail continues on to cross the base of a second falls at 2.3 mi. This falls is about 200 ft. high, with a sharp drop at the top and below it a long sloping area where a thin sheet

of water flows down. At the base of the falls is an interesting geological feature—a fault line cutting diagonally across
the slope. There is a conglomerate of knobby rocks above,
and very smooth slippery rock below.

Beyond the falls the trail soon crosses the last source of
water and begins a steeper ascent. It slabs left through an
area of many cherry trees and Dutchman's-pipe plants (a
vine having large, heart-shaped leaves). At 2.7 mi., as the
trail rounds the crest of a small ridge, there is a small heath
bald where mountain laurel and rhododendron grow. And
from here there are excellent views of the Gunter Fork and
Big Creek Valleys. The trail continues up a dry ridge, passing between two hemlocks about 3.5 ft. in diameter. Several small patches of brier may be encountered.

As the trail continues to ascend, the spruce-fir forest
gradually becomes predominant. Sphagnum moss covers the
ground. The trail slabs along the left side of the ridge for
some distance and at one point is very narrow where it
crosses a dry-wash area. It has little grade near the top and
at 4.5 mi. finally terminates at the Balsam Mtn. Trail (see p.
112). Fifty paces to the right down the Balsam Mtn. Trail
and a little over the crest, there is a very nice view of the
Big Creek Valley. At the junction, Tricorner Knob is 4.8
mi. to the right (NE) and Laurel Gap Shelter is 1.1 mi. to
the left (SE).

---

(6) YELLOW CREEK (Camel Gap) 5.2 mi.

Horse trail / Max. elev. gain 1,611
Start: Walnut Bottoms, 3,080 ft.
End: Camel Gap on A.T., 4,691 ft.
USGS quads: Luftee Knob, N.C. (trail not on map)
Trail connections: Big Creek, Swallow Fork, Low
   Gap, Gunter Fork, A.T.

This excellent, wide, graded trail connects the Walnut Bottoms valley to the A.T. at a point about 1.5 mi. west of Cosby Shelter. It follows the creek at the lower elevations and then an old railroad logging grade, passing through a second-growth forest. It provides access to within 2.2 mi. of the Maddron Bald Trail, which runs into the Cosby section.

Trailhead: The trail starts at the upper end of Walnut Bottoms, 5.8 mi. on the Big Creek Trail (see p. 69). At this point there is a trail sign reading, "Camel Gap, 5 mi." Walnut Bottoms is also the trailhead of the Low Gap Trail (see p. 74) and the Swallow Fork Trail (see p. 73).

Trail Details: The trail goes upstream along a railroad bed blasted in the rocks on the right. In a rhododendron patch at 0.5 mi. the Gunter Fork Trail (see p. 75) goes left and crosses Big Creek, while the Yellow Creek Trail goes straight along the main stream. (Some maps label Big Creek above its junction with Gunter Fork as Mt. Guyot Creek.) At 2.0 mi. the trail tops a bluff, and Mt. Guyot (6,621 ft., the second highest peak in the Great Smokies) lies ahead, while the Balsam Ridge with Luftee Knob bulks to the left. At 3.2 mi. the trail leaves Big Creek at its junction with Yellow Creek and makes a sharp turn to the right. There is a chestnut "lap," or downed treetop, at this point, which contains a den of rattlesnakes. The trail continues its ascent, offering beautiful views for the last mile before it arrives at Camel Gap, 9.5 mi. on the A.T. There is a trail sign at this junction.

Note: The new *Chestnut Branch Trail*, which provides trail access between Big Creek Ranger Station and the Appalachian Trail, has recently been opened up. It is 2.1 miles in length and is designated for use by both hikers and horses.

Cataloochee Section
(North Carolina)

Introduction

Cataloochee is one of those charming areas you don't want
to tell anyone about for fear it will be spoiled by popularity. Because it is isolated from the main tourist routes, it is
little visited by outsiders. Its character is not of wilderness,
however, but that of a pastoral mountain community. History and loyalty run deep. A few of the original families
lived in the cove as late as the 1960s; the Cataloochee
family clans still reside in the region and continue to use
the cove for worship and farming. Mark Hannah, whose
family settled there in the 1830s, retired from his job as
ranger of Cataloochee in 1971.

But the character of the area may not remain unspoiled
much longer. The Park Service has considered large-scale
recreational development for Cataloochee. It is building a
connecting road to link Cataloochee directly with I-40 a
few miles east of the park. Facilities for more than 500
people have been proposed, with parking for 300 cars, and
the usual amphitheater, visitor center, concessionaire store,
sanitary disposal station for trailers, etc. A proposed motor
nature trail would destroy the Little Cataloochee Trail. The
Park Service already uses one mountain cove—Cades Cove,
in the Tennessee section of the park—as a showcase. Cataloochee would have more developments than Cades Cove,
and in a smaller, narrower area. Unless the plans are modi-
fied, it is hard to imagine how it could survive intact.

The name Cataloochee comes from the Cherokee, *god-a-
lu-chee*, meaning "waves of mountains," or "wave upon

wave." It describes the wide expanse of mountain range viewed from the mountain crests.

The Cataloochee basin is bounded on the north by the Mount Sterling Ridge and the southeast by Cataloochee Divide. Both of these are major ridge systems extending out from the Balsam Mountain Range, which forms the western edge of Cataloochee basin, and runs northward to meet the Smokies Crest at Tricorner Knob. Within the basin there are many minor ridges, causing a complicated drainage system. The mainstream divides and subdivides many times, frequently changing its name. Thus the basin is not dominated by one major stream.

The trails of the Rough Creek and Caldwell Fork drainages run to Balsam Mountain and Cataloochee Divide, respectively. The trails of the Palmer Creek and Little Cataloochee areas form a complex which links with Balsam Mountain and Mount Sterling Ridge. From these ridges, there is access into the Big Creek and Raven Fork sections of the park. The Asbury Trail on the northeastern edge of the basin connects Mount Sterling Ridge with Cataloochee Divide; it is the route of Bishop Asbury, greatest of the traveling preachers.

Car camping is available at the Cataloochee Primitive Campground (28 sites and four pit toilets) on the Cataloochee Road. The campground is open spring to fall and may be full on weekends during the summer. Six backcountry campsites are located in this section—at Spruce Mountain, Mount Sterling, Pretty Hollow, Palmer Creek, Caldwell Fork and Rough Fork. (Pretty Hollow and Palmer Creek are horse camps and may be closed to hikers; check first with the ranger.) Hikers from Cataloochee may be using the Spruce Mountain Trail and campsite, but that trail is really part of the Balsam Mountain trail system and is therefore described in the Raven Fork section of this book.

The trails of Cataloochee Valley are used more heavily

by horseback riders than any other trails in Great Smoky Mountains National Park. The low trails, therefore, may be somewhat muddy and there may also be odors of horse manure. The horsemen, however, are generally most considerate of hikers. Many horses will shy when suddenly overtaking hikers, or when hikers make a sudden move. If you will move off the trail and remain quiet until the horses are aware of your presence, you may prevent an accident.

A direct access road is being built into Cataloochee from I-40 but the completion date is uncertain. At present the entrance is via old N.C. 284, immediately south of the Jonathan's Creek Intersection of I-40. If you are approaching from the south or east, take U.S. 276 to Dellwood, North Carolina, and go right, continuing on 276. After 5.0 miles take the Cove Creek Road (N.C. 284) to the left. This turnoff comes just 150 feet before the entrance from 276 to the I-40 interchange. Unfortunately, there is no sign marking Cove Creek Road. Cove Creek Road is narrow and can be dangerous to drive. The pavement ends at 0.4 mile, where a side road comes in from the right, but go straight ahead and cross the creek. At 0.9 mile there is a small grocery store on the left, and beyond it a road branching left to Suttontown. Continue on the right fork of the road, pass a church on the left and begin to climb. After this point you will see a few mountain homes but no more side roads.

At 5.8 miles Cove Creek Gap is located; it is the beginning of the national park. The Cataloochee Divide Trail is on the left to the west, and the Asbury Trail to the right (east). The road descends and at 7.5 miles intersects with the new Cataloochee Road at Sal Patch Gap. Cataloochee is to the left (west) on the new road, and the proposed connecting road to I-40 is to the right (east). (Old N.C. 284 continues straight on and connects with the old Cataloochee Road at 9.8 miles, Little Cataloochee at 14 miles,

Mount Sterling Gap at 16 miles, the Big Creek area at 23 miles and finally Cosby, Tennessee. It is an exhausting road to drive.)

Turn left onto the new road into Cataloochee (a wide, two-lane, black-topped road). After descending, you will cross a concrete bridge at 2.8 mi., where the Old Cataloochee Road goes to the right. Down this dirt road the group camp is located, on land once leased for a dude ranch. Camping arrangements must be made with the ranger.

Continuing on the new road, at 3.0 miles on the left you will arrive at the Cataloochee Primitive Campground beside a popular trout stream, Cataloochee Creek. At 3.1 miles Caldwell Fork Trail begins on the left at a trail sign. At 3.3 miles on the left the Old Palmer Chapel Road begins; a sign indicates a horse trail. At 3.5 miles on the right you will see the ranger station, which used to be an old valley home. It was built in 1916 by Hub Caldwell, with beams of entire chestnut logs, and chestnut paneling, all cut from local trees. The surrounding fields are still cut for hay, and old rail fences line the road. At 4.5 miles Palmer Chapel is located on the left, and the old church graveyard on the hill to the right. There is an excellent show of pink lady's-slipper at the cemetery in the springtime. The Palmer Creek Trail begins on the right at 4.6 miles. The road continues for 5.5 miles to a gate, where the Rough Fork and Big Fork Ridge Trails begin.

---

(7) **CALDWELL FORK** (Big Poplar) 5.8 mi.

Horse and gated jeep trail / Max. elev. gain 1,360
Start: Cataloochee Primitive Campground, 2,640 ft.
End: Rough Fork Trail, 4,000 ft.
USGS quads: Dellwood, Cove Creek Gap, Bunches
   Bald, N.C.
Trail connections: Booger Man, Big Fork Ridge, Mc-
   Kee Branch, Double Gap, Rough Fork

Caldwell Fork Trail follows the main stream and thus is a
valley trail. It is graced with an abundance of flowers—dog-
hobble, violets, hepatica, bloodroot, May-apple, wood
anemone, spring beauty, trillium and Solomon's-seal. The
largest single-stem rhododendron in the park can be seen
from this trail, as well as large hemlocks and maples.

This trail provides the only access to Booger Man Trail,
and also has connections leading to Rough Fork and the
ridges of Cataloochee Divide and Balsam Mtn. It is named
after one of the families who settled the valley. Three of
the houses built by the Caldwells are still standing.

Note: there is a new back-country campsite, Caldwell
Fork, located at approximately 4.4 mi. along this trail.

Trailhead: The trail starts on the left side of the new
Cataloochee Road at 3.1 mi., just beyond the primitive
campground. There is a trail sign; the trail register is located
to the left of the trail on the other side of the footbridge.
This is the longest footbridge in the park and the first of 14
spanning the stream on this trail.

Trail Details: At 0.8 mi. at Den Branch on the left (E) is the
beginning of the Booger Man Trail. The trail follows the
creek, frequently crossing the stream and climbing, until at
2.5 mi. at Snake Branch the Booger Man Trail comes in

from the left. At 3.0 mi. the Big Fork Ridge Trail terminates on the right at a Park Service sign (see p. 94). On the
left at 3.1 mi. is the beginning of the McKee Branch Trail,
which is not marked by a trail sign (see p. 87). This area
might be used for a backwoods camp, but there is a better
campsite 1.5 mi. farther up the trail near the junction with
the Double Gap Trail.

At 3.3 mi. a cleared path on the left leads up to an old
roadbed with two graves nearby. Two men, Elzie Caldwell
and Levi Shelton, are buried in one of them. They
were killed April 1, 1865, by the notorious federal raider,
Col. George Kirk. Kirk, who had deserted the Confederacy
and been given a commission by the North, was at the time
operating with mountain guerrilla forces out of eastern Tennessee. He and his 400 cavalry and 200 foot soldiers plun-
dered Cataloochee and then advanced down Jonathans
Creek and into Waynesville, where they were finally driven
back into Tennessee via Soco Gap.

The open area along the trail is known as the "Deadening Fields." Owner John Caldwell killed the virgin trees
there by "deadening" them: cutting the bark from around
the trunks about 18 inches above the ground. He then
cleared the area so he could farm it.

The trail continues through this relatively open area
(watch for yellow jackets) to 4.4 mi., where the Double
Gap Trail begins on the left (see p. 88). (There is a sign.)
This section has one of the largest shows in the park of
wakerobin trillium, as well as white trillium, galax, partridge-berry, Turk's-cap lily, azaleas, Indian-pipe and wood
sorrel. The trail crosses Double Gap Branch at 4.4 mi. On
the other side within a circle of trees is a cleared area which
may be used as a campsite. Creek water is available. After
passing through this area, the trail begins to climb and is
known thereafter as the Big Poplar Trail. Old rotting fences
and piled rocks here and there bear witness to early farming.

At 5.0 mi. an unmarked trail leads downhill to the right into a heavily wooded area along a small creek. At 300 yds. down this side trail grows the largest of three yellow poplar trees, which has given this section of trail its name. It takes seven men with arms outstretched to encircle this tree at its base. In 1968 a vandal cut his initials on the far side of the tree at six ft. above the ground, and it bled throughout that summer. The scar is healing, but it can still be seen.

Big Poplar Trail climbs gradually and circles to the right, passing areas of rich, old-growth timber, until it terminates at the Rough Fork Trail. The Cataloochee Road head is 3.8 mi. to the right on the Rough Fork Trail. To the left is Paul's Gap on Balsam Mtn.

---

(8) **BOOGER MAN** 3.8 mi.

Horse trail / Max. elev. gain 900
Start: Caldwell Fork Trail, 0.8 mi., 2,700 ft.
End: Caldwell Fork Trail, 2.5 mi., 3,000 ft.
USGS quads: Dellwood, N.C. (trail not on map)
Trail connections: Caldwell Fork

Booger Man is a side loop off the Caldwell Fork Trail. It has no other trail connections. In many places it is poorly graded and thus is more difficult to hike than others in this watershed. But it probably offers the best stand of poplars in the park—one poplar measures 6 ft. in diameter and 60 ft. to its first branch. Additionally, there are large oaks and chestnut trees, and an excellent display of rhododendron and laurel.

The trail is named after one Robert Palmer. As a youngster he was extremely shy and when asked his name at school, hid his face on his desk and replied, "Booger Man." So he became known as the Booger Man. It is said that he wanted to get away from the "crowded" valley; using hand tools he later built a road to his home on the mountainside. He never allowed the woods on his land to be cut during the logging days, which accounts for the excellent display of mature hardwoods. Booger Man Trail generally follows Palmer's hand-built road. It was restored by the Youth Conservation Corps.

Trailhead: The trail begins at 0.8 mi. on the Caldwell Fork Trail and ends at 2.5 mi. on that same trail. There are no signs to identify the Booger Man Trail at either spot, so both entrance and exit can be easily missed.

Trail Details: The trail leaves Caldwell Fork on the left, swings along the side of the mountain back toward the north, again turns south, and continues climbing. Robert Palmer built his house in a small clearing at 2.0 mi. Just before the clearing, as the trail tops the ridge, an old manway runs left to Panther Springs Gap at the park boundary. This is presently grown over. Near 3.0 mi. Booger Man Trail joins the drainage of Snake Branch, and descends 0.8 mi., passing the remains of an old barn building and a log house built by Carson Messer. At 3.8 mi. it rejoins the Caldwell Fork Trail.

---

 9 McKEE BRANCH 2.5 mi.

Horse trail / Max. elev. gain 1,710
Start: Caldwell Fork Trail, 3,090 ft.
End: Cataloochee Divide Trail, 4,800 ft.
USGS quads: Dellwood, N.C. (trail not on map)
Trail connections: Caldwell Fork, Big Fork Ridge, Cataloochee Divide

---

The residents of Caldwell Fork used this trail for years as a passway to Hemphill and Waynesville. It still provides the shortest route into the park from Maggie Valley and Jonathan's Creek trails, and is a major connection between the Caldwell Fork Valley and Cataloochee Divide ridge. It passes through pleasant forest, rhododendrons and wildflowers.

Trailhead: At 3.1 mi. on the Caldwell Fork Trail (see p. 84), this trail runs up a wide, grassy path to the southeast. There is no trail sign. The Big Fork Ridge Trail ends 0.1 mi. down the Caldwell Fork Trail (see p. 94).

Trail Details: To the left of the trail at 0.4 mi. is the roof of an early farm building; note the split shingles. The trail climbs the mountainside with only one switchback. Above this switchback the trail crosses a stream which provides the last water on the trail. After a steep climb, the trail slabs the right side of the mountain and comes out at Purchase Gap, where it terminates at the Cataloochee Divide Trail at 4.9 mi. on that trail (see p. 90). There is a rail fence between the park and private property; through a gateway is the trail to Purchase Knob. There is no trail sign.

---

10 DOUBLE GAP 2.2 mi.

Horse trail / Max. elev. gain 1,800
Start: Caldwell Fork Trail, 3,160 ft.
End: Double Gap on Cataloochee Divide, 4,960 ft.
USGS quads: Dellwood, N.C. (trail not on map)
Trail connections: Caldwell Fork, Cataloochee Divide

This trail passes through a very beautiful forest of many large oaks and poplar. Two superior trees (selected for their qualities as timber producing trees, *not* for their size) have been marked by the TVA Forestry Division, which will develop seed stock from them. This trail connects the valley trail, Caldwell Fork, with the Cataloochee Divide ridge trail.

Trailhead: The trail leaves the Caldwell Fork Trail (see p. 84) at 4.4 mi. and goes to the left (SW). Double Gap Branch is on the right as you enter this trail.

Trail Details: At 0.4 mi. the trail crosses the creek, and at 0.5 mi. to the left of the trail grows the first of the superior trees. It is marked by a line of green paint 2 feet above the ground. This is a northern red oak with a diameter of 5.5 ft. It measures 80 ft. to the first limb and 170 ft. to the top. Immediately beyond the tree is a creek crossing, after which the trail climbs the mountain.

At 1.8 mi. there is a spring. At 1.9 mi. to the right of the trail and 20 ft. below a 30-ft. rock, grows an outstanding black cherry tree. It is marked by another green line, and a metal tag identifies it as "TVA Superior Tree SP 2116." Measuring 11 ft. in circumference and 60 ft. to the first limb, it may amount to more board feet than any other cherry tree in the park.

At 2.2 mi. the trail terminates at the Cataloochee Divide Trail at Double Gap, at 6.2 mi. on that trail. The spot is marked by a trail sign and trail register. A wire gate gives entrance into Cataloochee Ranch, a privately owned ranch and ski area.

---

(11) **CATALOOCHEE DIVIDE** (Boundary, Hemphill
         Bald) 11.5 mi.

Horse trail / Max. elev. gain 1,470
Start: Cove Creek Gap, 4,070 ft.
End: Paul's Gap, 5,130 ft.
USGS quads: Cove Creek, Bunches Bald, Dellwood,
    N.C.
Trail connections: Asbury, McKee Branch, Double
    Gap, Spruce Mtn., Rough Fork

This is a trail to hike for especially good views of fall color.
It follows along a high ridge and provides views into Cataloochee Valley on the right, and Jonathan's Creek and
Maggie Valley on the left. The trail is the route of the
proposed Circle the Smokies Road. The middle section of
the trail is heavily used by horses and may be muddy.

Trailhead: The trailhead is located at Cove Creek Gap
where old N.C. 284 enters the park, 5.8 mi. from I-40.
Parking is limited at the gap; two or three cars at most can
be parked alongside the narrow dirt road. There is a trail
sign and a trail register. This is also the trailhead of the
Asbury Trail (see p. 103).

Trail Details: The trail starts in a southwesterly direction
from the trailhead. After a slow ascent for 1.3 mi., it
descends to Panther Spring Gap at 2.1 mi. There is water
here on the west side of the trail, 100 ft. from a gate in the
fence of the park boundary. (No sign.) Panther Spring was
named for the panthers that once roamed this area and
were said to scream like women in distress. The trail continues a slow climb, generally following the park boundary. At
4.9 mi. the McKee Branch Trail terminates from the right,
coming in from Caldwell Fork (see p. 87). To the left is a

gate which leads to Purchase Knob and Maggie Valley.

The trail follows a split-rail fence marking the park boundary, and passes near a private home. At 6.2 mi. it reaches Double Gap, where Double Gap Trail enters from the right and a trail to Cataloochee Ranch enters from the left. There is a trail sign and register. Cataloochee Ranch is a commercial guest ranch reached from Maggie Valley. Permission for camping on the ranch pastures may be obtained from Cataloochee Ranch, Route #4, Waynesville, N.C. 28786. There is a spring on the ranch property at the site of an old shack 0.2 mi. southeast from the park gate. Another spring is located about 100 yds. down the Double Gap Trail inside the park.

At Double Gap the rail fence is replaced by a wire one. The trail climbs to its highest point, Hemphill Bald (5,540 ft.), at 7.0 mi. The bald is an open pasture which gives excellent views to the south and east of the ranch and ski slopes of Cataloochee and Ghost Town, a "town" of simulated western shacks. Beyond Maggie Valley lies the Plott Balsam Range. At 7.6 mi. the trail passes through Pine Tree Gap, while descending gradually through hardwood second growth. It then resumes climbing and at 8.7 mi. passes to the north of Sheepback Knob, where another commercial development is in progress. At 9.1 mi. it passes through Maggot Spring Gap, where an early traveler thought a nearby spring had maggots in it. Probably they were nothing but juvenile aquatic insects. The spring can be found 0.2 mi. to the south, outside the park.

The trail continues west to 10.2 mi. at Garretts Gap, where it swings northwest and follows an old railroad grade to reach Paul's Gap at 11.5 mi. Paul's Gap is at mile 6.2 on the Blue Ridge Parkway spur road. At this point the Spruce Mtn. Trail begins and runs north along the Balsam range (see p. 110), and the Rough Fork Trail goes right to the Schoolhouse on the new Cataloochee Road. Flat Creek

Trail ends 0.9 mi. south on the spur road; from there it is
1.0 mi. to Flat Creek back-country campsite (see p. 109).

---

(12) **ROUGH FORK** (Paul's or Poll's Gap) 8.0 mi.

Gated jeep trail / Max. elev. gain 2,380
Start: End of new Cataloochee Road, 2,750 ft.
End: Paul's Gap (Blue Ridge Pkwy.), 5,130 ft.
USGS quads: Bunches Bald, Dellwood, Cove Creek,
     N.C.
Trail connections: Palmer Creek, Big Fork Ridge,
     Caldwell Fork, Cataloochee Divide, Spruce Mtn.

This trail is a continuation of the road into Cataloochee
Valley and connects the trails of the valley floor (Palmer
Creek, Caldwell Fork, Big Fork Ridge) to the ridge trails
(Spruce Mtn., Cataloochee Divide). A corridor along this
trail has been omitted from the wilderness proposal for the
park, "with the thought in mind that future public use of
the Cataloochee area might be so great that an outlet might
become necessary," according to the acting superintendent
in 1968. The trail begins in the cleared fields of the valley
floor and passes two old farm buildings. It runs through
early second growth and then old-growth timber of mountain magnolia, hemlock, mountain and striped maple, red
maple, oak and poplar. Many flowers may be seen: wakerobin trillium, jack-in-the-pulpit, Solomon's-seal, Clinton's
lily, trailing arbutus, galax, yellow lady's-slipper, mountain
laurel, rhododendron, azalea and Dutchman's-pipe. Near
the end the trail follows an old logging rail bed and joins
the Blue Ridge Parkway spur road.

Note: there is a new back-country campsite, Big Hemlock, located at approximately 2.1 mi. along this trail.

Trailhead: The trail starts near the Cataloochee Schoolhouse, which is also called Beech Grove School. To reach it, drive down the new Cataloochee Road past the gated road on the right (the Palmer Creek Trail—see p. 95) and over a bridge. The school is on the right. At present cars are allowed to drive 0.9 mi. beyond the school, but the Park Service will probably put up a gate near the school. For this reason the trail description begins there.

Trail Details: Proceed down the road. At 0.1 mi. there is a spring on the other side of a footbridge. To the right a rail fence separates the hayfields from the road; the creek flows on the left. At 0.4 mi. the Hiram Caldwell house stands on the left and is reached by a footbridge. It was built at the turn of the century with hand tools and water power from Ugly Creek (now called Rough Fork). It is paneled in chestnut and has a fitted circular staircase and an upstairs storage room over the kitchen where flour and other supplies were stored to keep them from freezing. Occupied by a Caldwell until the mid-1960s, it is now scheduled to be torn down in the Cataloochee development plan to make way for a maintenance area.

At 0.8 mi. the Big Fork Ridge Trail begins on the left at a trail marker. Showy orchis can be seen along this section of the trail. At 0.9 mi. just beyond the crossing of a small creek, a park gate closes the road. The trail continues on the other side of the gate, crossing Rough Fork three times on footbridges. At 1.9 mi. it enters the clearing of the Steve Woody house, an old log cabin which was later covered by board siding. The house is maintained by the Woody family but is not safe and should be left alone. Additionally, a springhouse and woodshed are still standing. This clearing makes an excellent picnic spot.

Continuing to run between old rail fences and the creek, the trail passes through a grove of large trees where excellent painted trilliums grow on the forest floor. Then it climbs away from the stream (your water supply). At 3.8

mi. the Big Poplar section of the Caldwell Fork Trail terminates on the left (see p. 84), marked by a trail sign. At 4.1 mi. after climbing sharply, the trail makes a switchback. At 4.7 mi. it joins an old railroad grade and follows it to terminate at Paul's Gap. You will occasionally see railroad ties, nails, cables and pieces of coal along the way. The trees are mostly second-growth beech and cherry. At Paul's Gap the Cataloochee Divide Trail terminates on the left, and the Spruce Mtn. Trail begins on the right (see p. 110). There is a trail register, a parking area for cars and a bank for unloading horses from vans. Paul's Gap can be reached via the Blue Ridge Parkway spur road.

---

(13) BIG FORK RIDGE (Fork Mountain) 2.8 mi.

Gated jeep trail / Max. elev. gain 820
Start: Rough Fork Trail, 0.8 mi., 2,800 ft.
End: Caldwell Fork Trail at McKee Branch Trail, 3,060 ft.
USGS quads: Dellwood, N.C.
Trail connections: Rough Fork, Caldwell Fork, McKee Branch

This graded jeep road connects the Cataloochee Road-Rough Fork Trail with the Caldwell Fork trail system. It crosses Big Fork Ridge, a long, low ridge separating Caldwell Fork and Rough Fork. It provides a fine show of purple fringed orchid, galax and trailing arbutus.

Trailhead: The trail starts at 0.8 mi. on the Rough Fork Trail. It is marked by a trail sign.

Trail Details: The trail leaves to the left and crosses Rough Fork on a footbridge. The area to the right has been cleared and still shows the effects of farming by one Steve Cove about 1918. On the left bank beautiful purple fringed orchids are growing.

The trail climbs. At 1.1 mi. it switches back to the left on Jim's Ridge; at 1.6 mi. it reaches the high point in a gap. Then it begins to go downhill, with Rabbit Ridge on the right. At 2.5 mi. it switchbacks to the left and arrives in a clearing. To the right was the former location of the Caldwell Fork Schoolhouse, one of three in the valley. This makes a good lunch stop but is more heavily wooded than the ideal campsite. At 2.7 mi. the trail crosses Caldwell Fork on a footbridge and after a climb of 100 yds., terminates at the Caldwell Fork Trail (see p. 84); the spot is marked by a trail sign. The McKee Branch Trail begins 0.1 mi. to the right, although there is no trail sign (see p. 87).

---

(14) **PALMER CREEK** (Trail Ridge, Balsam Mountain) 4.6 mi.

Gated jeep and horse trail / Max. elev. gain 1,770
Start: Cataloochee Schoolhouse, 2,740 ft.
End: Balsam Mtn. Road near Pin Oak Gap, 4,510 ft.
USGS quads: Cove Creek Gap, Luftee, N.C.
Trail connections: Rough Fork, Little Cataloochee, Pretty Hollow Gap, Balsam Mtn.

The first part of this trail is a gated, well-maintained old road. Soon it becomes a horse trail and follows Palmer Creek, which was once called Indian Creek. Then it climbs Trail Ridge to reach the Balsam Mtn. Road. Along the way there are trail connections with Mt. Sterling Ridge and Little Cataloochee.

While in the valley, the trail passes hepatica, violets, white fringed phacelia, rue anemone, bloodroot, trout lily and wild geranium, and while on the ridge (at 4.3 mi.), a large bed of yellow lady's-slipper. The upper section of the trail affords good views of Cataloochee Valley.

There is ample water along most of the trail, and the fishing is good. A horse camp is located 0.2 mi. from the trail at Turkey George.

Trailhead: Turn right off the new Cataloochee Road at 4.6 mi., just before the bridge crossing Palmer Creek. There is a sign, a park gate and a parking area nearby.

Trail Details: The trail follows a road along the right bank of Palmer Creek, a beautiful mountain stream with rapids and falls. At 0.7 mi. the Little Cataloochee Trail (see p. 98) terminates from the right between young trees. There is no trail sign.

The Palmer Creek Trail then curves to the left, still following the creek. At 1.5 mi. it enters a clearing where there is a trail junction with sign and register. The Pretty Hollow Gap Trail goes straight on the jeep road. The Turkey George Horse Camp is 0.2 mi. above the junction on the Pretty Hollow Gap Trail. Palmer Creek Trail goes to the left across a footbridge over Pretty Hollow Creek.

The trail then climbs the mountain, crossing Lost Bottom Creek at 2.6 mi. and Beech Creek at 3.1 mi. (last water). It continues to climb and at 4.5 mi. joins a jeep road which goes to a rainfall gauge. At 4.6 mi. the trail terminates at the one-way dirt road running from Heintooga picnic area to Round Bottom. To the right (NW) on this road at 0.7 mi. the Balsam Mtn. Trail begins at Pin Oak Gap (see p. 112). To the left (S) at 1.8 mi. is the Spruce Mtn. Trail (see p. 110). The Palmer Creek Trail is marked by signs calling it the Balsam Mtn. Trail at the lower end and Trail Ridge Trail at the upper end.

---

(15) **PRETTY HOLLOW GAP** (Indian Ridge) 4.0 mi.

Horse trail / Max. elev. gain 2,190
Start: Palmer Creek Trail, 2,990 ft.
End: Pretty Hollow Gap on Mt. Sterling Ridge, 5,180
   ft.
USGS quads: Luftee Knob, N.C.
Trail connections: Palmer Creek, Mt. Sterling Ridge,
   Swallow Fork

The Pretty Hollow Gap Trail is noted for its very large
horse camp, called Turkey George. The trail connects Cataloochee Valley trails, via the Palmer Creek Trail, with the
Mt. Sterling Ridge Trail and the Swallow Fork Trail to Big
Creek. It follows Pretty Hollow Creek, which is a lovely
stream, and passes through a fine forest. An excellent bed
of pink lady's-slipper grows on the right of the trail below
the campsite.

The horse camp got its name from young George Palmer,
one of the valley citizens, and his capture of a wild, elusive
tom turkey. After many attempts George finally caught the
bird by building a covered log pen and placing corn in a
trail leading into it. But then, in order to get the turkey
home, George had to crawl into the pen with it. The old
tom was almost as large as the boy and put up a terrific
fight. When George finally reached home with his trophy,
he was covered with bloody scratches. Thereafter the name
Turkey George followed him through life and was also
given to the present campsite.

Trailhead: The trail begins at 1.5 mi. on the Palmer Creek
Trail, just before that trail crosses Pretty Hollow Creek.

Trail Details: Turkey George Horse Camp is located at 0.2
mi. It has two pit toilets, a hitching rack for 36 horses, two

metal storage cans, a wooden supply box, lean-to poles for
shelters, pole supports for the kitchen area and a campfire
circle.

Beyond the camp the trail crosses the creek three times
on footbridges. At 3.0 mi. the trail crosses Onion Creek
without benefit of a footbridge. This is the last water on
the trail.

At 4.0 mi. the trail terminates at the Mt. Sterling Ridge
Trail at Pretty Hollow Gap (see p. 100), where there is a
small clearing with logs for sitting. The Mt. Sterling Fire
Tower is 1.6 mi. to the right, Walnut Bottoms is 3.8 mi.
straight ahead via the Swallow Fork Trail (see p. 73) and
Laurel Gap is 4.1 mi. to the left, despite the sign which says
it is 5.5 mi.

---

(16) LITTLE CATALOOCHEE (Davidson Branch)
     5.0 mi.

Gated jeep and horse trail / Max. elev. gain 900
Start: Old N.C. 284, 3,000 ft.
End: Palmer Creek Trail, 2,920 ft.
USGS quads: Cove Creek Gap, N.C.
Trail connections: Pig Pen, Palmer Creek

Little Cataloochee is a small subbasin of the Cataloochee
watershed. It was rather heavily settled in earlier times. The
oldest buildings in the Cataloochee area, badly in need of
repair, can be found in the basin. The trail follows the route
of old roads that once connected Little Cataloochee with
the upper section of Big Cataloochee, near the schoolhouse.
It is also the route of the proposed motor nature trail for
Cataloochee Valley.

There are no regular campsites along this trail.

Trailhead: Drive 14.1 mi. on old N.C. 284, or 4.4 mi. past the intersection of old Cataloochee Road and old 284. The trail is a gated roadway on the left and is marked by a sign reading, "Little Cataloochee, Baptist Church 2 mi."

Trail Details: The dirt road descends into Little Cataloochee and crosses Dude Branch, where large hemlocks grow on both sides of the trail. At 1.0 mi. on the right is the beginning of the Pig Pen Trail, which runs to Mt. Sterling Ridge. There is no trail marker, but the junction can be recognized because it is a jeep-sized road at this point. (More information on the Pig Pen Trail follows.)

At 1.1 mi. as the road curves to the left, the house built in 1862 by John Jackson Hannah is located on the right in a cove about 100 yds. from the road. The porch has rotted away but the fitted side logs still lie in place. The original roof has been replaced by a modern composition material in an effort to protect what remains of the rest of the house.

At 1.5 mi. the trail crosses a bridge over the Little Cataloochee Creek and enters an area where there used to be an old settlement called Ola. The rock foundations and ornamental shrubs can still be seen. At 2.0 mi. on the left is the Little Cataloochee Baptist Church, built in 1890 and still maintained by local families. Behind the church is an old graveyard. There are pit toilets at Ola.

The trail crosses Coggins Branch, continues up a rhododendron-lined road and at 2.3 mi. reaches a clearing. To the right of the trail is the oldest house in Cataloochee. Built by Daniel J. Cook in 1856, it is now in bad condition: the wooden-shingled roof is falling, and the loft has rotted away. Only one-half of the puncheon floor still exists. The building to the left, made of flat rocks held together by mud, is the old apple house.

The trail recrosses Coggins Branch, becomes a horse trail and begins to climb alongside the creek. At 2.8 mi. it passes through Noland Gap and continues to climb until Davidson

Gap—3,820 ft.—at 3.2 mi. Then it descends until it crosses Davidson Branch. At 3.8 mi. it turns left and follows an old roadbed alongside the creek. An old split-rail fence lies above the trail. After 1.2 mi. of following the creek, the trail terminates at the Palmer Creek Trail at 0.7 mi. on that trail (see p. 95). To the left the Palmer Creek Trail leads to the new Cataloochee Road where the Rough Fork Trail begins at the schoolhouse. To the right there is access to Pretty Hollow Gap and Balsam Mtn.

PIG PEN side trail (also called Long Bunk Trail) is a connection between Little Cataloochee Trail and the Mt. Sterling Ridge Trail. It is 3.6 mi. long. There is a large white oak at 0.4 mi. and, later on, mature poplar and hemlock. During the first 1.5 mi. the trail passes through the old domain of the Hannah clan. Look for a cemetery, a spring and the remains of barns, smokehouse and corncrib. Following Dude Creek, at 2.4 mi. the trail reaches a grown-over area where the remains of a pig shelter can be seen. After that the trail narrows and follows the hillside to the left until it terminates at the Mt. Sterling Ridge Trail at 0.4 mi. on that trail. If you are hiking along the Mt. Sterling Ridge Trail and intend to turn off it onto the Pig Pen Trail, you can easily miss the junction because there is no trail sign.

---

(17) MOUNT STERLING RIDGE (Mount Sterling Gap) 7.7 mi.

Gated jeep trail / Max. elev. gain 1,945
Start: Mt. Sterling Gap on old N.C. 284, 3,890 ft.
End: Near Laurel Gap on Balsam Mtn. Trail, 5,540 ft.
USGS quads: Cove Creek Gap, Luftee Knob, N.C.
Trail connections: Asbury, Pig Pen, Baxter Creek, Swallow Fork, Pretty Hollow Gap, Balsam Mtn.

Mt. Sterling Ridge is a major side ridge extending northeast from the Balsam Mtn. Range to the Pigeon River. The dominant peak is Mt. Sterling, 5,842 ft. high, where a fire tower offers an exceptionally good panoramic view. The Mt. Sterling Ridge Trail ascends the side of the ridge to the top very near Mt. Sterling peak. From there it travels southwest along the ridge top, from which you can see Cataloochee Valley on the left and Big Creek on the right. The trail ends on the Balsam Mtn. Trail. Balsam Corner is located where Balsam Mtn. and Mt. Sterling Ridge adjoin, about 0.3 mi. northwest of the trail junction.

The trail is steep during the first 2.0 mi. but the remainder is easy to hike. There is a back-country campsite near the fire tower; Laurel Gap Shelter is located 0.1 mi. south of the trail terminus. Because of its trail connections with Cataloochee and Big Creek, this ridge trail serves as a major route to the Balsam Mtn. Range.

Trailhead: The trail begins at Mt. Sterling Gap on old N.C. 284, a dirt road. Leave I-40 via the Waterville Exit, Number 122, and drive south 2.0 mi. to the village of Mt. Sterling. There make a left over a bridge and drive about 7 mi. south on old 284 to Mt. Sterling Gap. At the trailhead there is a small parking area, a trail register, a trail sign pointing out the Asbury Trail on the east, and a trail sign and park gate across the jeep supply road to the west. Beware: a contributor to this book has had gas siphoned from her auto at the parking area.

Trail Details: The trail ascends gradually on the right side of the ridge. At 0.4 mi. at a flat grassy area, there is a post on the left side of the trail where a small path forks away to the left. This is the easily missed terminus of the Pig Pen Trail.

At 0.7 mi. the trail switchbacks around to the east side of the mountain and then turns left on the right of the crest. Wide views can be seen to the east and north. The trail continues to climb, entering hemlock and spruce forests. At 1.7 mi. water is available by the trail. At 2.3 mi.

the trail reaches the ridge top. A side trail to the right leads 0.3 mi. to the Mt. Sterling Fire Tower.

The tower is not in use because the Park Service at present does its fire watching by air, but the view from the tower is outstanding. Mt. Cammerer and the Smokies Crest lie to the north, with most of the Big Creek basin visible below. To the west are the Balsam Mtn. Range and Mt. Guyot (6,621 ft.). Big and Little Cataloochee valleys can be seen to the south. The Pigeon River gorge is visible to the east, as well as the road scar of I-40.

Next to the fire tower is a well-built, locked CCC cabin. A horse rack and back-country campsite are located in the woods to the left (W) of the cabin. Water must be obtained several hundred feet down Baxter Creek Trail. Baxter Creek Trail ends to the northeast just beyond a sign saying "Big Creek 6 mi., no horses allowed" (see p. 71).

The main trail continues west along the ridge, descending a little-used jeep road. It leaves the evergreen forest and at 3.6 mi. arrives at Pretty Hollow Gap. The Swallow Fork Trail leads to the right 3.8 mi. to Walnut Bottoms in Big Creek (see p. 73). The Pretty Hollow Gap Trail leads to the left 5.5 mi. to the new Cataloochee Road (see p. 97). A trail sign indicates that Laurel Gap is 5.5 mi. straight ahead; actually it is 4.1 mi. In the gap is a small clearing which makes an excellent lunch stop. There is no water, but there are logs to sit on.

The trail continues to follow the ridge. Beneath the forest, deep grass covers the ground in many places, and there is a good show of mountain ash. The trail climbs somewhat and then runs nearly level for the last 3.0 mi., slabbing the left side of Big Cataloochee Mtn. The trail is somewhat muddy. It crosses creeks at 5.9, 6.4 and 7.0 mi. There are several cleared views of Pretty Hollow to the east and Spruce Mtn. to the south. At 7.7 mi. the trail joins the Balsam Mtn. Trail (see p. 112). Laurel Gap Shelter is 0.1

mi. to the left (S); Tricorner Knob and the A.T. are to the right (N).

---

(18) **ASBURY** 6.9 mi.

Unmaintained foot trail / Max. elev. gain 1,620
Start: Cove Creek Gap, 4,070 ft.
End: Mt. Sterling Gap, 3,890 ft.
USGS quads: Cove Creek Gap, N.C.
Trail connections: Cataloochee Divide, Mt. Sterling
   Ridge

Methodist preacher Bishop Asbury, the first and greatest of the circuit riders, traveled more than 200,000 miles in his preaching, most of it in the Appalachians. In 1810 he journeyed from Tenn. into western N.C. In his diary he described a flood, getting lost and how glad he was to arrive at the Shook residence in Clyde, N.C. The Asbury Trail generally follows the path of that eventful trip.

The trail is rough, frequently overgrown and poorly marked. It is occasionally cleared by boy scouts. (From Mt. Sterling Gap it follows old N.C. 284 into Davenport Gap; that segment is not described here.)

There is a back-country campsite at the Asbury Crossing, and a Park Service group campsite, about 2.0 mi. upstream from where the trail crosses the bridge over Big Cataloochee Creek. You *must* make arrangements ahead of time with the Park Service if you wish to use the latter. To reach it, go south (straight) on old N.C. 284 just as the trail reaches the roadway at trail mile 3.8. Do not cross the bridge. Go right at the next road intersection and continue on until you cross a bridge over Big Cataloochee Creek. Immediately beyond the bridge turn right through a gate and go downstream to reach the camp. Spring water is available there.

Trailhead: The trail starts at Cove Creek Gap, 5.8 mi. from I-40 along N.C. 284. There is a trail sign at the gap. Parking space is limited to two or three cars. This is also the trail-head of the Cataloochee Divide Trail (see p. 90).

Trail Details: The trail departs from the road going north to climb the ridge. It follows near the boundary of the park for 1.1 mi. as far as Hoglan Gap, where the new road into Cataloochee may be under construction. Turning left, the trail follows the boundary and then leaves it at 2.2 mi. to descend northwest into Cataloochee Valley. Big Cataloochee Creek is reached at 3.6 mi. This is old Asbury Crossing; a back-country campsite is located 0.2 mi. downstream. There is no footbridge at the spot where Bishop Asbury crossed, so the trail goes left upstream for 0.2 mi. to old N.C. 284. Cross the creek on 284's bridge, continue on the road for 0.1 mi. and cross another bridge (over Little Cataloochee Creek). Two hundred yds. past the second bridge, the trail leaves the road on the right. There is a trail sign at this point.

The trail climbs steeply to the top of Scottish Mtn. At 5.3 mi. it passes a mound of stones on the right, marking an Indian grave. There is water nearby. At Scottish Mtn. the trail joins a Forest Service jeep road which delineates the park boundary. Go downhill on this road 1.1 mi. to Mt. Sterling Gap and old N.C. 284, where there is a trail sign at 6.9 mi. The Mt. Sterling Ridge Trail also starts there. (You can continue on old 284 to Davenport Gap.)

Raven Fork Section
(North Carolina)

Introduction

The Raven Fork section is located adjacent to the Cherokee Indian Reservation in the southeastern portion of the park in North Carolina. A Cherokee war chief, *Kalanu* ("The Raven"), once lived on the river that now bears his name. The area is rich in the history of both the Cherokee Nation and white pioneers, yet it remains one of the least developed parts of the park.

The Raven Fork watershed is bounded by Hughes Ridge on the west and Balsam Mountain on the east. Balsam Mountain is part of a major, 40-mile-long range connecting the Smokies with the Blue Ridge Mountains. Hughes Ridge and Balsam Mountain (and Hyatt Ridge between them, forming two valleys) run north, approximately parallel, and terminate at the crest of the main Smokies Range. The Raven Fork River drains the western valley; Straight Fork drains the eastern one. Straight Fork converges with Raven Fork inside the Qualla Cherokee Indian Reservation, and then Raven Fork flows southwest to the Oconaluftee River.

Although the Cherokee Indians once inhabited all of the Appalachian region of North Carolina, Tennessee and Georgia, the heart of the Cherokee Nation was the Smokies, and its origin was the Kituhwa settlement, located next to the present Bryson City. But as white settlers moved southwestward along both sides of the mountains, the Cherokees were repeatedly driven from their lands until, in 1819, they lost the lands of the Smokies. After that they moved south to establish a new capital in Georgia.

The Cherokees were a progressive nation, and had made many cultural changes in an effort to become accepted by the white establishment. Most Cherokees lived on farms, some in mansions. They dressed like the white settlers, built schools, developed a written alphabet, published a national newspaper and established a republican form of government, complete with constitution and legislature. The Cherokee leaders were well-educated and capable of holding their own in treaty negotiations and before the Congress. But all these accomplishments meant nothing when gold was found on Cherokee lands in 1828. Georgia soon annexed all such lands within that state, and took away the Cherokees' personal legal rights as well. Even worse, in 1835 a sham treaty was arranged by the federal government in which the Cherokees were to lose all their territory east of the Mississippi. All 17,000 Cherokees were to be moved to Oklahoma. Sixteen thousand of them petitioned Congress, to no avail. They were ousted by force, put in stockades, then forced to walk—in winter—all the way to Oklahoma. The government called this operation The Removal. We refer to it now as the Trail of Tears. By any name, it was murder, for more than 4,000 people died during the journey. About a thousand Cherokees who had refused to leave became renegades in high, remote places in the Smokies where no federal soldiers were capable of hunting them down. Many starved or froze to death. But some survived to become the nucleus for the Eastern Band of the Cherokees. They were later given money to buy the land that is now the Qualla Boundary Reservation.

The white settlers who succeeded the Indians have left behind both their buildings and their names in many places. One family, the Enloes, settled in 1805 by the confluence of the Oconaluftee and Raven Fork rivers. Abraham Enloe became a community leader as well as the father of 16 children. A North Carolina mountain story dating back to

the early 1800s maintains that Abraham Enloe was the real
father of Abraham Lincoln. Nancy Hanks, Lincoln's
mother, was said to have worked as a hired girl in Enloe's
household. She became pregnant, so the story goes, and was
banished to Kentucky, where she married Thomas Lincoln
and gave birth to the son they named Abraham. In 1899
James Cathey, a local historian, went so far as to interview
Abraham Enloe's son Wesley. Apparently there was a strik-
ing resemblance between Wesley and the sixteenth president. In any case, the beautiful Enloe Creek area is worthy
of being named for a president's father. Old Abraham Enloe's homestead is now part of the museum complex at the
Oconaluftee Ranger Station on the Newfound Gap Road.

The first loggers who came into the Smokies sought out
the best single trees, especially fine specimens of cherry.
One way they got them out was by attaching the logs to
slings and having them ride a high cable from one ridge to
another ridge where there was a road or a railroad track. A
local person remembers watching logs "sail" from Hyatt
Ridge across the Straight Fork Valley to Balsam Mountain,
where they were taken to the log camp at Beech Gap.

Today the Blue Ridge Parkway straddles much of the
crest of Balsam Mountain, and a parkway spur road continues along the crest for 9 miles into the park. The Spruce
Mountain Trail covers about 5 miles of the Balsams before
it arrives at a gap in the trail system. A dirt road must be
used for 2.5 miles. Then the Balsam Mountain Trail starts
its 10-mile trip to the Smokies Crest. The only trails leading
up the two major streams in this section are rough ones, but
there are maintained trails on Hyatt and Hughes ridges. The
Beech Gap, Hyatt Bald and Enloe Creek trails serve as con-
nectors between the ridges and streams.

There are eight places to camp in the Raven Fork section. There is developed camping at the Balsam Mountain
Campground on the Blue Ridge Parkway spur road. Laurel

Gap Shelter is situated on the Balsam Mountain Trail, and a horse camp is located near Round Bottom. Five back-country campsites can be found at McGee Springs, Spruce Mountain, Flat Creek Trail, Enloe Creek and Raven Fork Manway. Additionally, several private campgrounds are located along the Big Cove Road.

There are two major routes of access to the trails of Raven Fork. 1) From the Blue Ridge Parkway: Near milepost 458 a spur road runs north into the Raven Fork section. The spur road begins 2.5 miles west of Soco Gap (U.S. 19) or 11 miles from the parkway's beginning near Cherokee inside the park. At 5.7 miles on the spur you come to the end of the Flat Creek Trail. Poll's (or Paul's) Gap is located at 6.2 miles at the convergence of three trails: Spruce Mountain to the north, Rough Fork to the east and Cataloochee Divide to the south. Balsam Mountain Developed Campground is located at 8.5 miles. The paved road ends at Heintooga picnic area (9 miles, head of the Flat Creek Trail) where the Balsam Mountain Road (one-way, dirt) begins. This road leads to Round Bottom, where it connects with the other route into this section. On the way at 5.9 miles on the Balsam Mountain Road, a jeep trail on the right goes to Spruce Mountain. At 7.7 miles the Palmer Creek (or Trail Ridge) Trail goes right, into Cataloochee. At 8.3 miles you come to Pin Oak Gap, where the Balsam Mountain Trail begins. Round Bottom, the end of the one-way, is reached at 13.5 miles. The Hyatt Bald and Beech Gap trails begin there.

2) From the Cherokee-Oconaluftee area: The approach to Raven Fork is via Big Cove Road. From Oconaluftee Ranger Station, drive south out of the park and pass the entrance to the Blue Ridge Parkway. Take the next left, cross the river and go left on Big Cove Road. (From Cherokee, drive toward the park, take the first right after passing the Boundary Tree Motel, cross the river and go left

on Big Cove Road.) Once on Big Cove Road, drive under the parkway and through the Qualla Reservation. At 7.3 miles pass a small store on the left. The paved road ends in a "T" junction at 9.1 miles; go right up Straight Fork Road. At 1.3 miles pass through a park gate. Hyatt Ridge Trail goes to the left at 12.8 miles, and Round Bottom (Hyatt Bald and Beech Gap trails) is reached at 13.9 miles.

---

(19) **FLAT CREEK** 2.6 mi.

Foot Trail / Max. elev. gain 100
Start: Heintooga picnic area, 5,340 ft.
End: Blue Ridge Parkway spur road, 4,900 ft.
USGS quads: Bunches Bald, N.C.
Trail connections: Bunches Creek Manway

Flat Creek makes a good, easy loop trip for campers at Balsam Mtn. Campground. The trail runs from Heintooga Overlook to Flat Creek Falls to the Blue Ridge Parkway spur road, where a car can be used to complete the circuit. This trail is popular with day hikers because it is short and pretty. Along the way a connection can be made with the unmaintained Bunches Creek Manway. There was once a backcountry campsite about midway on the trail.

Trailhead: The trail begins at a parking loop, Heintooga picnic area, at the end of the pavement on the spur from the Blue Ridge Parkway. There is ample room for cars; toilets and water are available. From the north end of the parking area, bear to the left on a flat trail to Heintooga Overlook (5,340 ft.). You will see a spectacular view to the north, looking out over many different ridges and peaks of the Smokies.

Trail Details: At 0.1 mi. pass a trail sign and enter a large stand of spruce. The trail descends moderately to a trail junction with signs at 0.7 mi., from which the unmaintained Bunches Creek Manway leads right 3.7 mi. to Bunches Creek Road in the Qualla Reservation. Flat Creek Trail continues straight ahead, crossing Flat Creek on log bridges three times in the next half-mile.

At 1.7 mi. you will arrive at Flat Creek campsite, a large grassy area extending on both sides of the trail, with a hitching rack for horses. At 1.8 mi. a trail sign indicates that a side trail leads right 0.2 mi. to Flat Creek Falls. The main trail continues straight ahead, gradually going uphill until 2.0 mi., then descending through birch, maple and rhododendron, with several good views to the south. At 2.3 mi. the trail crosses Bunches Creek on a log bridge. At 2.5 mi. there is a footbridge crossing a small stream. The trail climbs moderately until its end at the paved spur road at 2.6 mi. A sign points back toward Flat Creek Falls. To the right it is 5.3 mi. to the Blue Ridge Parkway; to the left, 3.7 mi. to the Heintooga picnic area.

---

20 **SPRUCE MOUNTAIN** (Poll's Gap) 4.8 mi.

Horse trail / Max. elev. gain 840
Start: Paul's (Poll's) Gap, Blue Ridge Pkwy. spur road, 5,130 ft.
End: Balsam Mtn. Road, 4,820 ft.
USGS quads: Bunches Bald, N.C.
Trail connections: Rough Fork, Cataloochee Divide

This trail runs north along a section of the Balsam Mtn. Range and could be considered part of the Balsam Mtn. Trail. But local custom calls it a separate trail. Beyond Spruce Mtn. a segment of trail is missing along the ridge. Until this is constructed, you must use the road nearby to reach the next trail. For information on how to continue north on the ridge beyond this trail, refer below and see also the Balsam Mtn. Trail description.

The trail passes through a rich conifer forest of spruce and hemlock. White rhododendron, blueberry, laurel and azalea grow along the trail, and wild turkey and grouse may be seen.

There is a campsite at the base of the fire tower on Spruce Mtn., and good views can be seen from the tower.

Trailhead: The trail starts at Paul's Gap at 6.2 mi. on the Blue Ridge Parkway spur road. Parking space is available. There is no sign for this trail, and two other trails are present (terminus of the Cataloochee Divide and Rough Fork trails, see pp. 90 and 92), so make sure you get started on the correct one—the trail going left (N) onto the ridge crest.

Trail Details: The trail climbs through spruce and fir forests. At 1.0 mi. on the left is the wreckage of a light plane which crashed there in 1969, killing the pilot. The trail is lined with tall blueberry bushes. At 1.8 mi. it goes over the top of Cataloochee Balsam Mtn. (5,970 ft.), the highest point on the trail. It goes downhill to a gap at 2.5 mi., then climbs to Chiltoes Mtn. at 3.1 mi. At 3.8 mi. on the right is an old campsite which is seldom used because it is very damp. At 4.0 mi. the trail merges with a jeep road coming from Spruce Mtn. Follow the jeep road to the left, cross a spring and at 4.8 mi. the trail ends at the Balsam Mtn. Road.

To reach the Spruce Mtn. firetower, continue straight ahead on the jeep road when you reach trail mile 4.0. Down that road 0.5 mi. is the firetower. The surrounding area has become overgrown because the tower is not being used for firewatching, but it still makes a satisfactory campsite. The lookout station itself is built of old spruce logs, some of which measure two feet thick.

Alternatives for further trail connections include Palmer Creek Trail and Balsam Mtn. Trail. To reach these, go back on the jeep road to the Balsam Mtn. Road. From there the Heintooga picnic area is 5.9 mi. to the left. The junction with the Palmer Creek Trail (see p. 95) is 1.8 mi. to the right (N). Seven-tenths of a mile farther north on the road are Pin Oak Gap and the start of the Balsam Mtn. Trail.

---

(21) **BALSAM MOUNTAIN** 9.9 mi.

Gated jeep and horse trail / Max. elev. gain 1,640
Start: Pin Oak Gap on Balsam Mtn. Road, 4,420 ft.
End: A.T. at Tricorner Knob, 5,960 ft.
USGS quads: Luftee Knob, Mt. Guyot, N.C.
Trail connections: Beech Gap, Mt. Sterling Ridge, Gunter Fork, Hyatt Ridge, A.T.

The Balsam Mtn. Trail provides an easy hike along the Balsam Mtn. Ridge, the major side ridge leaving the backbone of the Smokies range. The grades are gentle and the trail is generally in good condition, although it may be muddy in a few places. During the winter Balsam Mtn. gets very high winds. As a result there are more tree blow-downs across this trail than anywhere else in the park, and you should expect an extreme wind-chill factor in winter.

There is a shelter about halfway along the trail, at Laurel Gap. Side trails provide access to Mt. Sterling Ridge, Cataloochee, Big Creek, Round Bottom and the Hyatt Ridge trail system. The trail terminates at a point near Mt. Guyot.

Balsam Mtn. was logged in the early 1930s by the Suncrest Lumber Co., which had a logging camp at Beech Gap. In August the first part of the trail has very nice displays of Carolina lilies and some rather productive patches of wild blackberries. During the autumn the last 5.0 mi. display a colorful understory of yellow, orange or red hobblebush.

In the course of its last mile, the trail crosses Mt. Yona-guska, named for Chief Yonaguska, or Drowning Bear, one of the greatest Cherokee leaders. In 1819 when the Chero-kees lost their territory in the Smokies to the white people, Yonaguska was one of the few respected Cherokees who was allowed to stay behind and live on a personal reserva-tion of one square mile at the Kituhwa settlement near Bryson City. There he became a defender of ancient Chero-kee customs. Later, in 1838, Yonaguska and his followers formed the nucleus of the Cherokee renegades who hid from the federal troops instead of walking to Oklahoma. Their descendants now live in the Qualla Reservation adja-cent to the park.

Trailhead: Drive to mile 458 on the Blue Ridge Parkway and take the spur road north 9.0 mi. to the Heintooga picnic area. Continue on the one-way dirt road (Balsam Mtn. Road) for 8.3 mi. to Pin Oak Gap (no sign). At the gap the road takes a sharp left before going down the mountain. A gated jeep trail that goes uphill slightly on the right is the beginning of the Balsam Mtn. Trail. Because the Balsam Mtn. Road is closed during the winter season, the best access to this trail at that time is via the Beech Gap Trail (see p. 124).

Trail Details: The trail climbs through hardwood forest for the first 2.0 mi. until it reaches Ledge Bald at 5,184 ft. Then it descends a muddy slope to reach Beech Gap at 2.3 mi. There is a sign there saying that the Beech Gap Trail terminates on the left, having run 3.0 mi. from Round Bot-tom Horse Camp on Straight Fork (see p. 124). The Balsam Mtn. Trail continues to climb through a rich spruce-fir forest and reaches Balsam High Top at 3.6 mi. (5,640 ft.). Near the top of the mountain the Park Service has cleared space on the right to give an excellent panoramic view of the Cataloochee Valley. The trail crosses the level top of the mountain and then runs downhill to Laurel Gap at 4.1 mi., where there is a trail shelter built in 1969 by the Youth Conservation Corps at the site of an old CCC camp. The shelter contains 14 wire bunks, an indoor fireplace and a picnic table. The floor is frequently muddy from ground seepage. Outside there is a fireplace with grill and a pit toilet is behind the shelter. For fresh water follow the side trail from directly in front of the shelter as it angles left through a brier patch, leads over a hill and runs down a steep, slippery bank to a small stream about 200 yds. away. Firewood in this area is sparse; dead wood from nearby fir and yellow birch does not burn well.

Past the shelter, the trail climbs slightly. At 4.4 mi. it reaches a Park Service sign indicating Balsam Corner. At this point the Mt. Sterling Ridge Trail comes in from the right (see p. 100). It is a jeep road, infrequently used by vehicles, and gives access to Cataloochee, Big Creek or Mt. Sterling. The Balsam Mtn. Trail continues straight on as a horse trail, slabbing the left side of Balsam Corner and crossing a small creek (a possible year-round source of water). The trail is quite level and easy to hike. Horse use is no more than moderate. In this area grows a scattering of yellow birch, beech and conifers. During the autumn the orange-red leaves of the hobblebush present a beautiful understory and contrast with the moss on the ground. At 5.2 mi. the Gunter Fork Trail terminates from the right, providing access to Big Creek (see p. 75). About 50 paces beyond the sign to Gunter Fork, off the trail about 20 yds. to the right and over a ridge, there is a cleared view of the Big Creek Valley. Notice the ground cover of wood sorrel and asters roundabout.

The trail continues through a muddy area of numerous blow-downs. Then it moves to the right side of a small peak and ascends slowly. There is a good view on the right into Big Creek, and then the forest becomes more dense, and the moss on the ground more lush. Soon the trail moves to the left of the ridge, going below Luftee Knob at 7.2 mi. (6,200 ft.). It traverses several groves of young balsam fir and spruce and finally reaches Mt. Yonaguska and a trail junction at 9.4 mi. There an inaccurate sign indicates Pretty Hollow as being to the left at 9.3 mi., but Pretty Hollow *cannot* be reached in that direction. The sign should indicate instead that the terminus of the newly opened Hyatt Ridge Trail is straight ahead. That trail leads for 9.5 mi. down Hyatt Ridge and gives access to Round Bottom and the Raven Fork areas.

The Balsam Mtn. Trail turns right and runs across a level area to join the A.T. at Tricorner Knob at 9.9 mi. The Tricorner Knob Shelters are situated about 100 yds. to the left down the A.T. The new one has 12 wire bunks; the old one has 6. This area is the junction of two major mountain ranges, the Smoky and the Balsam, and was given its name by geographer Arnold Guyot. Guyot, a Swiss scholar, arrived in these mountains in 1859 and guided solely by Robert Collins (toll collector on the Oconaluftee Turnpike) began his painstaking measuring and mapping of the Smokies. Despite his elementary instruments, most of his measurements were extremely accurate and have not been disproved by more than a few feet. Mt. Guyot, the second highest mountain in the park, is located about 2.0 mi. to the north of Tricorner Knob on the A.T.

---

(22) HYATT RIDGE 9.5 mi.

Gated jeep and horse trail / Max. elev. gain 3,200
Start: Straight Fork Road, 2,935 ft.
End: Mt. Yonaguska on Balsam Mtn., 6,000 ft.
USGS quads: Bunches Bald, Luftee Knob, N.C.
Trail connections: Enloe Creek, Hyatt Bald, Raven
　　Fork, Balsam Mtn., A.T.

The first half of the Hyatt Ridge Trail is used as a jeep road
by the Park Service trail clearance crew. The last half is
maintained for horses, but because it is not heavily traveled,
the footing is pleasant. The Hyatt Ridge Trail once extended to the very end of the ridge near Big Cove, but the
Park Service no longer maintains that portion. Today hikers
reach the ridge by going up Hyatt Creek to Low Gap.

　　There are no outstanding views along this trail, but any
amateur biologist should enjoy hiking it because of the
variety of trees. At first there are cove hardwoods; then on
the ridge a dry-type forest with laurel and oak. Just past
McGee Springs there grows an outstanding grove of large
hardwoods. The trail ends in a balsam fir forest which is
carpeted with moss.

　　The back-country camping area at McGee Springs receives only light use.

Trailhead: Drive along the Big Cove and Straight Fork roads
to a point 12.8 mi. northeast of the Newfound Gap Road;
or drive along the Balsam Mtn. Road from the Blue Ridge
Parkway spur to 1.2 mi. below the gate at Round Bottom.
There is a trail sign on the northwest side of the road (on
the left, approaching via Straight Fork Road). Ample parking is available.

Trail Details: The trail leads left from the road through
cutover woods on a rough jeep track. The forest is open

with wide views of Hyatt Creek and consists mostly of poplar and maple with an understory of dogwood, chestnut, fern and various wildflowers. At 0.6 and 0.7 mi. the trail crosses intermittent watercourses. The gradient is easy until 0.9 mi., where a moderate climb begins. The small stream at 1.0 mi. is the last water for 3.4 mi. The jeep road is deeply rutted in some places. At 1.6 mi. the vegetation changes to oak and maple with some hemlock. This slope was once logged, and the forest is just recovering; note the large grapevines. Then the trail climbs steeply to Low Gap on Hyatt Ridge (4,425 ft.) at 1.9 mi. The Park Service signs here are inaccurate: McGee Springs is 2.5 mi. away, and Tricorner is 7.6 mi. The Enloe Creek Trail starts here and runs straight ahead to Raven Fork and Hughes Ridge. The old, graded, ridge trail can be seen going to the left.

The Hyatt Ridge Trail goes to the right. It ascends rather steeply for the first 0.5 mi. and leads to a dry ridge where there are laurel, some rhododendron, and abundant galax and arbutus. The trail continues along the ridge and reaches the junction with the Hyatt Bald Trail at 3.8 mi. (see p. 123). (Note: the Park Service sign calls this Beech Gap Trail, but it comes from Round Bottom.) The Hyatt Ridge Trail continues to climb slightly along the left side of Hyatt Bald, then crosses a level area on the ridge to a junction at 4.3 mi. About 0.1 mi. to the left along a maintained trail, a sign indicates that the McGee Springs campsite is located 0.1 mi. to the right, while the Raven Fork Manway terminates straight ahead (see p. 121). At McGee Springs (5,000 ft.) there is a horse camp with no facilities except a spring and abundant firewood. Completely level ground is scarce, but there are enough flat places for several tents.

At about 4.6 mi., the Hyatt Ridge Trail passes through a grove of large hardwoods. In this grove to the right there is a large yellow birch measuring approximately 4 ft. in diameter. Several large maples and oaks can also be seen. A bit farther on, immediately to the left of the trail, grows a cherry tree of probable near-record dimensions—4.5 feet in diameter. According to a local source, this tree was a cull—not worth cutting during the days of selective logging. Past these large trees, the jeep trail turns into a horse trail. It gains very little elevation until at 6.1 mi. it passes through Roses Gap, where it makes a jog to the left and begins a climb through a predominantly hardwood forest. After straightening out again it slabs the right side of the mountain and finally reaches an elevation of about 5,400 ft. There it levels off along the ridge top and the trail becomes somewhat muddy. The forest now passes through a transition from hardwoods to conifers. Several large conifers can be seen on the left, and the rhododendron bushes become so dense that there is no ground cover. At 7.1 mi. the trail is very muddy and unpleasant to hike.

The trail begins to climb through loose rock fragments and at 7.9 mi. crosses a small creek. A second small creek is soon crossed; it is the last source of water on the trail. The trail continues to ascend through dense stands of small conifers with an understory of moss and hobblebush. At about 9.0 mi. some fine examples of large oyster fungi grow on the left. The summit of Mt. Hardison (6,100 ft.) is finally reached at 9.2 mi. There the trail levels off along the top of the mountain and is enjoyable to walk on, being of soft duff. Moss carpets the ground roundabout. At 9.5 mi. the trail terminates on Mt. Yonaguska at the Balsam Mtn. Trail. Tricorner Knob and the A.T. are about 0.5 mi. to the left.

(23) **ENLOE CREEK** 3.6 mi.

Gated jeep and horse trail / Max. elev. gain 1,200
Start: Low Gap on Hyatt Ridge, 4,420 ft.
End: Hughes Ridge Trail, 4,820 ft.
USGS quads: Bunches Bald, Smokemont, N.C.
Trail connections: Hyatt Ridge, Raven Fork, Hughes
  Ridge, Chasteen Creek

Enloe Creek Trail is the sole connection between the Oconaluftee and Raven Fork sections of the park. It also
provides the only easy access to the headwaters of the
Raven Fork drainage: down the side of Hyatt Ridge to
Raven Fork, then upstream along Enloe Creek to Hughes
Ridge. It passes through an area of great beauty, which
largely compensates for the poor condition of the trail in
several locations, where heavy horse traffic has created
virtual quagmires. There is a potential campsite located on
the east bank of Raven Fork.

Note: there is a new back-country campsite, Enloe
Creek, located at 1.0 mi. on this trail.

Trailhead: The trail starts at Low Gap, at 1.9 mi. on the
Hyatt Ridge Trail.

Trail Details: The trail descends moderately on a jeep track
into the Raven Fork drainage and enters an old-growth
forest with many large specimens of hickory, oak, maple,
beech, hemlock and basswood. At 0.4 mi. it crosses from
very ancient igneous rocks to younger, sedimentary ones of
the Ocoee Series (see Geologic History, p. 23). At 0.5 mi.
there is a good view to the east, and the roar of Raven Fork
can be heard. There is another good view at 0.6 mi. At 0.7
mi. a stream crosses the trail in the midst of rhododendron

and large hemlocks; note the interesting fungi. About 75 ft. below the stream crossing, the obscure Raven Fork Manway begins on the right. A blaze on a fair-sized tree marks the junction. Enloe Creek Trail continues on past large boulders and reaches Raven Fork (3,620 ft.) at 1.0 mi.

Raven Fork is a rushing flow of water filled with multi-sized boulders—some measuring 30 ft. in diameter. In the sandstone upstream you can see large breached potholes, some 7 ft. deep. The bridge that used to span the stream has been washed away. Fording is difficult at best and could be impossible at times of high water and after summer thunderstorms. Seventy-five to 100 ft. downstream on the east side of the river, there is a primitive campsite under a rock overhang with enough room to shelter three people.

After the crossing, Enloe Creek Trail becomes a horse path. It climbs easily through a rich forest, passing a tulip poplar on the left (riddled with sapsucker holes) and a clump of the rattlesnake plantain orchid, which can be recognized by its showy rosette of leaves. As the trail makes its way west, it passes through a boulder field (at 1.4 mi.) and some muddy places, making for difficult walking. Enloe Creek comes into sight at 1.5 mi. Two small falls can be seen at 1.6 mi., and a sliding shoals (on Enloe Creek) at 1.8 mi. At 1.9 mi. another falls is passed, and shortly thereafter a major tributary crosses the trail. At 2.0 mi. you must ford Enloe Creek, which will seem easy after having coped with numerous muddy stretches. After crossing, wade 300 ft. through another quagmire of mud. The trickle at 2.2 mi. is the last water for some distance.

Then the trail begins a moderate climb toward Hughes Ridge. At 2.5 mi. it leaves the valley behind. The roar of Enloe Creek fades, but there is a good view out across Enloe Creek Valley. The trail climbs the mountainside, making several switchbacks. At 3.6 mi. it reaches the crest of Hughes Ridge (4,820 ft.) and its terminus. Park Service signs indicate that the A.T. at Pecks Corner is 6.0 mi. to the right (N) by the Hughes Ridge Trail. Actually it is 4.7 mi. instead. To the left (S) the Hughes Ridge and nearby Chasteen Creek trails lead to Smokemont Campground (see pp. 138 and 134).

---

(24) **RAVEN FORK** 6.4 mi.

Manway / Max. elev. gain 1,700
Start: Enloe Creek Trail, 3,840 ft.
End: McGee Springs, Hyatt Ridge Trail, 5,040 ft.
USGS quads: Smokemont, Mt. Guyot, Bunches Bald, Luftee Knob, N.C.
Trail connections: Enloe Creek, Hyatt Ridge

This trail should not be attempted by an inexperienced hiker because it is extremely difficult and passes through some of the most rugged wilderness in the Appalachians. It is no longer maintained by the Park Service, is not graded and is impassable at times of high water. Nevertheless, hiking it may not be a solitary experience because an amazing number of fishermen and wilderness enthusiasts find their way along it. Fishermen created the trail and are primarily those whose use keeps it open.

It generally follows the Raven Fork with little net gain in elevation until it reaches the Three Forks Big Pool (where there is a former back-country campsite). But within the next 0.8 mi. the trail climbs a steep 1,100 ft. up Breakneck Ridge, which is appropriately named. Slippery moss and algae growing on rocks and roots make for further difficulties. The possibility of a twisted ankle, or worse, is very likely.

The Raven Fork watershed is primarily a hemlock-tulip-poplar forest with heavy rhododendron in many places.

Although this area was never completely logged, selective cutting did remove the choice specimens so that you will see only a few exceptionally large trees. Raven Fork differs from the adjacent streams (Bradley and Straight forks) in that it has not cut down as deeply in its upper sections, possibly because its rock base is more resistant to weathering. Whatever the cause, the Raven Fork area amounts to a perched watershed. Downstream from its confluence with Enloe Creek, it finally drops its water through a steep gorge.

Trailhead: The trail leaves Enloe Creek Trail on the right (N) at 0.8 mi. It may be found by watching for a blaze on a hardwood tree about 75 ft. past the first stream crossing on the Enloe Creek Trail. The trailhead is 2.7 mi. from the Straight Fork Road via the Hyatt Ridge and Enloe Creek trails.

Trail Details: The trail goes downhill to Raven Fork (3,740 ft.) and crosses Jones Creek, which flows into Raven Fork from the right at 0.4 mi. During the first 2.5 mi., the trail is frequently obscure and rough, going up and down and occasionally merging with the stream bed. After that it runs fairly level and is not so hard to follow to the campsite, although a modern pack frame may be difficult to work through the thick brush. The campsite (no facilities) is located on the left (N) bank of Big Pool. You should use only already-established spots for building a fire, and be sure to boil water taken from Raven Fork.

About 150 ft. downstream from Big Pool, the trail cuts sharply to the right (S) and begins the ascent of Breakneck Ridge. It is a very steep climb through hardwoods and then spruce and fir in the upper half. There is a beautiful conifer forest on the ridge top (5,440 ft.) at 5.3 mi. Wood sorrel (which looks like four-leaf clover) and hobblebush (or candelabra bush) form a rich understory. The trail then de-

scends gradually to a junction at 6.3 mi., where there is a
Park Service sign. McGee Springs and campsite are about
700 ft. to the left. McGee Springs is a horse camp. Its only
facilities are a spring, abundant firewood and enough level
ground for several tents. Straight ahead at 6.4 mi. Raven
Fork Manway ends at the Hyatt Ridge Trail (see p. 116).

---

25 **HYATT BALD** (Hyatt Ridge, Beech Gap) 2.9 mi.

Horse trail / Max. elev. gain 1,880
Start: Round Bottom, 3,060 ft.
End: Hyatt Ridge, 4,940 ft.
USGS quads: Luftee Knob, Bunches Bald, N.C.
Trail connections: Beech Gap, Hyatt Ridge

The Hyatt Bald Trail provides the quickest access to the
middle of Hyatt Ridge and the McGee Springs campsite. It
is a graded horse trail (although not heavily used by horses)
and climbs steeply for the first 2.0 mi. A Park Service sign
at the lower end of the trail identifies it as Hyatt Ridge
Trail; a sign at the upper end calls it Beech Gap Trail. The
trail passes through a second-growth, mixed hardwood
forest of young oak and maple which has grown in since the
area was clearcut just prior to the creation of the national
park. Watch for wildflowers—the saprophyte, beech drops
and Indian cucumber root.

   Hyatt Bald, near the trail terminus, is no longer a bald
but is now covered by a second-growth hardwood forest.
According to Park Service employee Frank Hyatt, his family once grazed cattle in this area.

Trailhead: Drive 13.9 mi. on Big Cove and Straight Fork
roads from the Newfound Gap Road, or go on the Balsam
Mtn. Road until the end of the one-way road at Round
Bottom. There are plenty of parking spaces there. The trail

begins on the road to the north through the gate, as does the Beech Gap Trail. Note: several maps show a camping area at Round Bottom, but the Park Service does *not* allow any camping there.

Trail Details: At about 100 yds., on the left, the trail passes a free-flowing spring. At 0.2 mi. the trail goes left from the road, where a sign indicates the Hyatt Ridge Trail. At 0.8 mi. where the trail jogs first left, then right, there is a small grove of silverbell trees. Climbing steadily, at 2.2 mi. the trail takes a sharp left at what turns out to be a false gap. At 2.5 mi. it seems to approach another gap but instead continues to climb and meets the Hyatt Ridge Trail at 2.9 mi. (see p. 116). Low Gap is located 1.7 mi. away to the left down Hyatt Ridge Trail; McGee Springs is 0.9 mi. to the right. The Park Service sign at this junction calls the Hyatt Bald Trail the Beech Gap Trail.

---

(26)   **BEECH GAP** 3.0 mi.

Gated jeep trail / Max. elev. gain 2,010
Start: Round Bottom, 3,060 ft.
End: Beech Gap on Balsam Mtn., 5,070 ft.
USGS quads: Luftee Knob, Bunches Bald, N.C. (trail
    not on map)
Trail connections: Hyatt Bald, Balsam Mtn.

This old CCC trail was recently reopened to provide horse and jeep maintenance access to Balsam Mtn. It is steep, and the jeeps have made it rocky and hard. It passes close by the Round Bottom Horse Camp. Camping may be permitted there, but to be sure, check with the Park Service in advance. On the trail, water is available from several small creeks.

At one time Beech Gap was the site of a Suncrest

Lumber Co. logging camp; note several railroad grade
ing out along the topographical contours from the gap.
notice the proliferation of the American beech tree, which
has given the gap its name. One authority believes that the
beech has more ability to withstand strong winds than
other trees do, and that this accounts for the predominance
of the beech in high windy gaps.

Trailhead: Drive to Round Bottom, 13.9 mi. on Big Cove
and Straight Fork roads from the Newfound Gap Road, or
go to the end of the Balsam Mtn. Road from the Blue Ridge
Parkway spur. Ample parking is available at Round Bottom.
The trail begins on the gated road on the north side of the
area, as does the Hyatt Bald Trail.

Trail Details: At about 100 yds., on the left, the trail passes
a free-flowing spring. At 0.2 mi. the Hyatt Bald Trail leads
to the left; the Beech Gap Trail continues on the road. Just
past that spot, the road crosses Straight Fork. There is no
bridge, so you can expect to get wet at least to the ankles.
Continue on the road. At 0.4 mi. it curves to the right, and
just beyond that, a jeep trail leaves the road on the left (no
sign). About 300 ft. down the jeep trail, the Beech Gap
Trail departs on the right (again no sign), while a side trail
goes straight for about 200 ft. to the Round Bottom Horse
Camp. At the horse camp there are pole frames for two
lean-to's which will shelter six people each; also a table,
fireplace with grill, pit toilet and horse-hitching rack. Note:
the Park Service may not be willing to issue a camping
permit for this area.

Back on Beech Gap Trail, climb through a small lush
cove and cross a small creek. The trail then slabs the left
side of a ridge until at about 3.0 mi. it reaches Beech Gap
and terminates at the Balsam Mtn. Trail (see p. 112). Pin Oak
Gap is 2.3 mi. to the right (S), and Laurel Gap is 1.8 mi. to
the left (N).

Oconaluftee Section
(North Carolina)

Introduction

The word *Oconaluftee* means "by the river" in the Cherokee language. The Indians applied it to a series of small
Cherokee villages located on the banks of the impressive
river flowing southeastward from Newfound Gap in nearly
a straight line to the present-day Smokemont and then
south to the town of Cherokee. Gaining volume along the
way from several tributaries, notably the Raven Fork, it
eventually flows into the Tuckasegee River at a spot southwest of Cherokee. White settlers adopted *Oconaluftee* as
the name of the river itself. That straight upper section of
the river (from Newfound Gap to Smokemont) follows
along the location of the Oconaluftee Fault. This fracture
in the earth's crust created shattered rocks that were more
easily eroded, and so the Oconaluftee Valley formed along
the fault line.

The Newfound Gap Road follows the river upstream
from Cherokee to near the gap. Formerly called U.S. 441,
the road's name was changed when it was closed to commercial traffic. Despite that measure, traffic is heavy all
year around. On weekends in mid-October during the peak
of fall color, and in late April during the wildflower season,
traffic jams with hour-long waits are common. But in the
winter this road is always the first one cleared, and it can be
counted on except under very unusual conditions.

The Oconaluftee watershed is headed by Newfound Gap,
Mount Kephart and Pecks Corner. Thomas Divide is on the
west and Hughes Ridge on the east. Bradley Fork and the
Oconaluftee River are the major streams.

Many early pioneers settled in the river valleys in the Smokies. The soil was fertile, and the rivers provided them with good travel routes. In the late 1790s, the Hughes and Mingus families settled in the Oconaluftee Valley. John Mingus emigrated from Germany to establish his family along the creek which now bears his name. He later built a successful gristmill. The mill has now been restored and is open to the public. In 1805 Abraham Enloe made his homestead near the spot where the Raven Fork flows into the Oconaluftee. Enloe's farm is now part of the Pioneer Museum at the Oconaluftee Ranger Station on the New-found Gap Road. Other settlers—Bradley, Beck and Hyatt—gave their names to various localities nearby. Chasteen Creek, for instance, was named after Chastain Reagan, a colorful mountaineer and a natural hunter and trapper.

In 1831 the North Carolina General Assembly author-ized the Oconalufty Turnpike Company to build a wagon road up the Oconaluftee River and over the Smokies Crest to Sevierville, Tennessee, and one Will Thomas, a white man who had been appointed a Cherokee chief, set to work on the project. Although the Tennessee portion was not com-pleted until much later, the North Carolina section was soon being used for moving livestock over the mountain. Mount Collins and Collins Creek are named after toll collec-tor Robert Collins, who charged two cents per head of cattle traveling over the crest and later guided geographer Arnold Guyot through the mountains.

Despite the existence of the "turnpike," the valley changed very little until about 1900 when logging compa-nies moved into the area. First the Montvale Lumber Com-pany logged partway up the Oconaluftee Valley, using tracks made of wood. Then in 1917 the Champion Fibre Company logged almost the entire distance to Newfound Gap and soon acquired ownership of more than 90,000 acres in the heart of the mountains. A new community grew up around a large band mill in Smokemont. But in the end, getting the logs down from the mountains became uneconomical, and logging operations slowed to a halt. Fortunately, enough unscarred land remained to form the nucleus of a national park.

The Newfound Gap Road provides all vehicular access to the Oconaluftee trails and splits the trail system into two sections. On the east side of the highway, the Bradley Fork Trail serves as a focal point, with side trails running east to Hughes Ridge and west to Richland Mountain. Kephart Prong has its own set of three trails which connect with the Appalachian Trail and Bradley Fork. On the west side of the highway, four trails connect with the Thomas Divide Trail, which starts in Deep Creek and therefore is described in the Deep Creek section of this book. Camping is possible at the highly developed Smokemont complex, the Kephart Prong Shelter, Cabin Flats Horse Camp, and several back-country campsites.

Leaving Cherokee, the Newfound Gap Road (old U.S. 441) runs 3.5 miles north to the Oconaluftee Ranger Station. Mingus Creek Mill stands 0.5 mile farther up the road. At 3.2 miles past the ranger station, the road passes the entrance to Smokemont Campground and the Newton Bald Trail. At 5.3 miles past the ranger station, Collins Creek picnic area is located on the left; at 6.9 miles the Kephart Prong parking area is on the right. Soon after, at 7.1 miles, the Kanati Fork Trail begins on the left of the highway. Then the road doubles back on itself and starts to climb in earnest. At 12.0 mi. the Thomas Divide Trail terminates on the left. At 13.7 miles the Deep Creek Trail terminates, also on the left. The Clingmans Dome Road runs left at 15.3 miles. Newfound Gap is finally reached at 15.4 miles.

---

27 BRADLEY FORK (Ri

Gated roadway / Max. elev. g
Start: Upper end Smokemon
End: Cabin Flats, 3,140 ft.
USGS quads: Smokemont, N.(
Trail connections: Smokemont
   Taywa Creek, Richland Mtn

130

Fork. You wi
walnut, red
a view of
the tr
wo

Bradley Fork Trail runs from Smokemont Campground to a spot near the headwaters of Bradley Fork. It involves very little climbing and provides access to several easy trails which allow a short day hike or an overnight loop back to Smokemont. Summer hikers on the trail, which follows a service road for most of its length, will be passed around noontime any day by an auto caravan, for the road is the route of a popular nature tour conducted by the Park Service.

There is back-country camping available at Cabin Flats and Chasteen Creek. At the opposite pole, Smokemont Campground provides the ultimate in camping development—problem bears, no wood, crowding, and movies. History buffs may visit the nearby Bradley family cemetery.

Trailhead: The trail begins at Smokemont Campground on the Newfound Gap Road, 3.2 mi. north of the Oconaluftee Ranger Station. To reach the trailhead, turn right at the Smokemont sign from the Newfound Gap Road, cross the Oconaluftee River, turn left upriver and park (ample space) by a gate at the back end of the campground. Park Service signs call this section of trail the Richland Mtn. Trail. This is also the trailhead for the Smokemont Loop.

Trail Details: Go through the gate (note the large pool just above it) and follow the service road parallel to Bradley

be in a typical cove hardwood forest of
oak, scarlet oak and poplar. At 0.5 mi. there is
Mine Ridge (N) and Becks Bald (NE). At 0.7 mi.
il passes lobelia, asters and strawberry bush. Box-
ds and plum trees mark an old homesite at 0.8 mi. A
rge "bench" boulder on the right marks the 1.0-mi. point;
just past it on the left is a scenic hemlock grove. At 1.2 mi.
the Chasteen Creek Trail begins on the right and leads 4.0
mi. to Hughes Ridge (see p. 134). At 0.1 mi. up the Chasteen
Creek Trail, there is a back-country campsite, equipped
with hut and table, one large and six small lean-to frames,
two picnic tables, two iron grills, a campfire circle and pit
toilets.

The Bradley Fork Trail continues to follow Bradley
Fork upstream. At 1.7 mi. the Smokemont Loop Trail parts
company to the left and crosses Bradley Fork on a 60-foot
footbridge. At 2.5 mi. the Bradley Fork Trail passes a
waterfall and a pool. It crosses Bradley Fork twice on
motor bridges at 3.2 and 3.5 mi. At 4.1 mi. the Taywa
Creek Trail begins, leading right on a jeep road for 3.6 mi.
to the crest of Hughes Ridge (see p. 135).

The Bradley Fork Trail (still being identified as the
Richland Mtn. Trail) leads straight ahead. Soon it crosses
Bradley Fork a third time. At 4.3 mi. there is another
bridge over Tennessee Branch and a waterfall on the left.
One hundred ft. farther, the Richland Mtn. Trail begins,
running straight ahead to Dry Sluice Gap on the A.T. (see
p. 136). The Bradley Fork Trail goes right and soon crosses
a small stream. At 5.3 mi. the trail ends at Cabin Flats
Horse Camp, where there are water, tables, grills and pit
toilets. But hikers must check in advance with the Park
Service before using these facilities. A permit is necessary,
and it may or may not be issued.

(28) **SMOKEMONT LOOP** 5.9 mi.

Foot trail / Max. elev. gain 1,240
Start: Upper end Smokemont Campground, 2,220 ft.
End: Lower end Smokemont Campground, 2,200 ft.
USGS quads: Smokemont, N.C.
Trail connections: Bradley Fork, Chasteen Creek

This is a pleasant trail of moderate grade providing a good
opportunity to study the characteristics of cove hardwood
and oak forests. It circles from the Smokemont Campground to an elevation of 3,460 ft. on the slopes of Richland Mtn. and then returns to the campground. The grade is
approximately the same in both directions. The first 1.7 mi.
follows the Bradley Fork Trail.

Trailhead: The trail starts at Smokemont Campground on
the Newfound Gap Road, 3.2 mi. north of the Oconaluftee
Ranger Station. The trail begins at the service road gate at
the rear of the campground (see the Bradley Fork Trail for
details).

Trail Details: Follow the gravel road along the east bank of
Bradley Fork. The creek forms a picturesque pool 500 ft.
from the gate. The forest is typical of cove hardwood, with
walnut, red oak, poplar and scarlet oak predominating. The
trail enters a stand of rhododendron at 0.3 mi., then enters
a clearing and descends to creek level. Another clearing, at
0.5 mi., offers a view of Mine Ridge (N) and Becks Bald
(NE) on Hughes Ridge. Asters, lobelia, and strawberry bush
are prominent at 0.7 mi. At 0.8 mi. boxwoods and plum
trees mark an old homesite. A large "bench" boulder on the
right marks the end of 1.0 mi. Just beyond, between the
road and creek, is a scenic hemlock grove. The trail crosses
Chasteen Creek to reach, at 1.2 mi., a grassy meadow where
the Chasteen Creek Trail begins, and runs to the right.

Continuing to follow Bradley Fork, the road narrows and begins a gradual climb through hemlock and rhododendron. At 1.7 mi. it reaches a trail junction and sign: Bradley Fork Trail straight ahead, Smokemont Loop Trail to the left. The latter runs downhill and across Bradley Fork on a long footbridge. Shield ferns grow on the stream bank. After 500 ft. there is another "bridge," and the trail begins a moderately steep ascent of the lower slopes of Richland Mtn. Dutchman's-pipe vine climbs high on the right at 1.8 mi. At 1.9 mi. the trail leaves the branch (last water for 2.2 mi.). It passes through a heavy growth of hemlock, cherry and birch at 2.0 mi. After two switchbacks the forest community changes to pignut hickory, scarlet oak, white oak, sourwood and poplar. A downed chestnut log beside a mountain magnolia at 2.2 mi. makes a good resting spot.

At 2.6 mi. the trail is level, with Becks Bald appearing through the trees on the left (E). Then it climbs again briefly through typical dry-ridge vegetation—chestnut oak, scarlet oak, pignut hickory and laurel. Here also trailing arbutus is common. At 2.7 mi. the trail reaches the ridge of Richland Mtn., which lies between Bradley Fork and the Oconaluftee River. An old overgrown manway ascends the ridge to the right.

From the sign at the divide, Smokemont Loop Trail climbs moderately to the left (S), with a view through the trees of the Oconaluftee River and the Newfound Gap Road. The forest is a chestnut oak-heath community, with the wildflower galax edging the path. A stand of pitch pine can be seen up-slope at 2.7 mi. The trail runs downhill briefly, west of the ridge line, climbs to 3,460 ft. and then begins a gradual descent back to Smokemont.

Many large chestnut oaks grow at 3.5 mi., and Dutchman's-pipe is again prominent. At 3.6 mi. the trail passes a large chestnut snag and many downed chestnut logs which give testimony to the chestnut blight that ravaged the forest

during the twenties and thirties. A number of small chestnut sprouts are growing here and there, but close examina-
tion of their bark will reveal the scars characteristic of the
blight. Meanwhile, pignut hickory, scarlet oak and chestnut
oak vie for the predominant role once played by the chestnut.

Several large locust trees can be seen at 4.1 mi. At 4.2
mi., as you continue downhill, mosses, wintergreen and
mountain holly are growing. The trail once again runs
opposite Bradley Fork, affording a view to the right (E) of
Becks Bald. It passes springs at 4.2 mi. and 4.3 mi. Past the
second spring, opposite a steep rhododendron-covered
slope, grow several yellow poplars, the largest ones on this
trail. The trail passes through several stands of laurel and
through a pitch pine-heath community at 4.8 mi.

At 5.0 mi. a 100-ft. connector leads to the right, through
a barbed wire fence, to the Bradley family cemetery. Most
of the readable stones commemorate Bradleys, but other
family names appear, such as Wilson, Matthews, Clover,
Harvey and Reagan. Among the older graves, marked by
severely weathered fieldstones, the oldest readable date is
1885. There was a burial as recently as 1925. Continuing
through white pine and pitch pine, the trail joins a gravel
service road at 5.2 mi. Bear to the left and pass two
maintenance buildings. The road first parallels the Oconaluftee River and then crosses Bradley Fork at 5.3 mi. on a
concrete bridge into the south end of Smokemont Campground. You close the loop by walking north through the
campground to the starting point, for a total hike of 5.9 mi.

(29) **CHASTEEN CREEK** 4.0 mi.

Gated jeep and horse trail / Max. elev. gain 2,300
Start: Bradley Fork Trail, 2,360 ft.
End: Hughes Ridge, 4,660 ft.
USGS quads: Smokemont, N.C.
Trail connections: Bradley Fork, Hughes Ridge, En-
    loe Creek

The Chasteen Creek Trail serves as a major connection
between Smokemont Campground and the Raven Fork
area. It follows Chasteen Creek from Bradley Fork to the
crest of Hughes Ridge. More than half of it runs on a jeep
road; the remainder is a graded trail with a well-maintained,
dug footway. Because the Chasteen Creek watershed was
completely logged from valley floor to ridge top, the forest
now consists mostly of second-growth oak and poplar. You
can camp at a back-country campsite located near the beginning of the trail.

Note: there is a new back-country campsite, Upper Chasteen Creek, located at 2.2 mi. along the trail.

Trailhead: The trail starts on the right at 1.2 mi. on the
Bradley Fork Trail (see p. 129) and is a jeep road.

Trail Details: At 0.1 mi. the trail reaches a back-country
campsite where there are pit toilets, tables, grills, a lean-to
frame and walnut trees. Following the right bank of Chasteen Creek, at 0.8 mi. it passes a 15-ft. waterfall. There is a
good view at 1.0 mi. The trail crosses a bold stream at 2.4
mi. At 2.8 mi. the jeep road ends with a turnaround, and a
graded horse trail takes over, climbing moderately. The
small stream at 3.1 mi. may be a permanent source of
water; at any rate, it is the last source on this trail. There is
another view available around 3.8 mi. At 4.0 mi. the trail

arrives at the crest of Hughes Ridge and terminates at the
Hughes Ridge Trail (see p. 138). Hughes Ridge Trail leads
0.5 mi. to the left (N) to meet the Enloe Creek Trail (see p.
119). To the right (S) Hughes Ridge Trail leads back down
to Smokemont Campground.

---

(30) TAYWA CREEK (Upper Creek) 3.6 mi.

Gated jeep trail / Max. elev. gain 2,130
Start: Bradley Fork Trail turnaround, 2,930 ft.
End: Hughes Ridge, 5,060 ft.
USGS quads: Smokemont, Mt. Guyot, N.C.
Trail connections: Bradley Fork, Richland Mtn.,
    Hughes Ridge

This trail climbs along Taywa Creek, a good source of
water, and connects the Bradley Fork Valley with Hughes
Ridge. It is a frequently used jeep road with some steep
places. *Taywa* means "flying squirrel" in the Cherokee
language.

Trailhead: The trail starts at 4.1 mi. on the Bradley Fork
Trail (see p. 129) with a sharp turn to the right. A sign
marks the spot. The Richland Mtn. Trail begins 0.2 mi.
farther up the Bradley Fork Trail.

Trail Details: The trail slabs around the side of Long Ridge,
climbing easily. It reaches a scenic overlook at 0.4 mi. From
there on it is moderately steep for the remainder of its
length. At 0.5 mi. there is a view of Taywa Creek below.
The trail enters a dense forest where there are frequent rock
outcrops. There is a bridge at 0.7 mi., and then two bridges
over Taywa Creek, very close together, at 1.0 mi.
    At 1.7 mi. the trail crosses a fourth bridge over Taywa
Creek, the last good source of water. Becoming steeper, it

switchbacks up the mountain. The footing is muddy, and rocks make it rough in some places. The trail reaches the crest of Hughes Ridge at 3.5 mi., and a trail junction in a gap at 3.6 mi. Hughes Ridge Trail (see p. 138) runs to the left for 2.0 mi. to the A.T. at Pecks Corner, where there is a nearby shelter. To the right it runs for 9.6 mi. to Smokemont Campground, with connections along the way to Enloe Creek and Chasteen Creek trails.

---

(31) RICHLAND MOUNTAIN (Dry Sluice Gap, Tennessee Branch) 4.3 mi.

Horse trail / Max. elev. gain 2,540
Start: Bradley Fork Trail, 3,080 ft.
End: Dry Sluice Gap on A.T., 5,380 ft.
USGS quads: Smokemont, Mt. Guyot, N.C.
Trail connections: Bradley Fork, Taywa Creek, Grassy Branch, A.T., Porters Creek

---

The Richland Mtn. Trail connects the Bradley Fork Valley with the ridge of Richland Mtn. and finally the A.T. In the course of its length, there is access to the Kephart Prong and Greenbrier areas. The trail gains most of its elevation during the first 3.0 mi., where the grade is considerable. Several large hardwood trees grow along the lower portion of the trail.

Trailhead: The trail starts at 4.3 mi. on the Bradley Fork Trail (see p. 129), just past a bridge crossing Tennessee Branch. There is a trail sign. The trailhead of the Taywa Creek Trail is 0.2 mi. away.

Trail Details: The trail climbs along the right bank of Tennessee Branch and crosses it on a bridge at 0.1 mi., within sight of a waterfall. Soon it crosses a tributary and at

0.3 mi. it recrosses Tennessee Branch on a tree cut down across the stream. Then there is a steep climb to 0.4 mi. At 0.5 mi. the trail again crosses Tennessee Branch. At 0.6 mi. it crosses a tributary creek near a poplar so large it takes four people to reach around it. Within 200 ft. the trail recrosses the tributary and continues up the left bank of Tennessee Branch. It crosses Tennessee Branch for the last time at 0.9 mi.—the last reliable water source.

Climbing with a moderate grade, the trail rounds the point of a ridge at 1.2 mi., coming into a maple-sourgum forest. At 1.7 mi. it passes through a zone of oak-maple forest with a few large specimens. The condition of the trail deteriorates at 1.8 mi., becoming rough where heavy horse traffic has accelerated erosion. Continuing to climb moderately, it reaches the ridge of Richland Mtn. and at 2.9 mi. the terminus of Grassy Branch Trail (see p. 142) on the left. There is a small stream 0.2 mi. down that trail.

The Richland Mtn. Trail climbs easily along the ridge crest through young beech and birch and lush grass. In July blueberries and blackberries are plentiful. There are excellent views of Kephart Prong and Thomas Divide on the left. The trail reaches a wooded knob at 3.8 mi. and then descends an easy grade to the A.T. at 4.3 mi. in Dry Sluice Gap. To the right (E) the A.T. leads 2.0 mi. to False Gap, where there is a nearby shelter. A few yards to the left (W) on the A.T. is the terminus of the Porters Creek Trail, which has climbed 5.7 mi. from the Porters Creek Road in the Greenbrier section in Tennessee (see p. 244). At 0.5 mi. to the left on the A.T. is Charlies Bunion, at 2.0 mi. the Ice Water Spring Shelter and at 4.6 mi. Newfound Gap.

---

(32) **HUGHES RIDGE** 11.8 mi.

Horse and gated jeep trail / Max. elev. gain 3,340
Start: Smokemont Chapel, 2,220 ft.
End: Pecks Corner at A.T., 5,560 ft.
USGS quads: Smokemont, Mt. Guyot, N.C.
Trail connections: Becks Branch, Queen Mtn., Chasteen Creek, Enloe Creek, Taywa Creek, A.T.

This trail climbs along the crest of Hughes Ridge, connecting Smokemont Campground with the crest of the Smokies. It gains most of its elevation in the first 5.0 mi., but the remainder is easy walking along a high ridge. The first half of the trail receives moderate to heavy horse use, and so it is muddy in several places. Because the first mile of this trail is part of a complex of horse trails, it is easy to make a false start. Water is scarce along this trail; carry a canteen.

Trailhead: The trail starts next to the chapel at the entrance to Smokemont Campground. Turn right off the Newfound Gap Road at the Smokemont sign. Cross the river and park immediately to the right of the "T" intersection. The chapel is located on the hill directly ahead. Climb the path to the chapel and intersect a well-used trail. Hughes Ridge Trail runs straight ahead.

Trail Details: At 0.1 mi. a horse trail continues on and Hughes Ridge Trail turns left. It climbs to an intersection at 0.6 mi. with the Becks Branch Trail. At that junction it goes left and climbs farther to intersect the Queen Mtn. Trail at 1.0 mi. (That horse trail goes left for 1.3 muddy miles to meet the Bradley Fork Trail just above the campground.) From the Queen Mtn. Trail intersection, the Hughes Ridge Trail runs to the right and ascends through several switchbacks. It climbs along the right side of a dry ridge where laurel, pines, galax and arbutus grow. After passing through two clearings with views of the Bradley Fork Valley (the second at 2.3 mi.), it tunnels through rhododendrons and makes two switchbacks. At the second switchback, unmaintained Tow String Trail goes straight and leads to the church on Tow String Road. Hughes Ridge Trail continues to climb the ridge, alternating between dry and moist forest types. At 4.5 mi. it crosses the last source of water for the entire trail. Then it skirts the top of Becks Bald and finally reaches the ridge top.

Along the ridge there is a forest of young chestnut oaks, locust, cherry and a few large old oaks. This area was probably once used as a pasture. At about 5.4 mi. there is a cleared view to the right of Big Cove in the Qualla Reservation. The trail along this section is often muddy because of heavy horse traffic. At 6.6 mi. the Chasteen Creek Trail terminates on the left (see p. 134); at 7.1 mi. Enloe Creek Trail terminates on the right from Raven Fork (see p. 119).

The Hughes Ridge Trail continues on as a well-maintained, wide pathway, running up and down generally to the left of the ridge crest. Occasionally, in the gaps, there are views to the right of nearby Katalsta Ridge. At 9.0 mi. where the ridge top is level, there is a USGS bench mark in the trail. The laurel grows thick roundabout, and galax and teaberry cover the ground. During autumn the Smokies Crest may be seen to the left. At 9.6 mi. the Taywa Creek Trail terminates on the left from Bradley Fork (see p. 135).

Past this junction the trail is used by jeeps in the maintenance of the A.T. shelter and therefore may be muddy or rutted. After several gaps the trail climbs into a conifer forest growing along a wide ridge top. At 10.9 mi. a horse patrol cabin is situated on the right. (The patrol no longer operates because of lack of funds.) The trail curves left; signs indicate a horse campsite to the right. At 11.3 mi. the trail enters a gap where Hughes Ridge Shelter is located (12 bunks, indoor and outdoor fireplace, table inside). There is a good source of water below the shelter, but firewood is very scarce. A mutilated sign indicates that Smokemont is 19.5 mi. away; actually it is 11.3 mi.

Past the shelter the trail climbs from the gap to reach the A.T. on Pecks Corner at 11.8 mi. False Gap Shelter is located 3.8 mi. to the left; Tricorner Knob is to the right.

---

(33) KEPHART PRONG 2.1 mi.

Gated jeep trail / Max. elev. gain 830
Start: Newfound Gap Road, 6.9 mi. north of Ocona-
   luftee Ranger Station, 2,730 ft.
End: Kephart Prong Shelter, 3,560 ft.
USGS quads: Smokemont, N.C.
Trail connections: Kanati Fork, Grassy Branch, Sweat
   Heifer

Kephart Prong flows south from Mt. Kephart to meet the Oconaluftee River near its headwaters along the Newfound Gap Road. Kephart Prong Trail follows the creek upstream, running along a gated maintenance road. It has been compacted by jeeps and is muddy in several places. This easy hike is the route of access to a heavily used shelter located in a hardwood cove.

Horace Kephart was a nationally known outdoors writer who lived on Hazel Creek. His book *Our Southern Highlanders* is the classic description of frontier mountain life in the southern Appalachians.

Champion Fibre Co. used to run one of its major logging railroads up Kephart Prong and had a logging camp near the present shelter at the head of the cove. Other developments in the past were a large CCC camp near the head of the trail, and a Park Service fish hatchery (trout and bass) above it. Remains of the small rearing ponds, as well as a few buildings, may still be seen.

April-blooming wildflowers in the basin include spring beauty and trout lily, and the flowering tree, serviceberry; trilliums, many orchids, and the silverbell and black locust trees flower during the month of May.

Trailhead: The trail starts at a parking area to the right off the Newfound Gap Road, 3.7 mi. north of Smokemont Campground. The Kanati Fork Trail begins 0.2 mi. farther up the road on the opposite side (see p. 149).

Trail Details: The trail crosses the Oconaluftee River on a bridge and soon passes the old CCC camp; a fancy stone sign marks the entrance. At 0.2 mi. the jeep road turns left and fords Kephart Prong, while the hiking trail goes straight for 65 paces and then turns left. (If you don't walk to the left, you will find yourself at a dead end.) The trail crosses the creek on a foot log and turns right onto the road. This is the general area of the hatchery; there is a small dam on the stream nearby. The trail passes an old cistern on the left and then proceeds through a hemlock forest. At 0.8 mi. it crosses the creek on another foot log. At 1.1 mi. the trail turns right while the road fords the stream. Follow the trail to a foot log over the stream and rejoin the road. The last foot log spans the stream at 1.7 mi.; the trail ends at the Kephart Prong Shelter at 2.1 mi.

This area has been overused and abused. Firewood is scarce. The shelter has 16 bunks, a table, and both indoor and outdoor fireplaces. You can get water from the adjacent stream. There is a pit toilet nearby. At the shelter, the Grassy Branch Trail begins and goes right to the Richland Mountain Trail. The shelter is also the trailhead for the Sweat Heifer Trail (see p. 143), which runs straight ahead using old railroad grades to join the A.T. between Mt. Kephart and Newfound Gap.

---

(34) **GRASSY BRANCH** 2.3 mi.

Foot trail / Max. elev. gain 1,740
Start: Kephart Prong Shelter, 3,560 ft.
End: Richland Mtn. Trail, 5,300 ft.
USGS quads: Smokemont, Mt. Guyot, N.C.
Trail connections: Kephart Prong, Sweat Heifer,
   Richland Mtn.

This is a graded trail which climbs the west side of Richland Mtn. to connect the Kephart Prong Shelter with the Richland Mtn. Trail. In the lower parts it crosses several moist ravines, but in the higher elevations it runs through the rich grassy areas that give the trail its name. There is ample water along the way.

Trailhead: The trail starts at the Kephart Prong Shelter which also is the terminus of the Kephart Prong Trail, and the head of the Sweat Heifer Trail. A sign identifies Grassy Branch as the trail running to the right.

Trail Details: The trail climbs moderately, running parallel to Kephart Prong, whose roar can be heard below. After crossing an unnamed branch, the trail crosses Lower Grassy Branch at 0.8 mi., where it cascades through a rich ravine. Continuing to climb, the trail makes a sharp right at 1.4 mi. and then runs parallel to Lower Grassy Branch. The forest consists of young hardwoods, but near the upper end of the stream, the trees thin and the grass gets thicker. At 2.1 mi. the trail crosses the last water, in an open grassy area where there are good views to the west of the Kephart Prong Valley and Thomas Divide. At 2.3 mi. it reaches the ridge and terminates at the Richland Mtn. Trail (see p. 136). To the left it is 1.4 mi. to the A.T. Bradley Fork is straight ahead in the next valley to the east.

---

(35) **SWEAT HEIFER** 3.6 mi.

Foot trail / Max. elev. gain 2,270
Start: Kephart Prong Shelter, 3,560 ft.
End: A.T. 1.6 mi. east of Newfound Gap, 5,830 ft.
USGS quads: Smokemont, Clingmans Dome, N.C.
Trail connections: Kephart Prong, Grassy Branch,
    A.T.

This little-used trail connects the Kephart Prong Shelter area with the main crest of the Smokies. It roughly parallels the Newfound Gap Road and makes a pleasant 7-mi. day hike from Newfound Gap down Kephart Prong to the highway. After the turn of the century, this region was completely cut over by the Champion Fibre Co., which operated a logging camp near the present shelter site. Champion's old railroad grade forms a part of the trail. Bluets (wildflowers) are common along this trail, and water is plentiful. The name Sweat Heifer is probably derived from the old-time practice of driving cattle up steep trails to high grassy pastures.

Trailhead: The trail starts in front of the Kephart Prong Shelter. The shelter also is the terminus of the Kephart Prong Trail (see p. 140) and the head of the Grassy Branch Trail. The Sweat Heifer Trail is marked by a sign indicating the direction of the State Line. The trail starts to the north.

Trail Details: The trail immediately crosses a stream on a footbridge and enters a flat, open area—the site of the former logging camp; note the old cables. It then passes through a rich bed of partridge-berry, crosses a small creek and starts to climb. It slabs the left side of a mountain to merge with a railroad grade at 0.8 mi. Ascending gradually along the grade, it crosses a beautiful cascading stream and at 1.8 mi. passes the base of a small waterfall.

There is a right turn where the rail bed was blasted through the rocks. The trail then climbs steeply through silverbell and cherry trees. Toothwort (*Dentaria*), with its deep-green pointed leaves, can be seen on the right of the trail. At 2.2 mi. the trail cuts sharply to the right and tops a small ridge. Just beyond, the railroad grade goes left; the trail ascends straight ahead, sometimes through tall rhododendron.

The forest consists of second-growth hardwoods, mainly cherry. Large clumps of rattlesnake plantain, an orchid, may be found on the right. At 2.9 mi. the trail runs through a grassy glade and crosses the last real stream. There is a small seepage at 3.3 mi. The ridge top and the A.T. are reached at 3.6 mi. in the midst of a stunted beech grove. To the left it is 1.6 mi. on the A.T. to Newfound Gap. Mt. Kephart is to the right.

(36) MINGUS CREEK 5.6 mi.

Gated jeep and foot trail / Max. elev. gain 3,030
Start: Mingus Mill on Newfound Gap Road, 2,050 ft.
End: Newton Bald, 5,080 ft.
USGS quads: Smokemont, N.C.
Trail connections: Cooper Creek, Newton Bald

Beginning near the Oconaluftee Ranger Station on the Newfound Gap Road, this trail crisscrosses Madcap Branch several times. At 2.8 mi. it is possible to follow linking trails into the Deep Creek watershed or make a loop via the Newton Bald Trail. There is a campsite near Newton Bald, which makes this trail, in combination with a number of others, suitable for an overnight trip.

Trailhead: The trail starts at the Mingus Mill parking area on the Newfound Gap Road, 0.5 mi. north of the Oconaluftee Ranger Station.

Trail Details: Go through the gate and walk up Mingus Creek on a gravel service road. The trail crosses the creek twice in the first 0.5 mi. At 0.4 mi. there is a target range to the right of the trail. At 0.8 mi. an explosives cache may be seen, also on the right. Then the trail crosses to the left side of the creek. It passes a water-supply treatment plant at 1.0 mi. and crosses Madcap Branch just above the point where it flows into Mingus Creek. At 1.2 mi. the road forks and the trail runs left up the right bank of Madcap Branch on a rough jeep track. It recrosses Madcap Branch at 1.3 mi. and begins to climb a moderate grade. At 1.5 mi. it crosses a large spring branch. At 1.6 mi. the climb becomes steep. At 1.8 mi. the trail crosses a tributary and passes two very large hemlocks on the right. The crossing to the right side of Madcap Branch at 2.1 mi. is the last place to get water for miles. The jeep trail ends there, and a graded foot trail takes over.

The trail climbs moderately upward through a cove and at 2.2 mi. turns right to begin a series of switchbacks. At 2.4 mi. there is a zone of dry upland hardwoods: oak, maple and sourwood. The trail reaches a gap and a trail intersection at 2.8 mi. The signs there are difficult to read and, additionally, inaccurate. Actually, to the left (S) it is 0.5 mi. to Adams Creek Road. Cooper Creek Trail (see p. 160) terminates straight ahead, leading down Cooper Creek and then up Little Creek to the Thomas Divide Trail.

The Mingus Creek Trail runs to the right (N). It continues to climb at a moderate grade up the ridge. The vegetation roundabout is primarily oak forest. If you are quiet you may surprise a ruffed grouse. Along this stretch there are occasional views, but there is no water. At 5.6 mi. the trail reaches the Newton Bald Trail at a spot just below the top of Newton Bald. To the right (E) the Newton Bald Trail leads 4.2 mi. to the Newfound Gap Road at the entrance to Smokemont Campground. To the left (W) it is 0.6 mi. to the Thomas Divide Trail and a nearby campsite.

---

(37) **NEWTON BALD** 4.8 mi.

Horse trail / Max. elev. gain 2,900
Start: Smokemont, 2,200 ft.
End: Thomas Divide Trail, 5,000 ft.
USGS quads: Smokemont, N.C.
Trail connections: Hughes Ridge, Mingus Creek,
    Thomas Divide, Sunkota Ridge, Collins Creek

This trail leads from the Newfound Gap Road to Newton Bald and Thomas Divide. It gives access into the Deep Creek drainage or can be used as part of a loop, with the return portion via the Mingus Creek Trail to Oconaluftee Ranger Station. Horse use of this trail is moderate to heavy. There is no water at the campsite.

Trailhead: The trail starts on the Newfound Gap Road, opposite the entrance to Smokemont Campground. The Hughes Ridge Trail also begins nearby (see p. 138). There is ample parking on the left side of the highway. From a point opposite the bridge into Smokemont, walk upstream (N) on the left side of the road for 0.1 mi. to the end of a field. A sign there marks the beginning of the trail.

Trail Details: The trail climbs moderately on an old road through pole timber, mostly poplar. At 0.3 mi. a horse trail enters from the left. At 0.4 mi. in a gap another horse trail enters from the left. Newton Bald Trail runs straight ahead with a steady, moderate, uphill grade. It passes under dry rock overhangs at 1.3 and 1.8 mi. and crosses a bold stream at 2.8 mi. This is the last source of water.

At 3.8 mi. the trail reaches the crest of a ridge, from which there is a good view. Then it follows the ridge through an oak forest. At 4.2 mi. the Mingus Creek Trail enters on the left. (Down the Mingus Creek Trail, it is 6.1

mi. to the Oconaluftee Ranger Station on the Newfound
Gap Road.) At 4.7 mi. there is a campsite with a fire pit,
and at 4.8 mi. the junction with the Thomas Divide Trail
(see p. 157). To the right on the Thomas Divide Trail it is
0.5 mi. to the Sunkota Ridge Trail (see p. 168) and Collins
Creek Trail. To the left it is 8.9 mi. to Deep Creek Campground.

---

(38) **COLLINS CREEK** 4.2 mi.

Manway / Max. elev. gain 2,300
Start: Collins Creek picnic area, 2,500 ft.
End: Thomas Divide Trail, 4,800 ft.
USGS quads: Smokemont, N.C.
Trail connections: Thomas Divide, Sunkota Ridge,
    Newton Bald.

This difficult trail leads from Collins Creek picnic area up
Collins Creek to the crest of Thomas Divide. At that point a
loop trip can be fashioned by ascending or descending along
the divide on the Kanati Fork, Newton Bald or Mingus
Creek Trail and returning to the Newfound Gap Road. To
the west of the divide there is access to the Deep Creek trail
system. However, the Collins Creek Trail is not maintained,
so its use by backpackers, except for very strong ones, is
discouraged. The first half of the trail follows the bed of
an abandoned logging railroad; the second half follows a
graded and dug footway.

Trailhead: The trail starts at the Collins Creek picnic area
on the Newfound Gap Road, approximately 5.3 mi. north
of the Oconaluftee Ranger Station. The area is equipped
with ample parking spaces, water and toilets.

Trail Details: The trail is unmarked. Leave the paved loop
road on the most southerly of the gravel service roads,

passing around the gate. It is a level walk until 0.1 mi., where the road turns right in front of a pumphouse and climbs about 50 ft. Then it turns left onto an old railroad grade running parallel to Collins Creek. At 0.2 mi. it crosses a tributary on an old bridge and begins to climb gently. At 0.5 mi. it crosses the stream on a rotten foot log and leaves the railroad grade, temporarily. It rejoins the railroad bed at 0.7 mi. At 0.9 mi. it reaches a small meadow where it turns left at an acute angle, in second-growth beech and poplar.

At 1.0 mi. it makes a sharp right switchback, passes big vines and emerges at the upper end of an old field. For the next mile it runs through masses of hepatica. At 1.2 mi. it makes a sharp left switchback, past several jack-in-the-pulpit and then through open groves of poplar pole timber. It crosses Newton Branch at 1.8 mi. and reaches the end of the railroad grade at 2.3 mi.

At this point the grade of the trail increases. It crosses Collins Creek at 2.5 mi., makes one short switchback and climbs along the right bank of the stream. At 2.6 mi. it reaches the edge of a virgin forest: the contrast between the logged and uncut areas is immediately apparent. The trail crosses a spring branch at 2.8 mi. near large maples. It is the last sure source of water on the trail. Trilliums flower abundantly there in late April and early May.

At 3.1 mi. the trail crosses a watercourse in a "V" by a buckeye tree. At 3.4 mi., after a switchback, an exceptionally large black gum tree is growing on the right. The surrounding forest is mostly oak and several chestnut logs block the trail. There is a view to the left at 3.6 mi. At 4.2 mi. the trail reaches the crest of the Thomas Divide where it terminates at the Thomas Divide Trail, at 9.4 mi. on the latter (see p. 157). A little to the right is the beginning of the Sunkota Ridge Trail, marked with a sign (see p. 168). Farther right, up the Thomas Divide Trail, it is 4.7 mi. to

the Newfound Gap Road; to the left it is 0.5 mi. to the
junction where the Newton Bald Trail ends.

---

(39) KANATI FORK 3.0 mi.

Foot trail / Max. elev. gain 2,115
Start: Newfound Gap Road, 7.1 mi. north of Ocona-
     luftee Ranger Station, 2,860 ft.
End: Thomas Divide Trail, 4,975 ft.
USGS quads: Smokemont, Clingmans Dome, N.C.
Trail connections: Kephart Prong, Thomas Divide

This trail is a connector between the Newfound Gap Road
and the Thomas Divide Trail, ascending the valley of Kanati
Fork. It is well maintained, graded and has the advantage of
passing through several vegetation zones in its short length.
Kanati means "Lucky Hunter" in the Cherokee language.

Trailhead: The trail starts on the left of the Newfound Gap
Road, just where Kanati Fork flows under the highway.
This point is 3.9 mi. past the entrance to Smokemont
Campground. There is a large parking area. The Kephart
Prong Trail starts 0.2 mi. down the road on the opposite
side (see p. 140).

Trail Details: The trail climbs a moderate grade on the right
side of Kanati Fork through cove hardwoods. At 0.2 mi. an
old unmaintained trail leads left and runs parallel to the
main trail. Kanati Fork Trail crosses a small branch at 0.3
mi. and two more at 0.5 mi.
    At 0.9 mi. the trail leaves the cove hardwoods and begins
a series of switchbacks through a hemlock forest. It crosses
three small branches, the third flowing through a pile of
rocks. At 1.4 mi. it leaves the hemlocks behind and enters
an area of maples and oaks.

A small branch is crossed at 1.6 mi. This is the last source of water. At 1.8 mi. the trail enters a rhododendron thicket; magnolia, black gum and sourwood may be seen on the other side. At 1.9 mi. it enters a thicket of laurel. At 2.4 mi. a remarkable beech tree grows out of a rock pile on the right. The trail is climbing moderately on the right side of a valley. It passes through mixed hardwoods, mostly oak and maple, and emerges on the crest of a ridge at 3.0 mi. A sign marks its terminus at the Thomas Divide Trail, at a point 12.3 mi. from the Thomas Divide trailhead (see p. 157). To the right (N) it is 1.8 mi. to the Newfound Gap Road. To the left (S) the Thomas Divide Trail follows the ridge to Deep Creek.

Deep Creek Section
(North Carolina)

Introduction

The drainage in the Deep Creek Valley generally flows from the north to the south. In the north, its boundaries extend from Luftee Gap (near the intersection of the Newfound Gap and the Clingmans Dome roads) west along the state line ridge crest, past Mount Collins, to Webb Overlook on the Clingmans Dome Road. On the east the valley is bounded by Thomas Divide. On the west it is bounded by Noland Divide and Beaugard Ridge. Deep Creek eventually flows through the campground of the same name and then empties into the Tuckasegee River at the edge of Bryson City. Deep Creek is probably no deeper than other streams in the Smokies, but since it was the deepest creek the valley residents knew they gave it that name.

Major trails beginning in the vicinity of the Deep Creek Campground follow both the Thomas and Noland-Beaugard ridges to end high in the center of the park. Other trails provide access to Sunkota Ridge and the Appalachian Trail at a point near Mount Collins or make loops within the Deep Creek watershed.

Bryson Place, on Deep Creek, was the location of a hunting lodge belonging to the Bryson family at the turn of the century. A wagon road ran upstream from Bryson City to the lodge, crossing the creek 15 times. (The present trail fortunately does not follow the original route, but is located entirely on the east side of the stream.) Jenkins Place, about halfway between Bryson City and Bryson Place, is the homeplace of the Jenkins family; the outlines of several old fields can still be seen there. Most tributary streams in the vicinity bear family names of other early settlers. But Keg Drive Branch was the favorite hunting spot of Jim Keg, an Indian, and Poke Patch was originally the location of a patch of pokeweed.

During the late nineteenth century the Deep Creek watershed was selectively cut for poplar and basswood, two lightweight varieties of tree. The timber was later floated downstream to Bryson City. The procedure was to let the logs accumulate at splash dams—one at the mouth of Pole Road Creek (some remains are apparent) and the other just below the mouth of Keg Drive Branch. Then after heavy rains the logs would be released from the dams, and the swollen streams would carry them to their destination. Other trees, such as oak, chestnut and maple, were left standing because the green wood was too heavy to float. Hemlock was bypassed, also, because it was a less valuable species. Pole Road Creek received its name in the logging days when a "skid trail" extended up it: poles were laid crossways in the trail at intervals of several feet so logs could be skidded along on the poles rather than on the ground. This technique kept the logs from catching on rocks and sinking into the mud.

Deep Creek Campground today is a large, developed area located just inside the park boundary. Its facilities include water, areas for picnicking and camping (including camper vehicles) and toilets. To reach the campground, enter Bryson City on U.S. 19 and turn north at the Swain County Courthouse. Follow the signs for three miles to the campground. The road continues straight ahead but is blocked and must be hiked. Starting at the campground, the Deep Creek Road Trail continues straight and at 0.1 mi. reaches the Galbraith Road, which goes right. At 0.4 mile a sign marks Tom's Branch Falls, on the right. Indian Creek Trail and Falls, and the Thomas Divide Trail, are to the

right at 0.9 mile. Jenkins Place and the start of a loop trail
to Indian Creek are located at 1.9 miles. At 2.2 miles there
is a parking area and the beginning of the Deep Creek Trail.

   In addition to the developed campground, camping areas
in Deep Creek Valley include a large horse camp at Bryson
Place and smaller back-country campsites at Pole Road
Creek, Poke Patch and Deep Creek. Other, newer back-
country sites are listed as notes.

---

(40) **DEEP CREEK** 12.0 mi.

   Gated jeep and horse trail / Max. elev. gain 2,820
   Start: Parking loop at end of Deep Creek Road, 1,990
      ft.
   End: Overlook on Newfound Gap Road, 1.7 mi.
      south of Newfound Gap, 4,810 ft.
   USGS quads: Bryson City, Clingmans Dome, N.C.
   Trail connections: Indian Creek, Pole Road Creek,
      Fork Ridge

Deep Creek Trail follows cascading Deep Creek from the
valley floor all the way to the Newfound Gap Road on
Thomas Divide. The average hiking time for day hikers,
including a stop for lunch, is seven hours. There is a large
horse camp at Bryson Place, and several back-country
campsites. Water is abundant everywhere except the last
mile. This trail climbs gradually for most of its entire
length. Additionally, it is graded and well maintained, so it
should not be difficult to hike.

   Note: there are four new back-country campsites along
this trail—approximate mileages are: Bumgardner Branch
campsite at 0.5 mi., McCracken Branch at 3.0 mi., Nicks
Nest Branch at 3.5 mi. and Nettle Creek at 5.7 mi.

Trailhead: The trailhead is the parking loop at the end of the Deep Creek Road. To reach the loop, drive into Deep Creek Campground, bear to the left (W) on a gravel road and pass between the campground proper and the Assembly Building. You will be on the Deep Creek Road Trail. Hike for 2.2 mi. to the parking loop, crossing Deep Creek three times along the way on one-way bridges. At the loop, a sign points toward the Deep Creek Trail.

Trail Details: The graded trail climbs 0.1 mi. to an intersection with a jeep road, turns left onto it and follows it as far as Bryson Place at 3.9 mi. In general during the first 3.0 mi. it runs uphill and downhill, crossing nine spurs leading down from Sunkota Ridge. The top of each spur affords a view of the Deep Creek Valley. On the way to Bryson Place, the cove forest is mostly second growth, with river birch, yellow poplar, Fraser magnolia, basswood, maple and white pine being the dominant species. But there are many magnificent towering eastern hemlocks and a few large oaks and maples. In the fall the fruit of the strawberry bush is a bright pink and orange.

At 0.4 mi. the trail crosses Bumgardner Branch on a foot log, where an old unmaintained manway can be seen leading upstream. The trail then leaves Deep Creek and starts a steep climb to cross the highest spur at 1.0 mi., several hundred feet above the stream, from which there is a view. After passing a rock spring at 1.2 mi., the trail crosses over three spurs and then runs downhill to pass a grove of big hemlocks at 2.1 mi. It follows the creek and then climbs again to cross four more spurs before reaching Bryson Place at 3.9 mi.

Just before crossing the stream into Bryson Place, a sign points to the left to a spot 200 ft. off the trail where there is a brass memorial plaque mounted on an old millstone. It reads:

On this spot Horace Kephart—dean of American Campers and one of the principal founders of the

Great Smoky Mountains National Park—pitched his
last permanent camp. — Erected May 30, 1931, by
Horace Kephart Troop, Boy Scouts of America, Bryson City, North Carolina.

Horace Kephart used to set up permanent camps in the
Smokies and live in them for months at a time. This, then,
was the site of his last one. He lost his life in an automobile
collision near Bryson City and is buried in the cemetery
there. A boulder from Kephart Prong serves as his grave
marker.

Bryson Place (2,400 ft.) is a large horse camp with
plenty of water, several concrete picnic tables, lean-to shelter frames, open fireplaces with iron grills, and hitching
racks. There also are two bear-proof barrels and one pit
toilet. Because this camp is heavily used by horse riders, it
may be closed to hikers. At Bryson Place several signs stand
at the junction with the Indian Creek Trail (see p. 169).
That trail leads right (E) to Martin's Gap on Sunkota Ridge
and then loops back south toward Deep Creek Campground.

The Deep Creek Trail continues upstream, as a horse
trail, on an easy grade. At 4.6 mi. the Pole Road Creek Trail
begins on the left (leading 3.2 mi. to Upper Sassafras Gap
on Noland Divide, see p. 166) and at this junction Pole
Road back-country campsite is located on Deep Creek.
There are no facilities there except for water and level
ground.

The trail continues up the right side of Deep Creek,
where there are beautiful views of its tumbling water. Several tributaries enter from the right, crossing the trail, but
they should present no problems to the hiker. Beginning at
5.9 mi. hemlock and tulip poplar trees grow as large as four
ft. in diameter.

At 8.0 mi. the trail reaches Poke Patch back-country
campsite (3,000 ft.). It may be recognized by its level
grassy area, two iron-grilled fireplaces, tables made from

hewn logs, and a hollow buckeye tree with two rocks jammed in the hollow. There is room for four to six tents. The creek furnishes the water supply. At Poke Patch the Fork Ridge Trail exits to the left (see p. 171). That trail leads 4.9 mi. to the Clingmans Dome Road near Mt. Collins where there is a connection to the A.T. 0.1 mi. beyond.

Deep Creek Trail continues to climb along the right bank of Deep Creek. Shot Beech Ridge runs parallel and to the right of the trail. This ridge was named after an old beech tree which once grew on the crest. The tree was a favorite target for local hunters and had many scars to prove it.

At 9.4 mi. the trail passes a flat area beside the creek. At 10.0 mi. it runs down to the edge of the stream to cross an open bog-like area of low foliage and strawberry plants. At 10.5 mi. it turns right, away from Deep Creek, and starts to climb up out of the valley. The grade becomes steeper as the trail winds through a hemlock forest. At 10.9 mi. it passes a spring branch which is the last source of water on the trail. An unmarked, unmaintained but graded trail exits to the left at 11.2 mi. Deep Creek Trail then commences a stretch where it has been newly established. It climbs, at a good grade, up a series of switchbacks to the Newfound Gap Road at 11.9 mi. A sign there marks the trail. Continue 600 ft. further to the parking area, which is the trail terminus (12.0 mi.). This spot is situated 1.7 mi. south of Newfound Gap.

---

(41) **THOMAS DIVIDE** 14.1 mi.

Gated road, horse and foot trail / Max. elev. gain
   3,310
Start: Deep Creek Road (0.9 mi.), 1,900 ft.
End: Newfound Gap Road, 3.5 mi. south of New-
   found Gap, 4,650 ft.
USGS quads: Bryson City, Clingmans Dome, Smoke-
   mont, N.C.
Trail connections: Indian Creek, Deeplow Gap, New-
   ton Bald, Sunkota Ridge, Collins Creek, Kanati
   Fork

Thomas Divide is a long ridge which arcs in a half-circle
from the vicinity of Deep Creek Campground to the crest
of the Smokies. The Thomas Divide Trail, although beginning in the valley where Indian Creek empties into Deep
Creek, is mostly a ridge-top path, following Thomas Divide
all the way to the Newfound Gap Road. It is well graded,
open, well maintained and well marked. Five overlooks
have been cleared to show broad vistas. Being a ridge route,
it is generally dry, but there are a few sources of water
along the way. Although there is no designated campsite on
this trail, a suitable location may be found along the way
near the end of the Newton Bald Trail. The proposed Indian
Creek Motor Nature Trail would have caused the closing of
a part of the lower section of the Thomas Divide Trail, but
the Motor Nature Trail has been abandoned (as of 1977 up-
date). You should check with the ranger at Deep Creek
Campground for the latest information.

    Thomas Divide takes its name from William Thomas, a
white man and a native of Haywood County, N.C. He had
been adopted by the great Cherokee chief Yonaguska and
given the name *Wil-Usdi* or "Little Will." In 1839 Yona-

guska died, and Thomas was elected chief of the Eastern Cherokees. During his early years as chief, he fought hard before Congress to gain the Indians their just rights, earning the reputation of their savior. He was, on the other hand, quite an operator, and was much criticized for his involvement in land speculation (at one time owning more than 100,000 acres in N.C.) and for promoting road and railroad construction in Indian territory. During the Civil War he was the leader of "Thomas's Legion of Indians and Highlanders," which was organized to guard the Smokies from attack by the North. Later his power waned and he lost control over his vast empire. He died in 1893, leaving his estate in terrible confusion.

Trailhead: The trail starts at a gate on the right, 0.9 mi. above the Deep Creek Campground, on the Deep Creek Road. This is also the head of Indian Creek Trail (see p. 169). There is limited parking.

Trail Details: Walk through the gate up Indian Creek Trail, which is a jeep road. At 0.1 mi. Indian Creek Falls is on the left. The trail crosses Indian Creek on a jeep bridge at 0.2 mi. and reaches a trail junction, with sign, at 0.5 mi. The Thomas Divide Trail goes to the right and immediately crosses Indian Creek on a foot log. Then it starts to climb at a moderate grade but with rough, washed out stretches, alongside a small branch, whose water is silted and unsuitable for drinking. At 0.8 mi. the trail turns sharply to the left, crosses a branch and ascends a small dry ridge. At 0.9 mi. it turns sharply to the right; note an old, unmaintained trail running to the left. The Thomas Divide Trail climbs on the right side of the ridge line. At 1.2 mi. it crosses a silted spring branch. Continuing its moderate climb, it leaves the zone of cove hardwoods behind and at 1.4 mi. reaches the crest of Thomas Divide at Stone Pile Gap.

At Stone Pile Gap the trail runs into construction for the

Indian Creek Motor Nature Trail. For the next 2.0 mi. the
trail has been affected by road work. Follow the road as it
climbs gradually along the left side of the ridge line, which
incidentally marks the park boundary. At 3.4 mi. (watch
out; no sign) the trail leaves the road to bear right in a low
gap. (The road bears left and leaves the ridge.) The trail
continues to climb at a moderate grade along the crest of
the Thomas Divide. At 3.5 mi. there is a small knoll and the
park line veers to the right. The trail continues uphill on the
crest through second-growth oak and dry-ridge hardwoods.
At 4.4 mi. there is a view to the right into the valley of
Cooper Creek. After passing over a wooded knob at 4.9 mi.,
the trail descends moderately down the crest, slabs to the
right and reaches a good, small spring at 5.2 mi. At 5.8 mi.
it arrives at an intersection at Deeplow Gap. To the left
(W) the Deeplow Gap Trail leads 2.3 mi. to the Indian
Creek Trail. To the right (E) the Deeplow Gap Trail leads
first past a small spring (400 ft.), then past Little Creek
Falls and on to Cooper Creek (see p. 162).

From the gap the Thomas Divide Trail continues straight
on a moderate upgrade along the crest of Thomas Divide.
At 8.9 mi. the Newton Bald Trail (see p. 146) terminates on
the right (E) having come 4.8 mi. from the Newfound Gap
Road. Along that trail a short distance is a campsite with a
firepit and a spring.

At 9.4 mi., along a level area of the ridge, there is a sign
and two trail intersections. To the left (W) the Sunkota
Ridge Trail (see p. 168) leads 4.8 mi. to Martins Gap. To
the right (E), about 150 ft. before reaching the trail sign,
the unmaintained Collins Creek Trail leads east 4.2 mi. to
the Collins Creek picnic area (see p. 147).

The Thomas Divide Trail continues along the ridge,
crosses a wooded knob and descends into Tuskee Gap. It
then climbs again to crest at Nettle Creek Bald, where there
is a sign, at 11.8 mi. At 12.3 mi. the Kanati Fork Trail

terminates from the right. A sign indicates that that trail leads east 3.0 mi. to the Newfound Gap Road. There is water 1.4 mi. down the Kanati Fork Trail (see p. 149).

Continuing along the crest of Thomas Divide, at 13.0 mi. the trail arrives at its highest point, 5,160 ft., in a clearing where there are extensive views to the east of Mt. Kephart and Charlies Bunion. This general area is known as Turkey Flyup: hunters used to flush wild turkeys there, causing them to "fly up." The trail then follows a knife edge to the crest of Beetree Ridge at 13.4 mi. It crosses the nose of the ridge through a birch forest and runs downhill, reaching a gap at 13.9 mi. Then it again climbs, moderately, to reach a large grassy area and the Newfound Gap Road at 14.1 mi. There is a trail sign at the upper edge of the grassy area, but it is hard to see from the highway because it is 250 ft. away. To the right 0.25 mi. down the highway, there is an overlook, with parking. Driving northbound, it is the first overlook on the left after crossing Beech Flats Prong. To the left Newfound Gap is 3.5 mi. away.

---

(42) COOPER CREEK 2.3 mi.

Gated jeep trail / Max. elev. gain 1,430
Start: Deeplow Gap Trail and Cooper Creek Road, 2,190 ft.
End: Mingus Creek Trail, 3,620 ft.
USGS quads: Smokemont, N.C.
Trail connections: Deeplow Gap, Mingus Creek

This short trail is an important segment in the lateral trail system leading from the Deep Creek Campground to the Oconaluftee Ranger Station. It connects the Deeplow Gap Trail, of which it amounts to a continuation, to the Mingus Creek Trail. Mostly, it follows the course of Cooper Creek, but it ends on an unnamed ridge leading south from Newton Bald. Water is abundant along the way.

Trailhead: The trailhead is the Deeplow Gap Trail where it ends at Cooper Creek. Cooper Creek is 1.5 mi. east of Deeplow Gap on Thomas Divide. From the trailhead a jeep trail runs to the south, downstream on Cooper Creek, about 0.33 mi. to the Cooper Creek Road, which connects with U.S. 19.

Trail Details: The trail runs upstream (E) along Cooper Creek. The ford of Cooper Creek at 0.2 mi. is difficult for backpackers, as is the second one at 0.3 mi. The trail crosses a tributary at 0.8 mi. At 0.9 mi. it enters a large cleared area with views out to the ridge top, and another tributary crossing at the upper end. It crosses Cooper Creek for the last time at 1.2 mi. There is a potential campsite in a cove at 1.3 mi. The trail turns hard right at 1.7 mi., leaving Cooper Creek (last water source) and begins to climb at a moderate grade up to the ridge. (Note: an unmaintained manway continues up Cooper Creek.) At 1.9 mi. there is a view to the right. At 2.3 mi. the trail reaches the crest of the ridge and ends at a trail junction. The signs there are hard to read and inaccurate. To the left (N) the Mingus Creek Trail leads up the ridge to Newton Bald and Thomas Divide at 3.4 mi. Straight ahead the Mingus Creek Trail runs down to its trailhead at Oconaluftee Ranger Station, also 2.8 mi. away (see p. 144). To the right (S) an unmaintained trail runs for 0.6 mi. to Adams Creek Road.

---

(43) **DEEPLOW GAP** (Georges Branch, Little Creek, Little Creek Falls) 3.8 mi.

Horse trail / Max. elev. gain 1,275
Start: Indian Creek Trail, 2,440 ft.
End: Cooper Creek Road and Trail, 2,190 ft.
USGS quads: Clingmans Dome, Smokemont, N.C.
Trail connections: Indian Creek, Thomas Divide, Cooper Creek

Deeplow Gap Trail is part of an important lateral trail system between the Deep Creek and the Oconaluftee areas. Starting at Indian Creek, it runs up and over the Thomas Divide at Deeplow Gap and then follows Little Creek down to Cooper Creek. From there the Cooper Creek Trail climbs to the Mingus Creek Trail, which leads to the Oconaluftee Ranger Station. Deeplow Gap Trail also serves as the main route from Deep Creek Campground to the Little Creek Falls. The first 0.5 mi. of it will be destroyed by the Indian Creek Motor Nature Trail, which is now under construction.

If this trail is hiked in a westerly direction, the maximum elevation gain is 1,525 ft.

Trailhead: The trail starts at 3.0 mi. on the Indian Creek Trail (see p. 169). There is no trail sign.

Trail Details: The trail turns right (E) on a jeep road and immediately crosses Indian Creek on a bridge just above the mouth of Georges Branch. The road follows Georges Branch, crossing it at 0.2 mi. At 0.5 mi. the jeep road angles to the right, leaving the branch, while the graded Deeplow Gap Trail (no sign) bears to the left. (When the new roadway is completed in 1974, this spot will probably be the start of the trail.) The trail enters a hemlock forest in the valley of Georges Branch, climbing moderately up-slope on a good grade. Up to 1.8 mi. there are several sources of water. At 2.3 mi. the trail reaches Deeplow Gap on Thomas Divide and an intersection. To the left (N) the Thomas Divide Trail leads 8.3 mi. to the Newfound Gap Road, with several side-trail connections. To the right (S) the Thomas Divide Trail leads 5.8 mi. to the confluence of Indian Creek and Deep Creek (see p. 157).

Deeplow Gap Trail runs straight ahead (E), descending moderately on a graded footpath. About 400 ft. below the gap it passes a small spring branch which is a good source of water. The trail slabs along a south facing slope and enters a cove at 2.8 mi. It crosses Little Creek and then runs downhill through pine and hemlock to reach the base of the Little Creek Falls at 3.1 mi. The falls are about 80 ft. high and very beautiful. The trail crosses the creek at the base of the falls and switchbacks downhill at a moderate grade. At 3.8 mi. it terminates at the Cooper Creek Trail, which is a jeep road. To the left (E) the Cooper Creek Trail runs 2.3 mi. to the crest of the ridge to end at the Mingus Creek Trail. To the right (S) a road follows Cooper Creek downstream to U.S. 19 near Bryson City, N.C.

 NOLAND DIVIDE 11.5 mi.

Horse trail / Max. elev. gain 4,150
Start: Deep Creek Campground, 1,780 ft.
End: Clingmans Dome Road near Webb Overlook, 5,929 ft.
USGS quads: Bryson City, Clingmans Dome, N.C.
Trail connections: Noland Creek, Pole Road Creek

Noland Divide, which runs north-south, separates the drainages of Deep Creek and Noland Creek. South of Coburn Knob, the divide splits: the western ridge, bordering Noland Creek, retains the name of Noland Divide, while the eastern ridge, bordering the Deep Creek watershed, is called Beaugard Ridge. Noland Divide Trail runs from Deep Creek Campground up to and along Beaugard Ridge and then along Noland Divide to the Clingmans Dome Road. Along the way it passes over or around three prominent peaks: Coburn Knob, Sassafras Knob, and Roundtop Knob.

The average day hiker should allow seven hours to cover this trail, including time for a lunch stop. He should carry plenty of water because there are few sources of water along the trail, and none at all in the upper half. The first 5.0 mi. are a steep and sometimes rough climb, but the remainder is much easier. Several delightful side trails, in combination with the Noland Divide Trail, provide loop trips of varying lengths within the Deep Creek and Noland Creek valleys.

Trailhead: The trail starts near the entrance to the Deep Creek Campground—on the left (W) side of the entrance road, immediately opposite the bridge leading to the ranger station and the campground sign-in station. A signpost marks the start of the trail.

Trail Details: Initially the trail follows a fairly level course as it ascends gently along a wide ridge. But at 0.4 mi. it begins a moderately steep ascent, rising around the headwaters of Juney Whank Branch. The slope into the Juney Whank drainage is very steep—in places a sheer drop from the trail. At 1.7 mi. a small stream flows under the trail. The trail continues to climb steeply up Beaugard Ridge. Pine trees are prevalent along this section. There are occasional views of the lower Deep Creek Valley to the right.

The trail then follows the crest of Beaugard Ridge, crossing at 3.5 mi. a very narrow gap, which has been built up to provide a level passage. From this spot there is an excellent view of Deep Creek Valley to the east, and to the west, the small valley of Lands Creek, which lies between

Beaugard Ridge and the southern end of Noland Divide. Looking south, one can see Bryson City about 5.0 mi. away. From this gap the trail climbs steadily to Coburn Knob. At 3.8 mi. it passes through a cleared area, possibly burned over in the recent past. Fairly thick undergrowth lines the trail. The trail reaches a spring on the right at 4.8 mi. At 4.9 mi. there is another spring, this time on the left. It is the last water on the trail, and its source is Coburn Knob (4,600 ft.), which the trail then slabs around on the right to join Noland Divide.

From Coburn Knob up the Noland Divide to the Clingmans Dome Road, the grade is easy. At 7.3 mi. the trail reaches Lower Sassafras Gap (4,040 ft.), and then slabs left (W) around Sassafras Knob. There are good views of Noland Creek watershed to the left; blueberries abound in season. At 7.9 mi. the trail reaches Upper Sassafras Gap (4,240 ft.) and a trail junction, marked by a sign. To the left (W) the Noland Creek Trail terminates (see p. 175). It is about 1.0 mi. down Sassafras Branch to the Bald Creek campsite on Noland Creek and thence down Noland Creek to the North Shore Road. To the right (E) is the terminus of the Pole Road Creek Trail, down which it is 3.2 mi. to Deep Creek. If you are desperate for water, you can find it by following the Noland Creek Trail down to the spot where a spring flows into Sassafras Branch, but you will have a steep climb back up to the gap.

Leaving Sassafras Gap the Noland Divide Trail climbs moderately along the ridge. At 8.6 mi. green galax leaves carpet the path as it passes through a laurel tunnel. The trail slabs to the left (W) around Roundtop Knob. Hardwoods, mostly oak, grow in this area. The trail passes another laurel slick and at 1.5 mi. descends slightly, only to climb again. Moss-covered coniferous trees begin to predominate—many spruce, with a ground cover of blackberry, asters and fern. At 11.1 mi. the trail reaches a gravel road to a pumping

station; you should follow the road to the right. To the left
it is 0.3 mi. to a small stream. The trail terminates at the
Clingmans Dome Road at 11.5 mi. To the left 1.5 mi. away
at the end of the Clingmans Dome Road is Forney Ridge
parking area. To the right at 0.2 mi. is Webb Overlook. The
A.T. may be reached by continuing about 0.5 mi. past the
overlook to Collins Gap. There go left through the woods
(no trail) for about 100 ft. and you will find the A.T.

---

45 **POLE ROAD CREEK** (Upper Sassafras Gap) 3.2
    mi.

Horse trail / Max. elev. gain 1,800
Start: Near Bryson Place on Deep Creek Trail, 2,440
    ft.
End: Upper Sassafras Gap on Noland Divide Trail,
    4,240 ft.
USGS quads: Bryson City, Clingmans Dome, N.C.
Trail connections: Deep Creek, Noland Divide, No-
    land Creek

This is a connecting trail between the Deep Creek and the
Noland Divide trails. In the upper sections, it passes through
a rich hardwood forest. It is a graded four-foot-wide bridle
path, and there is plenty of water available. Pole Road
back-country campsite is located on Deep Creek at the start
of this trail.

Trailhead: The trail starts 0.7 mi. north of (upstream from)
Bryson Place or 4.6 mi. on the Deep Creek Trail (see p.
153). The trail turns left (W) off the Deep Creek Trail.

Trail Details: The trail immediately fords Deep Creek. (The
bridge that once stood there has been washed away.) After
the crossing, about 200 ft. upstream, there is the undevel-

oped campsite. The trail runs through a broad valley and at
0.1 mi. crosses Pole Road Creek. It turns left to parallel the
creek and at 0.2 mi. runs on a man-made platform directly
above the channel. After 1.2 mi. three crossings of Pole
Road Creek occur in quick succession. Several hundred feet
beyond the third crossing, a large dead tree stands immediately to the right of the trail. The trail ascends moderately,
with the creek to the left. The final crossing (and last water
source) is at 2.0 mi.

The trail then begins to climb to Upper Sassafras Gap. A
grove of very large hemlocks to the left at 2.2 mi. is but one
feature in a forest of magnificent trees. At 2.3 mi. the trail
runs up a series of small switchbacks and then ascends
alongside a ravine, with Sassafras Knob occasionally visible
to the left. At 2.6 mi. the trail passes through rhododendron, followed by an open, attractive hardwood forest. At
3.2 mi. it terminates at the Noland Divide Trail in Upper
Sassafras Gap. From there the Noland Divide Trail leads
north 3.6 mi. to end at the Clingmans Dome Road and
south 7.9 mi. to its trailhead at Deep Creek Campground.
This junction also is the terminus of the Noland Creek
Trail, which runs straight ahead (W) down Sassafras Branch
(see p. 175).

---

46 **SUNKOTA RIDGE** 4.8 mi.

Horse trail / Max. elev. gain 1,370
Start: Martins Gap on Indian Creek Trail, 3,430 ft.
End: Thomas Divide Trail near Newton Bald Trail,
    4,780 ft.
USGS quads: Clingmans Dome, Smokemont, N.C.
Trail connections: Indian Creek, Thomas Divide, Collins Creek, Newton Bald

---

This trail leads from Martins Gap, about midway along
Sunkota Ridge above Bryson Place, to the crest of Thomas
Divide. Formerly there was a graded trail along the entire
length of Sunkota Ridge. In 1972 the Park Service was to
reopen the lower section. With that work completed, Sunkota Ridge Trail will begin at the roadway between the
Deep Creek Campground and Jenkins Place and will be
about 5.0 mi. longer.

Sunkota is believed to be a rather inaccurate rendition of
the Cherokee word for "apple." Apparently apple trees
used to grow on the ridge. Nowadays, an open forest of
mature oak offers a magnificent display of colors in the fall
and allows for fine views in the winter. The banks of the
trail, where dug out, are lined with trailing arbutus.

The grade is a steady, moderate uphill. You should carry
enough water for the entire trip because there is no reliable
source along the way.

Trailhead: The trail starts at Martins Gap, 5.2 mi. on the
Indian Creek Trail or 1.6 mi. east of Bryson Place.

Trail Details: At first the trail climbs gently along the crest
of Sunkota Ridge. At 0.1 mi. it passes several clawed pines.
In a zone of white pine at 0.4 mi. there is a good view to
the south. At 0.5 mi. the trail crosses an intermittent spring

branch in a hemlock grove. At 0.8 mi. it enters a rhododendron tunnel which leads up to a low gap. Another intermittent spring, at 1.4 mi., is the last certain source of water
on the trail. The trail passes through another gap at 2.1 mi.,
where many chestnut logs lie on the ground. To the south
there are many good views of the Indian Creek Valley and
Thomas Divide.

At 3.5 mi. the trail climbs steeply directly up the crest
of the ridge but soon levels out. It then crosses from one
side of the ridge to the other, climbing moderately. A patch
of trout lilies grows at 4.4 mi., as the trail levels out once
again. At 4.8 mi. it terminates at the Thomas Divide Trail
(see p. 157). To the left along the Thomas Divide Trail, it is
4.7 mi. to the Newfound Gap Road, while to the right at
0.5 mi. is a junction with the Newton Bald Trail (see p.
146). Immediately to the right, 150 ft. away, is the end of
the unmarked and unmaintained Collins Creek Trail, which
leads east 4.2 mi. to the Collins Creek picnic area (see p.
147).

---

(47) **INDIAN CREEK** 6.8 mi.

Gated roadway, horse trail / Max. elev. gain 1,530
Start: Deep Creek Road (0.9 mi.), 1,900 ft.
End: Bryson Place on Deep Creek Trail, 2,400 ft.
USGS quads: Bryson City, Clingmans Dome, N.C.
Trail connections: Thomas Divide, Deeplow Gap,
   Sunkota Ridge, Deep Creek

The Indian Creek Trail follows Indian Creek upstream for
awhile and then crosses Sunkota Ridge at Martins Gap. The
heads of several major trails are situated along it. The Indian
Creek Motor Nature Trail would have eliminated a portion
of this trail as well, but since its abandonment, the integrity

of the trail is assured, at least for the present. There is a horse camp at Bryson Place.

Trailhead: The trail begins where the Deep Creek Road crosses the mouth of Indian Creek, 0.9 mi. above the campground. It goes to the right, following a gated jeep road. There is a trail sign here, but parking space is limited.

Trail Details: Pass through a gate. At 0.1 mi. the road passes the Indian Creek Falls, which cascade about 60 ft. over a rock ledge. The Thomas Divide Trail parts company to the right at 0.5 mi. At 0.8 mi. a loop trail runs left for 1.2 mi. to the Deep Creek Road at Jenkins Place. An unmarked jeep trail exits on the right at 2.7 mi. and leads 0.3 mi. to the old Queen Cemetery. At 3.0 mi. Deeplow Gap Trail begins on the right as a jeep road (see p. 162). There is no sign there. The Indian Creek Trail continues to follow the road along Indian Creek and ascends gradually to 3.7 mi. where the road ends in a loop. The trail goes northwest, beside the main stream, to a sharp left turn at 4.3 mi. and crosses Indian Creek (the last source of water).

The trail makes several switchbacks, climbing steeply in a few places, and reaches Martins Gap (3,430 ft.) and a trail junction at 5.2 mi. The Sunkota Ridge Trail begins there and leads to the right 4.8 mi. to Thomas Divide. In the future a new trail will run to the left (S) along Sunkota Ridge and end at the Deep Creek Road.

Indian Creek Trail continues straight ahead to go steeply downhill from the gap. After it passes through a rhododendron tunnel, there is a view of the Deep Creek Valley to the right at 5.4 mi. The trail descends along a spur ridge and at 6.0 mi. turns right and begins to slab the left side of the mountain, entering a mixed pine and oak forest. At 6.4 mi. it crosses a bridge over a stream and runs downhill gradually through pines and hemlocks to terminate at Bryson Place at 6.8 mi. From there Deep Creek Trail goes to the left 3.9 mi.

to the Deep Creek Road and right to its terminus at the Newfound Gap Road (see p. 153). There is a large horse camp with many facilities at Bryson Place.

---

48 FORK RIDGE 4.9 mi.

Foot trail / Max. elev. gain 2,880
Start: Poke Patch primitive campsite on Deep Creek Trail, 3,000 ft.
End: Mt. Collins area on Clingmans Dome Road, 5,880 ft.
USGS quads: Clingmans Dome, N.C.
Trail connections: Deep Creek, A.T., Sugarland Mtn.

This is a connecting trail between the Deep Creek Valley and the Clingmans Dome Road. There is a graded, well-maintained footway the entire distance. The climb is steep for the first 0.3 mi. to Deep Creek Gap but thereafter is moderate, though steady, as the trail follows Fork Ridge. At its midpoint the trail passes through a grove of large hemlock trees. There are two springs toward the end of the trail, and beyond it, a shelter nearby on the A.T.

Trailhead: The trailhead is Poke Patch campsite at 8.0 mi. on the Deep Creek Trail (see p. 153). Downstream it is 4.1 mi. to Bryson Place. Upstream on the Deep Creek Trail it is 4.0 mi. to the Newfound Gap Road. There is no sign to mark the Fork Ridge Trail.

Trail Details: The trail proceeds upstream and to the left (W), passing out of the grassy area. Within 150 ft. it descends to and fords Deep Creek, which is about 20 ft. wide at this point. It crosses a bottom area through big trees and at 0.3 mi. begins a steep ascent, slabbing toward the south. At 0.4 mi. it reaches the ridge crest at Deep

Creek Gap. The remainder of the trail, up Fork Ridge, is a moderate-to-easy hike.

At the gap the trail makes a right turn where white pines grow and continues through a pine forest to 0.8 mi. At 0.9 mi. there is a good view to the left up Hermit Branch. After reaching the crest at 1.0 mi., the trail follows it for some distance. There is a view of Bearpen Ridge to the left at 1.4 mi. The trail soon passes clumps of wild azalea and heavy vines. At 1.7 mi. it crosses the nose of the ridge and enters a second-growth forest, with a ground cover of trailing arbutus. At 2.1 mi. blue gentian blooms in the fall, and trillium in the spring. Beginning at 2.4 mi., the trail enters a grove of hemlocks, with several very large specimens, and continues through it for more than a half mile. At 3.1 mi. it makes a sharp right turn and leaves the grove.

At 3.2 mi. the forest is maple and beech, and at 3.3 mi., predominately beech. The trail passes a white quartz out-crop at 3.4 mi. and at 3.6 mi. reaches a good spring. The trail then slabs along the right side of Fork Ridge, reaching the crest at 4.3 mi. At 4.5 mi. there are massive upthrust boulders on the left. At 4.7 mi. the grade levels off, and the trail soon passes another spring. From this point the trail runs through virgin fir forest with a lush ground cover of ferns, mosses and violets. At 4.9 mi. it terminates at the Clingmans Dome Road, where a sign marks the trail. The parking area for the Spruce Fir Nature Trail is located 450 ft. to the left. A connecting trail leads straight ahead for 0.1 mi. to the A.T. If you walk 0.3 mi. to the left on the A.T., and then 0.4 mi. to the right (N) on the Sugarland Mtn. Trail (see p. 260), you will arrive at the Mt. Collins Shelter. It has room for 12 people.

Noland and
Forney Creeks Section
(North Carolina)

Introduction

The adjacent valleys of Noland and Forney creeks are situated immediately west of the Deep Creek basin, and both orient generally north to south.

Noland Creek is the smaller of the two basins, bounded on the west by Forney Ridge and on the east by Noland Divide. It is a pleasant valley which was once heavily settled. Today it is roadless except for the North Shore Road which invades the lower end of the valley, providing easy access. The valley is moderately to heavily used, especially by local horseback riders and fishermen. Access to the Noland Creek area is available via Clingmans Dome Road, North Shore Road or Lake Fontana. The Noland Divide Trail is described in the Deep Creek section of this book because it originates at the Deep Creek Campground. This leaves only two trails entirely within the basin—a valley trail and a connector to Forney Ridge. There are five back-country campsites and one horse camp located in the valley.

The Forney Creek watershed is bounded on the east by Forney Ridge and on the west by Welch Ridge. It is noteworthy for being one of the major roadless valleys remaining in the Smokies and is accessible by road only at its extreme northern end near Clingmans Dome. Trails from the Noland and Hazel creek areas lead into it, however, and the southern end is often approached by boat on Fontana Lake. (For boat information, see p. 195 in Introduction to Hazel Creek section.) The six designated campsites in the Forney basin all are located along Forney Creek.

The Forney Creek Valley was settled by families named Crisp, Monteith, Cole and Welch. They farmed in the creek bottoms and raised cattle which they drove to summer pastures on the high balds—the best known one being Andrews Bald, just south of Clingmans Dome on the Forney Ridge Trail. This bald was the grazing pasture used by the Anders family and it is still referred to as "Anders Bald" by the local residents. Unfortunately, the written name has everywhere become "Andrews" throughout Smokies literature. When the Clingmans Dome Road was built, grass seed was gathered from Andrews (or Anders) Bald and used to seed the road banks so that no alien species of grass were introduced to the area.

From 1909 into the 1920s the Norwood Lumber Company removed virtually all the standing timber from the Forney Creek Valley. Logging extended to within a mile of Clingmans Dome; old railroad grades may be seen today up to that point. In 1925 a bad forest fire, fueled by the slash left behind from logging operations, devastated the valley. There are still fire scars on the trees just west of Clingmans Dome. During the 1930s a CCC camp was located near the mouth of Bee Gum Branch on Forney Creek. Its crews built many miles of trail throughout the area.

Nowadays, maintained trails run along both Welch and Forney ridges, while the Forney Creek Trail goes up the middle of the basin and then curves northeast to climb Forney Ridge. Three other trails connect the valley floor with the ridge tops. Many other trails have been abandoned in the Forney and Noland Creek watersheds, so hikers using old maps should be very wary.

---

49 **NOLAND CREEK** 9.5 mi.

Gated jeep and horse trail / Max. elev. gain 2,440
Start: Noland Creek bridge on North Shore Road,
    1,800 ft.
End: Upper Sassafras Gap on Noland Divide, 4,240
    ft.
USGS quads: Noland Creek, Bryson City, Clingmans
    Dome, N.C.
Trail connections: Springhouse Branch, Noland Di-
    vide, Pole Road Creek

This trail runs north alongside Noland Creek as far as the
Bald Creek back-country campsite, where it turns east and
climbs abruptly to Upper Sassafras Gap on the crest of
Noland Divide.

The Noland Creek Valley takes its name from the
Noland family who formerly resided there. Once, it was
thickly populated; today many old fields, open meadows
and the chimneys of several old homesites can still be seen.
Although the early settlers cut and cleared a large part of
the valley for their farms, logging after the turn of the
century was limited to the removal of pole timber, chestnut, oak and acid wood. Therefore, a nearly virgin forest
clothes the upper slopes of the watershed. There are several
places to camp along the trail, and water is abundant.

Note: three new back-country campsites have been
established along the Noland Creek Trail—Jerry Flat campsite at about 5.5 mi., Upper Ripshin campsite at about 6.4
mi. and Noland Creek campsite about 1.0 mi. below the
trailhead.

Trailhead: The trail starts at the Noland Creek bridge and
parking lot on the North Shore Road. To reach the
trailhead, drive to Bryson City, N.C., on U.S. 19. Once

there, turn north alongside the Swain County Courthouse, crossing the Tuckasegee River and railroad tracks at Bryson Depot. Continue straight ahead on the main road for a distance of 7.1 mi. from the edge of town. You will recognize Noland Creek bridge by its long, high span, which has a curve built into it. There is ample parking on the left before the bridge. From the parking lot, walk uphill 200 ft., around a gate and down a steep paved jeep road to the right.

Trail Details: The trail reaches an old road on the edge of Noland Creek at 0.2 mi. To the left the road goes about 1.0 mi. downstream to the shore of Fontana Lake. Make an abrupt turn to the right and walk along this gravel jeep road. Pass under the highway bridge at 0.5 mi. and immediately cross Noland Creek on a bridge. There is a spring at 1.1 mi. in a forest of cove hardwoods. At 1.7 mi. a sign points left up a trail which leads along the left bank of Bearpen Branch to a back-country campsite equipped with tables, fireplaces and a pit toilet. At 2.3 mi. the trail passes an old clearing and enters a grove of white pine; on the right Noland Creek pours over large flat rocks. In this area old homesites can be identified by boxwoods growing next to what used to be front walks.

After a jeep bridge over Noland Creek at 3.1 mi., the road forks. The trail takes the right branch, following Noland Creek, and then climbs a gentle slope to about 100 ft. above the stream. A TVA water-gauging station can be seen below at 3.3 mi. There is a view across the creek of the steep mountainsides and hills beyond. The trail passes by a large rock outcrop about 100 ft. above the trail and, shortly thereafter, there are old split-rail fences on both sides of Noland Creek. At 3.9 mi. an unmarked and unmaintained trail leads left to the upper end of Indian Creek and on to Forney Ridge. It is difficult to locate and now nearly impossible to hike because of the undergrowth, although it was originally a good graded trail.

The Noland Creek Trail soon descends gently into a large clearing where many walnut trees grow. This is Solola Valley, which was heavily settled in the days before the park was established. It takes its name from the Cherokee word for "squirrel." You will be in the valley for about a half-mile. Note the remains of an old grist mill foundation on the edge of Noland Creek, upstream from the bridge at 4.4 mi. At 4.6 mi. Springhouse Branch Trail begins on the left (N) and runs 2.8 mi. to the crest of Forney Ridge. This junction is the site of the Mill Creek Horse Camp where there are five picnic tables, horse feed racks and a pit toilet. The camp is heavily used by horseback riders and therefore usually closed to hikers. If you do stop, be sure to boil all water you take from Mill Creek (the camp's source of water). The Noland Creek Trail, still following the jeep road, passes a spring branch about 200 ft. beyond the camp and then a Park Service fire tool cabin and the ruins of several buildings, including cabins and a springhouse. In the days when the Park Service received enough funds to maintain adequate back-country surveillance, there was a ranger stationed there.

Leaving Solola Valley, the jeep road becomes somewhat rougher, but the grade stays gentle. At 4.9 mi. there is a picturesque waterfall on Noland Creek. The trail fords the creek to continue on the west bank. It passes an old homesite with very young trees at 5.8 mi. and then fords Noland Creek twice within 0.4 mi. The trail next climbs gradually through cove hardwoods—magnolia, silverbell, red and sugar maple, hemlock, beech, buckeye, oak, hickory, basswood and yellow poplar.

The trail narrows to a graded horse trail and crosses Upper Ripshin Branch on a springy footbridge at 7.2 mi. Just beyond, it fords Noland Creek for the last time. Dog-hobble bush and spikemoss are common there. The trail ascends moderately to cross Sassafras Branch at 8.6 mi. (fill canteens for the Noland Divide Trail) and then turns

sharp right at a junction. Six hundred ft. to the left (W), by
a particularly fast section of Noland Creek, is the Bald
Creek back-country campsite (3,560 ft.) where there is a
table and room for about eight tents.

The trail now climbs steadily and steeply along Sassafras
Branch to 9.1 mi., where it leaves the branch and climbs
even more steeply to end at Upper Sassafras Gap and a trail
intersection at 9.5 mi. To the left (N) along the Noland Divide Trail it is 3.6 mi. to the Clingmans Dome Road. Straight
ahead is the terminus of the Pole Road Creek Trail, down
which it is 3.2 mi. to the Deep Creek Trail (see p. 166). To
the right Noland Divide Trail leads 7.9 mi. to Deep Creek
Campground.

---

(50) SPRINGHOUSE BRANCH 2.8 mi.

Horse trail / Max. elev. gain 1,350
Start: Solola Valley on Noland Creek Trail, 2,550 ft.
End: Board Camp Gap on Forney Ridge, 3,900 ft.
USGS quads: Noland Creek, Silers Bald, N.C.
Trail connections: Noland Creek, Forney Ridge

This trail leads from Noland Creek to the crest of Forney
Ridge, and is the *only* open connection between the Noland
and Forney areas. All other trails shown on topographic
maps as giving access to Forney Ridge from the east are
unmaintained and impassable, or, in the case of one trail
appearing on the 1971 Park Service handout map, nonexistent. Additionally, there is no direct connection between
Mill Creek and Andrews Bald.

Trailhead: The trail starts at the Mill Creek Horse Camp in
the Solola Valley at 4.6 mi. on the Noland Creek Trail.

Trail Details: Leaving the campsite, walk past a shelter and

proceed north on the right bank of Mill Creek. The first few
hundred ft. of trail are in a rocky, dried-up creek bed, then
on an old wagon road. At 0.5 mi. the trail passes the ruins
of an old house. Then it enters a region of old fields which
are growing up in pole timber. At 0.6 mi. there are eight
pyramids of rocks, piled there by the settlers who cleared
the fields. On the N.C. side of the Smokies, rocks from the
fields were piled together haphazardly like this, whereas on
the Tenn. side, they were usually built into fences. The trail
crosses a rotten foot log over Mill Creek at 0.7 mi. and
continues through old fields. It then enters a stand of virgin
timber where there are many downed chestnut trees. It
crosses several small streams and begins a moderate climb
on a well-maintained trail. At 2.0 mi. it crosses the crest of
a side ridge. Ladies' tresses, a kind of orchid, grow there. At
2.4 mi., two springs, 200 ft. apart, supply the last water on
the trail. The trail reaches the crest of Forney Ridge and its
terminus at Board Camp Gap at 2.8 mi. To the left (S) the
Forney Ridge Trail leads 1.3 mi. from its trailhead at the
end of the Bee Gum Branch Trail. To the right (N) the
Forney Ridge Trail runs 5.5 mi. to terminate at the
Clingmans Dome Road (see p. 190). There is a flat area
suitable for camping in Board Camp Gap, but you would
have to carry water up from the springs you passed at 2.4
mi.

(51) **FORNEY CREEK** 11.4 mi.

Horse and foot trail / Max. elev. gain 4,030
Start: Fontana Lake, 1,710 ft.
End: Forney Ridge, 0.6 mi. north of Andrews Bald,
  5,740 ft.
USGS quads: Noland Creek, Silers Bald, Clingmans
  Dome, N.C.
Trail connections: Jumpup Ridge, Bee Gum Branch,
  Jonas Creek, Forney Ridge

The Forney Creek Trail is the major trail in the Forney
Creek Valley. It runs from Fontana Lake upstream along
Forney Creek and on to Forney Ridge. The first 9.0 mi.
follow an old logging railroad grade. The creek must be
forded repeatedly because most of its bridges have long
since washed away, so you can expect to get your feet wet.
The remainder of the route is on a graded foot trail which is
adequately maintained for hikers. There are several designated camping areas along the trail, and there is plenty of
water.
  Note: there are three new back-country campsites along
the Forney Creek Trail—Whiteoak Branch campsite at
about 1.5 mi., Jonas Creek campsite at about 4.1 mi. and
Steeltrap campsite at about 6.6 mi.

Trailhead: The trail starts where Forney Creek empties into
Fontana Lake. Look for the old railroad grade at the edge
of the high-water mark. Boats may be chartered at most of
the landings on the lake to deliver hikers to the trailhead or,
by prearrangement, pick them up there.

Trail Details: Just past the edge of the tree line, at 0.1 mi.,
the trail reaches Lower Forney Creek campsite, which has
picnic tables, grills and a pit toilet. Signs there mark the
trail and warn campers to boil all drinking water. The trail

continues on a jeep road up the west side of Forney Creek, which it crosses on a bridge at 0.2 mi. At 0.6 mi. the Jumpup Ridge Trail begins on the left on a railroad grade and leads northwest 5.8 mi. to Welch Ridge.

Forney Creek Trail, still on the main railroad grade, continues straight ahead up the east bank of Forney Creek. At 0.7 mi. a connector leads left to the Jumpup Ridge Trail. At 1.5 mi. the trail fords an old channel to an island where there is a railroad grade. At 1.6 mi. it again crosses Forney Creek, in an easy ford. It fords the creek again at 1.7 mi., just above Whiteoak Branch, where an unmarked trail in good condition leads to the right up the branch. Forney Creek Trail continues up the east side of Forney Creek, making an easy ford to the west side at 2.4 mi. At 2.6 mi. there is another easy ford, to a large island opposite Bee Gum Branch. The trail soon reaches the end of the island and makes a moderately difficult ford to the east bank and at 2.8 mi. arrives at the site of the old CCC camp. Farm machinery, a gas pump and 50-gallon drums lie about.

At the north end of the camp there is a difficult ford across an old channel and beyond it a trail junction with signs. Bee Gum Branch Trail begins at this spot and leads to the right 2.9 mi. to Forney Ridge, from which there is access to the Noland Creek area (see p. 185). Upper Forney Creek campsite is located just north of the trail junction. Beyond the camp there is an old homesite.

The trail passes a USGS benchmark at 2.9 mi. and immediately makes a wet, difficult crossing of the creek. At 3.3 mi. it crosses Slab Camp Branch on a fallen log bridge. ("Slab Camp" refers to an old hunting cabin that was built of slabs.) At 3.6 mi. there is a difficult rock hop across the creek. At 4.1 mi. the Jonas Creek Trail begins on the left and leads 3.5 mi. to Welch Ridge (see p. 186).

The Forney Creek Trail continues to the right as a foot trail on an old railroad grade along the creek. It crosses Board Camp Branch at 4.3 mi. There is a moderate ford across to the west bank of Forney Creek at 4.6 mi. At 5.0 mi. the trail fords to the east bank, just above the mouth of Chokeberry Branch. It fords back to the west bank at 5.3 mi., at the mouth of Huggins Creek, to reach Monteith camp (also known as Huggins Creek back-country campsite). Alas, early in 1972 this camp was a garbage collector's dream. It would be delightful if it were kept clean. Meanwhile, most hikers choose to pass it by.

The trail fords Forney Creek at 5.5 mi. with a moderately difficult crossing. The railroad grade then climbs several switchbacks. At a sharp left, an unmaintained trail leads right toward Board Camp Gap. Forney Creek Trail follows an easy grade through a forest of sourwood, maple, tulip, chestnut oak, sassafras and rhododendron. At 6.9 mi. the trail crosses Buckhorn Branch (an overgrown trail leads to the right) and immediately fords Forney Creek. Note the sign which indicates a campsite downstream. The trail now curves to the left and fords Little Steeltrap Creek at 7.0 mi. Climbing, it crosses three small bridges. It switchbacks to the right and again crosses Little Steeltrap Creek beside a caved-in trestle at 7.3 mi. The trail goes through two more switchbacks and then ascends gently along the side of Wild Cherry Ridge through a mixed forest of poplar, magnolia, maple and locust. It crosses Steeltrap Creek at 8.8 mi. on a fallen trestle to reach the end of the railroad grade at 9.0 mi. The rate of climb to this point has been barely perceptible, and the walking easy except for the many creek crossings, where you will inevitably get your feet wet.

The trail continues up Forney Creek and goes through two short switchbacks. At 9.1 mi. it begins to follow an old logging road, climbing moderately. At 9.5 mi. it leaves the logging road for a graded trail, switchbacks abruptly left and right, and at 9.6 mi. crosses Forney Creek easily as it cascades down a steep ravine.

The trail then climbs with moderate steepness on a

graded footpath above the creek. Forest growth has changed
to maple, beech, birch and hemlock. The trail reaches the
bank of a creek in a deep cove at 10.1 mi. and turns sharply
to the left (NW). It makes a turn to the right at 10.6 mi.
through balsam and beech. At 11.2 mi. it crosses several
small spring branches—the last water on the trail. In this
area several trees have fallen across the path. The trail ends
at a junction in a flat saddle at 11.4 mi. The trail coming
from the right is the Forney Ridge Trail, leading past
Andrews Bald. To the left it is 1.0 mi. along the Forney
Ridge Trail to the Clingmans Dome Road (see p. 190).

---

(52) **JUMPUP RIDGE** (Bear Creek) 5.8 mi.

Gated jeep trail / Max. elev. gain 3,100
Start: Forney Creek Trail, 1,800 ft.
End: Welch Ridge near High Rocks, 4,900 ft.
USGS quads: Noland Creek, Silers Bald, N.C.
Trail connections: Forney Creek, Welch Ridge, Cold
    Spring Branch

This trail follows an old railroad grade up Bear Creek and
then Jumpup Ridge to the crest of Welch Ridge. An
additional 0.6 mi. takes the hiker to the High Rocks Fire
Tower and a spectacular view. From near High Rocks the
Cold Spring Branch Trail may be followed into the Hazel
Creek watershed. The first half of the trail climbs moderately, but the second half is steep—so much so that a
climber topping the ridge appears to have "jumped up."
The day hiker should allow four hours to cover the trail.

Trailhead: The trail angles to the left at 0.6 mi. on the
Forney Creek Trail, 0.5 mi. upstream from the Lower
Forney Creek campsite. There is a trail sign at the spot.

Trail Details: After 200 ft. the trail crosses Forney Creek on a wooden bridge. At the far end of the bridge there is an old abandoned campsite with table and fireplace on the left.

The trail passes through bottom land and then crosses Bear Creek on a wooden motor bridge into a small meadow. At the upper end the trail turns right and ascends gently along Welch Branch. At 0.5 mi. it crosses Welch Branch in a loop, doubling back on itself, and enters a hemlock forest, climbing gently but steadily. It slabs along the south side of Jumpup Ridge, high above Bear Creek. To the south there are occasional views of Pilot Knob and Pilot Ridge, which were named for the large number of pilot snakes found there. According to local legend, pilot snakes (known elsewhere as copperheads) travel in front of rattlesnakes, leading the way.

At 1.9 mi. the trail crosses a wooden motor bridge over Bear Creek. At 2.0 mi. an unmaintained graded trail starts on the left and runs to the crest of Pilot Ridge, then up over Bee Knob to High Rocks. At 2.1 mi. the Jumpup Ridge Trail again crosses Bear Creek on a wooden motor bridge and continues upstream on the right bank. At 2.8 mi. it reaches Poplar Flats, a flat place where much poplar pole-timber grows. There the railroad grade makes a loop around a rough campsite on the bank of Bear Creek. This is the last easy source of water on the trail.

At Poplar Flats the trail takes the right fork of the railroad grade and makes a right-angle turn onto a jeep road. At once the trail begins a moderate to steep, and steady, climb through a giant "S" curve, which ends at 3.3 mi. on top of Jumpup Ridge. At 3.4 mi. there is a view of High Rocks to the left, up Bear Creek. At 3.6 mi. the trail enters a gap where an unmaintained trail enters on the right, coming from Advalorem Branch. Just above the gap to the left there is a view of Bear Creek Valley and Fontana Lake.

The trail slabs along the east side of the ridge in open woods and at 4.4 mi. negotiates a switchback. At 5.3 mi. it reaches another gap and the beginning of a zone of mature timber. The trail slabs left (W) and climbs on a moderate grade to terminate on the crest of Welch Ridge at 5.8 mi. (The mileages given for the Jumpup Ridge Trail on the trail sign are incorrect.) At this spot Welch Ridge Trail leads right 6.2 mi. to the A.T. at Silers Bald (see p. 187). To reach High Rocks, turn left onto the Welch Ridge Trail along a grassy ridge. (In 0.3 mi. a graded, unmarked trail enters from the left. It is the Cold Spring Branch Trail, having run 3.9 mi. from Hazel Creek, see p. 200). Keep to the right and after 0.6 mi. you will reach the rocks and a fire tower, from which there is a superb view.

---

(53) **BEE GUM BRANCH** 2.9 mi.

Horse trail / Max. elev. gain 1,640
Start: Old CCC camp on Forney Creek Trail, 2,160 ft.
End: Forney Ridge, 3,800 ft.
USGS quads: Noland Creek, Silers Bald, N.C.
Trail connections: Forney Creek, Forney Ridge

This is the only open trail connecting the lower end of Forney Creek with Forney Ridge. Many other trails once ran between Forney Creek and Forney Ridge, but they are now all overgrown. Therefore this trail must be used in any reasonable connection between the two watersheds. It is well maintained and graded.

Trailhead: The trail starts to the right at 2.8 mi. on the Forney Creek Trail, immediately north of the Upper Forney Creek campsite and the site of an old CCC camp (see p. 180).

Trail Details: The trail climbs at a moderate grade, crossing two spring branches at 0.2 mi. and a tributary stream at 0.5 mi. There is a good view of High Rocks Fire Tower directly to the west across Forney Creek at 1.7 mi. The trail follows the left side of Bee Gum Branch for a while and crosses that creek at 2.3 mi. in the head of a cove. There is a sharp bend at 2.8 mi., and then the trail ends on the crest of Forney Ridge. There is a trail sign. Forney Ridge Trail starts on the left, and runs 6.8 mi. to a parking area at the end of the Clingmans Dome Road, passing a junction with the Spring-house Branch Trail at 1.3 mi. (see p. 171). To the right (S) and directly ahead, unmaintained and impassable abandoned trails lead to Noland and Forney creeks.

---

(54) **JONAS CREEK** 3.5 mi.

Horse trail / Max. elev. gain 2,200
Start: Forney Creek Trail, 2,400 ft.
End: Welch Ridge, 4,600 ft.
USGS quads: Silers Bald, N.C.
Trail connections: Forney Creek, Welch Ridge

This trail, in combination with others, makes a major route between Forney Creek and the A.T. (or Hazel Creek) via Welch Ridge. The grade is moderate but steady, with a series of switchbacks. The trail follows an old railroad bed to its midway point, and then climbs a well-maintained horse trail.

Trailhead: The trail starts at mile 4.1 on the Forney Creek Trail on the east bank of Forney Creek (see p. 180), and runs to the left (W).

Trail Details: The trail immediately fords Forney Creek, just above the mouth of Jonas Creek and, at the end of the flood plain, begins a moderate climb. It crosses Jonas Creek on a log bridge at 1.2 mi. and recrosses it at 1.3 mi. Note the moss-covered rocks in the stream. Birch, poplar, maple and beech trees grow roundabout. The trail turns up the valley of Little Jonas Creek, bearing west. It crosses a small tributary at 1.4 mi., reaches the end of the old railroad grade and recrosses Little Jonas Creek at 1.6 mi. At 1.7 mi. it makes a scenic crossing of Yanu Branch on a log bridge and begins a series of switchbacks. At 1.8 mi. there is a view of the creek, the talus-filled valley and a poplar grove. After the switchbacks, at 2.7 mi. the trail runs to within 50 ft. of Yanu Branch—the last chance for water on the trail. Then the trail environment changes from an open valley to steep mountain slopes. The path runs at a moderate upgrade through oak, poplar, black locust and maple. There is a good view to the east at 3.0 mi. At 3.5 mi. the trail terminates on Welch Ridge at a junction with the Welch Ridge Trail. To the right (N) it is 2.4 mi. to the A.T. at Silers Bald. To the left (SW) it is 4.4 mi. to the head of the Welch Ridge Trail at High Rocks.

---

(55) **WELCH RIDGE** 6.8 mi.

Gated jeep and horse trail / Max. elev. gain 210
Start: High Rocks, 5,190 ft.
End: A.T. at Silers Bald, 5,400 ft.
USGS quads: Noland Creek, Silers Bald, N.C.
Trail connections: Cold Spring Branch, Jumpup Ridge, Jonas Creek, Hazel Creek, A.T.

Welch Ridge Trail, graded and well maintained, climbs along the crest of Welch Ridge. The first stretch is dug out and about four ft. wide; the remainder is more narrow. Two side trails connect with Hazel Creek, and two with Forney Creek. Along much of the trail you can see the path cut by cattle driven by the Siler family to summer pastures on

Silers Bald. Hiking time for this trail, without a load, is about 3.5 hours, including a stop for lunch. There is only one good source of water.

Trailhead: The trail starts at the rock outcrop known as High Rocks. The steel High Rocks Fire Tower can be climbed for spectacular views, but good views, particularly to the south, can be seen even from the rocks. There is also an old warden's cabin at High Rocks. It offers some shelter but no water.

Trail Details: The trail leaves the rocks and descends the nose of the ridge. It passes through rhododendron and then down stone stairs to a jeep road. It follows the road downhill at a moderate grade. At 0.3 mi. an unmarked trail terminates on the right. This is the Cold Spring Branch Trail, having run 3.9 mi. from Hazel Creek (see p. 200).

Welch Ridge Trail continues straight ahead on the jeep road, passing some large rocks on the right. At 0.6 mi. there is a trail junction—the jeep road turns right down Jumpup Ridge Trail to Forney Creek (see p. 183). The sign there is incorrect: actually, from the junction it is 5.8 mi. to Forney Creek, and 6.4 mi. to Fontana Lake at the mouth of Forney Creek.

Welch Ridge Trail runs straight and soon reaches Bearwallow Bald, an open area measuring 10 or 15 acres. The trail then descends to a gap at 1.2 mi. It slabs left leaving the gap and reaches a spring, walled up with rock, at 1.6 mi. This is the only easily accessible water on the trail. The trail climbs gently, crossing the nose of Hawk Ridge at 1.8 mi. Hawk Knob is directly to the right. These features get their names from the abundance of hawks in the region. At 2.0 mi. the four-foot-wide path narrows in the gap between Hawk Knob and Mt. Glory, whose top it reaches at 2.1 mi. The "glory" in Mt. Glory and White Man's Glory Creek (which tumbles down its slopes) originally described the ease of traveling on the mountain. I.e., Mt. Glory is open and not steep. At the top of the mountain, a graded but unmaintained and unmarked trail leads right down Slab Camp Branch to Forney Creek.

Welch Ridge Trail descends steeply, passing through a rhododendron tunnel, to a low gap at 2.4 mi. From there it generally continues along the ridge top. It passes a rock outcrop at 3.0 mi. and then slabs left around Scarlet Ridge. A high point is reached at 4.2 mi. The trail now descends on a moderate grade to a trail junction on the right at 4.4 mi. This is the end of the Jonas Creek Trail, which has come 3.5 mi. from Forney Creek.

Welch Ridge Trail climbs on the east side of the ridge to a gap at 4.7 mi. It climbs some more, gently, and then travels on the level to Mule Gap at 5.4 mi., where there is a sign. Water can be found on the southeast side of the gap, about 150 yds. down the very steep slope (no trail). To the left an unmarked trail leads down into Hazel Creek.

The trail next climbs by a series of switchbacks which end at 5.8 mi. in an oak forest. The oaks soon give way to beech as the trail ascends gently. It then follows the crest, passing for some distance along the west side of a meadow. At 6.3 mi. the marked Hazel Creek Trail terminates on the left, having run 15.0 mi. from Fontana Lake (see p. 196). At 6.5 mi. the Welch Ridge Trail reaches a meadow on the side of Silers Bald. An unmarked path leads to the left through grass for about 0.2 mi. to Silers Bald Shelters and Spring. The main trail slabs to the right, entering woods, and at 6.8 mi. terminates at the A.T. To the right it is 1.2 mi. to Double Springs Gap and Shelter, and 4.5 mi. to the parking lot at the end of the Clingmans Dome Road.

---

56 **FORNEY RIDGE** 6.8 mi.

Foot trail / Max. elev. gain 2,500
Start: Bee Gum Branch Trail, 3,800 ft.
End: Clingmans Dome Road end, 6,300 ft.
USGS quads: Noland Creek, Silers Bald, Clingmans
    Dome, N.C.
Trail connections: Bee Gum Branch, Springhouse
    Branch, Forney Creek, A.T.

This trail runs along the crest of Forney Ridge from the Bee
Gum Branch Trail to the Forney Ridge parking area at the
end of the road to Clingmans Dome, the highest mountain
in the national park. It was named for Thomas Lanier
Clingman (U.S. senator, mining prospector, Civil War general) who explored these mountains during the 1850s and
thereafter never stopped extolling their virtues. At one time
an old CCC trail continued southwest along Forney Ridge
from the trailhead to connect with the lower ends of
both Noland and Forney creeks, but lack of maintenance
has closed these trails. The Forney Ridge Trail climbs
steadily for most of its length, through beautiful open
woods. It is well maintained and generally free of litter.
Water is available along the way.

Trailhead: The trail starts where the Bee Gum Branch Trail
ends on Forney Ridge (see p. 185). There is a sign there.
Facing northeast up the Forney Ridge Trail, the following
trails can be seen at this junction: To the left (W) the
well-maintained Bee Gum Branch Trail leads 2.9 mi. to
Forney Creek. To the right (E) a graded but unmaintained
and unmarked trail leads to Noland Creek; this trail is
currently impassable. Directly to the rear (SW) a graded but
unmaintained trail leads down the crest of Forney Ridge
1.6 mi. to a junction with the Gray Wolf Creek and Laurel

Branch trails, both of which are graded but unmaintained and nearly impassable.

Trail Details: From the junction the trail slabs the left side of a knob. There is a fine view of the High Rocks Fire Tower to the west at 0.3 mi. The trail climbs easily to a small knob and then passes through several small gaps. At 0.9 mi. it runs along a level crest and then descends gently, reaching Board Camp Gap at 1.3 mi., where there is a marked trail junction. Springhouse Branch Trail terminates on the right (E), having come 2.8 mi. from Noland Creek at Mill Creek Horse Camp (see p. 178). Water is available at a spring 0.4 mi. down this side trail. To the left (W) a manway leads to Chokeberry Branch on Forney Creek. Board Camp Gap is named after a hunters' cabin that once stood there, constructed of rough boards.

The Forney Ridge Trail proceeds north and slabs left while climbing steadily, sometimes on switchbacks. It crosses the nose of the ridge at 2.0 mi. and continues to climb. Then it levels off and descends gently to a gap at 2.5 mi. This is an area of second-growth forest with occasional oaks scattered through it. Just beyond the gap, a large oak grows on the right, measuring 17 ft. in circumference. The trail slabs left, passes Buckhorn Bald and reaches a gap at 3.3 mi. There an unmaintained manway leads left down Buckhorn Branch to Forney Creek. The Forney Ridge Trail ascends along the ridge on a moderate to steep grade, curling around a spur at 3.8 mi. After passing through a small gap, the trail becomes rocky as the hardwoods thin out. It continues up a moderate to steep grade and at about 4.6 mi. crosses several springs.

At 5.0 mi. the trail enters the lower edge of Andrews Bald Meadows, a large grassy bald surrounded by spruce and fir trees. An outstanding display of flame azalea and purple rhododendron blooms at Andrews Bald during the last two weeks of June. At anytime, there are beautiful vistas to the south and southwest of the Little Tennessee River Valley and the Nantahala Mtns. Because this bald is reasonably close to an open road, it makes an easy and popular day hike throughout the warm months.

The trail leaves the upper end of the meadow at 5.2 mi. and enters a spruce and balsam fir forest which is accentuated by mosses and ferns. At 5.8 mi. the Forney Creek Trail terminates on the left, having come 11.4 mi. from Fontana Lake (see p. 180). The Forney Ridge Trail continues north on a well-used but rough, rocky path through a fir forest. At 6.7 mi. at a trail junction, it turns right (E) and climbs through jumbled rocks to its terminus at the Forney Ridge parking area on the Clingmans Dome Road (6.8 mi.). At the parking area there are water and restrooms. To reach the A.T., go back to the trail junction at 6.7 mi. and continue straight (NW) for about 0.4 mi.

Hazel Creek Section
(North Carolina)

Introduction

Hazel Creek is probably the most popular and widely publi-
cized of all the creeks in the Great Smoky Mountains, for it
has been written about as a trout stream in many outdoors
magazines. Its headwaters are formed by several springs
rising in a relatively small area just below the state line ridge
crest, southwest of Silers Bald. These spring trickles join
together to form a well-defined stream course which flows
in a southwesterly direction for 15 miles before emptying
into Fontana Lake. The main stream has several major
tributaries, the better-known ones being Cold Spring
Branch, Bone Valley Creek and Sugar Fork.

The major trail, the Hazel Creek Trail, extends from
Fontana Lake to Welch Ridge at a point one mile from
Silers Bald on the Appalachian Trail. All side trails leading
out of the Hazel Creek drainage follow one of the major
tributaries. The Sugar Fork Trail runs west to Pickens Gap
where it connects with both the Jenkins Ridge Trail (which
leads to the Appalachian Trail) and the Pinnacle Creek Trail
(which leads to Eagle Creek). The Bone Valley Trail begins
at Hazel Creek and runs to a dead end at an historical site,
the Hall Cabin. The Cold Spring Branch Trail runs east to
reach High Rocks on Welch Ridge. There are seven back-
country campsites on the Hazel Creek Trail, and one on the
Jenkins Ridge Trail.

As in other areas of the Smokies, streams and specific
locations have taken the name of a local family, often the
original settler, e.g., Walker, Proctor and Huggins creeks.

Occasionally an incident provided a name, as was the case with Bone Valley Creek. According to Horace Kephart, a severe and unexpected late spring blizzard hit the Smokies (probably in the 1880s). The cattle had already been herded to higher elevations for summer grazing on the grass balds. With the intense cold the stock crowded together for warmth, actually piling on top of one another. They died in the storm, leaving a huge pile of bones—and a geographical name—behind.

The Hazel Creek drainage was probably one of the most completely logged drainages in the park. The Ritter Lumber Company carried on extensive logging operations for nearly 20 years, removing virtually every stick of salable, accessible timber. During this period the town of Ritter sprang up on the Little Tennessee River at the mouth of Hazel Creek, where there were railway shipping connections. (The site of the town has been drowned by Fontana Lake.) At the peak of the lumbering, Proctor, 1 mile up the present Hazel Creek jeep road, was a boom town with a population exceeding 1,000, nearly all employed directly or indirectly by lumber companies in processing, storing and shipping. Today the remains of the old dry kiln, the depression and face of the log holding pond, and two or three small concrete pumping stations which can be seen on the left of the trail, about one mile above Fontana Lake, are all that is left of Proctor. Evidence of the old logging railroads may be found up Hazel Creek as far as the cascades (13 miles). Today the evenly spaced bumps you'll notice in the trail grade are the result of the rotting of cross ties. There are a switchback and some twisted sections of track just below the Hazel Creek Cascades.

As the timber supply began to dwindle in the mid-thirties, so did the population. After the lumber companies left, some people went to work in the copper mines on the Ecoah Branch of Eagle Creek. These were in operation from

1927 to the early forties. Residents of the Proctor area walked all the way to and from the mines each day. Then Fontana Dam was built (completed in 1945), and Fontana Lake filled up behind it. When the lake eliminated all road access to Hazel Creek, the basin began to recover from man's depredations.

The varied plants of Hazel Creek served as a medicine cabinet to the early inhabitants, who ate them raw, boiled, dried, squeezed, or made poultices of them to cure their aches and ills. Today, examples of nearly every flower, vine, shrub and tree growing anywhere in the Smokies may be found in the Hazel Creek drainage—although many of the small wild herbaceous plants, having been overpicked for their medicinal value, cannot be found near Proctor or other once-populated locations. Some beautiful domestic plants still grow at the sites of old houses.

The permanent residents of Hazel Creek nowadays are the wild animals. Beaver dams can be found a short distance up Possum Hollow along Shehan Branch. While the animal itself is seldom seen, its mark is easy to find on trees. Black bear and European wild boar (*Sus scrofa*) are common. The bears frequently get much too friendly to suit campers and will occasionally try to move right in and help themselves to the goodies. The wild boar is less of a nuisance to campers but considerably more destructive to the land because of its habit of rooting in the ground.

The Hazel Creek section can be reached only by hiking in from adjacent areas or by riding in a boat across Fontana Lake. The closest boat dock is Fontana Boat Dock, which is located about 1.5 miles east of Fontana Village on a short side road running north from N.C. 28. Boats and motors may be rented there; shuttle service to and from Hazel Creek is also available. The water distance from Fontana Dock to Hazel Creek is approximately 6 miles, depending on the level of the lake, which fluctuates considerably, but as a general rule is up during summer and down during winter.

---

(57) **HAZEL CREEK** 15.0 mi.

Gated jeep and foot trail / Max. elev. gain 3,583
Start: Fontana Lake at Hazel Creek, 1,742 ft.
End: Welch Ridge, 0.5 mi. south of Silers Bald, 5,325 ft.
USGS quads: Tuskeegee, Thunderhead Mtn., Silers Bald, N.C.
Trail connections: Sugar Fork, Bone Valley, Cold Spring Branch, Welch Ridge

---

Hazel Creek Trail follows Hazel Creek from Fontana Lake northeast to its headwaters near Silers Bald. At first the trail follows a maintenance jeep road, parts of which were county road during the logging era. This road is hard packed and has a rough gravel surface in many places but is generally in good condition as far as the Bone Valley campsite (5.6 mi.). Beyond Bone Valley the road becomes a jeep trail. There is little, if any, evidence that any surfacing work was ever undertaken. It is very rough with many mud holes and large rocks. The last 4.5 mi. are on a foot trail with no bridges and frequent wet fords. (Extra socks are in order.) The grade is gentle along the lower and middle sections, but the last part is quite steep in places.

Many beautiful flowers grow along this trail. White azalea may be seen along the banks and on the little islands of Hazel Creek—particularly from the old mill pond to north of Proctor, between the second and third bridges and beside the "Brown" pool above Sawdust Pile campsite. If you fail to notice them, their lovely fragrance will reveal their presence. In late summer fine displays of brilliant red cardinal flower, and pale pink and white turtlehead, bloom in wet areas all along the creek.

This trail is popular with trout fishermen, who usually stay at one of the back-country campsites located at fairly even intervals along the creek. Use of these camps is moderate and there is usually an adequate supply of firewood. With the exception of the Cascades campsite, all established campsites on Hazel Creek are equipped with tables, pit toilets, at least one bear-proof food cache and fireplaces (most of the latter in bad repair).

Note: there are two new back-country campsites on the Hazel Creek Trail—Sugar Fork at 4.9 mi. and Proctor Creek at 10.5 mi.

Trailhead: The trail begins at the head of the Hazel Creek bay on Fontana Lake. It can be reached only by boat from one of the docks along the south shore of the lake (see the general introduction to this section). The first informational sign is located a short distance from the lake along the jeep road. Two-tenths of a mile beyond the sign, there is a spring and a trail register box.

Trail Details: The trail follows the maintenance road until reaching the first campsite, Proctor, at 0.3 mi. In a fairly large area between the trail and the creek there are five tables, a bear-proof food cache and two pit toilets. A hitching rack for horses is located on the other side of the trail. Although this campsite is situated only a short distance from the lake, it seems to be no more heavily used than others on Hazel Creek. A rare "yellow berried" dogwood grows just above the campsite, a few feet to the left of the road in the south corner of a field.

The trail continues upstream, going through a giant curve called The Horseshoe. (Avoid all jeep trails leading away from Hazel Creek.) At 3.3 mi. the trail arrives at the Sawdust Pile campsite, which has three tables, a bear-proof food cache, two pit toilets and a hitching rack on the other side of the road. There is a spring (no sign) located beyond and above the hitching rack; wood is available.

The trail continues along the road. At 3.5 mi. a few beautiful showy orchis are growing on the left. They are difficult to find but worth the effort. At 4.9 mi. the Sugar Fork Trail begins on the left, with connections to the Jenkins Ridge Trail and Eagle Creek (see p. 202).

The Bone Valley campsite at 5.6 mi. has three tables (well separated to accommodate three parties), two bear-proof food caches, two pit toilets and a horse rack across the bridge and above the fork in the road. Good spring water flows from a pipe just upstream from the table closest to the bridge. Fire wood is available nearby. Across the bridge from the campsite, the Bone Valley Trail begins and runs north 1.7 mi. to the Hall Cabin (see p. 205).

The road becomes much rougher—a jeep trail. For the next 5.0 mi., it follows the left bank of Hazel Creek, where for about half that distance it is elevated 100 ft. or more above the creek. At about 6.1 mi. a particularly attractive display of yellow iris grows on the other side of the creek at the old Burlingame homesite. During the spring hundreds of these beautiful yellow flowers bloom along a spring seep, covering an area measuring more than 20 ft. wide and 100 ft. long. At 6.8 mi. the Cold Spring Branch Trail begins on the right and climbs to a spot near High Rocks on Welch Ridge. At 8.6 mi. the Hazel Creek Trail arrives at the Calhoun Place campsite, which has one table, a bear-proof food cache, two pit toilets and a hitching rack located a short distance beyond it on the upper side of the trail. Water may be had from a small branch a few yards below the campsite. There is plenty of wood close-by. At the Josh Calhoun homesite on the upper side of the trail from the campsite, a fine kerria bush survives and blooms profusely in season.

The trail continues upstream and crosses Walker Creek. A short distance beyond, at 9.5 mi., it fords the main creek, and then after 250 ft., fords it back again. These are very wet crossings at any time of year and may be avoided by following a section of foot trail that leaves the main trail at the water's edge. The jeep trail ends by a sign reading "Proctor Creek" at 10.4 mi. Just a few feet before the sign, the confluence of Hazel and Proctor creeks is practically obscured in thick rhododendron. The entire trail to this point has been on an easy grade with no steep climbs and with a total gain in elevation of only 1,333 ft.

Fifty ft. beyond and to the right of the Proctor Creek sign, a foot log with hand rail spans Proctor Creek, and then the trail picks up the old railroad grade. The trail becomes a footpath, but a fairly wide one, which is also used by horse traffic. The grade is gradual and pleasant for hiking. During the next 3.5 mi. there is an elevation gain of 1,425 ft., and there are 19 fords of the main creek, at least half of which are wet ones.

At 13.3 mi. the trail passes the Cascades campsite (4,000 ft.), which has no facilities. The wood supply, however, is adequate, and water may be had from the nearby creek. As a reward for those hiking this far up the trail, high-elevation flowers such as bluebead-lily (*Clintonia borealis*) and the wild monkshood can be seen above the Cascades campsite.

At about 14.1 mi., the trail becomes very steep for the remaining 0.9 mi. to Welch Ridge. While running up rocky and rough terrain, it is difficult to follow in many places and gains more than 600 ft. in elevation. Approximately halfway up there is an abandoned horse camp which is no longer used because this section of trail has been closed to horse travel. Present plans call for the eventual abandonment of the last 1.5 mi. of this trail and a rerouting into Mule Gap on Welch Ridge for the sake of a more gradual ascent.

At 15.0 mi. the trail finally ends on the top of Welch Ridge. The Welch Ridge Trail leads left (N) for 0.5 mi. to its terminus at Silers Bald on the A.T. (see p. 187). To the right (S) it is about 1.9 mi. to the end of the Jonas Creek Trail, which may be followed into the Forney Creek watershed.

---

(58) **COLD SPRING BRANCH** (High Rocks Fire Tower) 3.9 mi.

Horse and foot trail / Max. elev. gain 2,450
Start: Hazel Creek Trail, 2,480 ft.
End: Welch Ridge, 0.3 mi. from High Rocks, 4,910 ft.
USGS quads: Thunderhead Mtn., Tuskeegee, Noland Creek, Silers Bald, N.C.
Trail connections: Hazel Creek, Welch Ridge, Jumpup Ridge

This trail provides the only connection between the middle sections of Hazel Creek and Forney Creek. It generally follows an old railroad grade, but there is a very steep, short section for 0.2 mi. before Cold Spring Gap. The creek is forded many times. Near the top there are good springs. High Rocks Fire Tower, located about 0.3 mi. beyond the trail terminus, provides outstanding views of the Hazel and Forney Creek basins; see the Welch Ridge Trail for details.

Trailhead: The trail starts on the right at 6.8 mi. on the Hazel Creek Trail. There is no trail sign.

Trail Details: The trail climbs gradually to Hazel Creek, and fords it at 0.2 mi. After the ford it bears left through an old field grown up with small trees and shrubs. It reaches an old railroad grade at 0.3 mi. and turns right. At 0.5 mi. an obscure side trail on the right leads down a fairly steep bank to an old homesite on the flat below, believed to be the home, once, of a man who tended an old grinding mill. The remains of the mill may be seen a short distance above the mouth of Cold Spring. At 1.0 mi. the trail passes through an old homesite, grown up with blackberry bushes.

The trail fords Cold Spring Branch to the right at 1.1 mi. Then it leads straight away from the branch for a short distance, bends left a few feet, and back to the right, where the railroad grade is again obvious. At 1.3 mi. there is a sharp switchback to the left on the railroad grade. At 1.5 mi. wild ginger (*Asarum acuminatum*) grows in a rocky, wet area. This wildflower is not uncommon but is difficult to locate. For the next 0.3 mi., yellow lady's-slipper may be seen along the right side of the trail. The trail cuts to the right, up the bank, to continue along the right side of the branch. At 2.2 mi. it leaves the railroad grade to the left and fords the branch.

Soon the improved jeep trail ends, and a horse trail continues, crossing the branch three times in the next mile. A trickle on the left of the trail at 3.2 mi. is a good source of water. Immediately past it all signs of the railroad grade end. From there to the gap, the trail is very steep. It is scheduled for improvement in the future. The trail reaches Cold Spring Gap at 3.4 mi. Clingmans Dome is visible to the northeast on the far left of the horizon. Straight ahead, note the road scars of the Blue Ridge Parkway on the farthest ridge.

The trail turns left (NE) at the gap and follows along the right side of Welch Ridge. At 3.7 mi. there is a spring about 30 ft. below the trail on the right. It is marked by a large rock on the left of the trail. At 3.9 mi. the trail ends on Welch Ridge. The Welch Ridge Trail goes sharp left 0.3 mi. to reach High Rocks and runs to the right for 6.5 mi. to reach the A.T. (see p. 187). About 0.3 mi. down the Welch

Ridge Trail, the Jumpup Ridge Trail leaves on the right and runs 5.8 mi. to Forney Creek (see p. 183).

---

(59) SUGAR FORK 2.4 mi.

Gated jeep trail / Max. elev. gain 775
Start: Hazel Creek Trail, 2,189 ft.
End: Pickens Gap on Jenkins Trail Ridge, 2,964 ft.
USGS quads: Tuskeegee, Thunderhead Mtn., N.C.
Trail connections: Hazel Creek, Jenkins Ridge, Pinna-
   cle Creek

Sugar Fork was the site of the small mountain settlement of Medlin, where Granville Calhoun once lived. This famous mountaineer and bear hunter nursed writer Horace Kephart when Kephart first arrived in the Smokies in 1904 in a state of advanced alcoholism. Kephart eventually recovered and moved into a cabin by an abandoned copper mine on the Little Fork of Sugar Fork, where he lived for three years and absorbed almost every detail of pioneer life.

Once, this area was crisscrossed with trails. Today only the main trail up Sugar Fork remains, serving as the sole connection between Hazel Creek and points to the west— Jenkins Trail Ridge and Eagle Creek.

Note: there is a new back-country campsite, Sugar Fork, located at the trailhead.

Trailhead: The trail starts at 4.9 mi. on the Hazel Creek Trail (see p. 196) by the bridge at the mouth of Sugar Fork. It runs to the left (NW); a sign indicates the trail.

Trail Details: At 0.1 mi. the trail passes wisteria vines. A side trail at 0.5 mi. leads left a short distance to the Higdon Cemetery. Immediately past the junction, the unmaintained Haw Gap Branch Trail runs to the right to ford Sugar Fork.

At 1.5 mi. Copper Mine Branch flows into Sugar Fork on the right. At 1.7 mi. the Little Fork of Sugar Fork enters the main stream, also from the right. Note the old Johnson homesite there.

The trail then climbs to its terminus at Pickens Gap. Just before the gap, there is a bed of yellow lady's-slippers in the head of a hollow on the left. At the gap the Jenkins Ridge Trail begins and runs to the right 5.9 mi. to the A.T., while the Pinnacle Creek Trail descends westward 3.5 mi. to its trailhead on Eagle Creek (see p. 209).

---

(60) JENKINS RIDGE (Blockhouse Mountain) 5.9 mi.

Horse and foot trail / Max. elev. gain 2,076
Start: Pickens Gap, 2,964 ft.
End: A.T. at Spence Field, 4,958 ft.
USGS quads: Thunderhead Mtn., N.C.
Trail connections: Sugar Fork, Pinnacle Creek, A.T.,
    Bote Mtn., Eagle Creek

This trail provides the only connection between the A.T. and the middle and lower sections of the Hazel Creek area. It follows the main ridge separating the Eagle and Hazel Creek watersheds. The first 2.0 mi. are rather steep, but after that the grade is gentle. There are some good views, especially during the winter. A back-country campsite is located at Haw Gap.

Trailhead: The trail starts at Pickens Gap on Jenkins Ridge. This is the terminus of the Sugar Fork Trail from Hazel Creek and the Pinnacle Creek Trail from Eagle Creek (see p. 209).

Trail Details: Proceed north from the gap on a steep trail. It soon levels off somewhat, but at 0.5 mi. the truly steep section begins. Within the next 0.4 mi., climbing up Woodward Knob, it gains 800 ft. in elevation. Just before and after the knob, there are good views of Shuckstack to the southwest and High Rocks to the southeast. After the knob the trail climbs more moderately. At 1.6 mi. to the left down Pinnacle Creek there is a good view of Fontana Dam and Village. The trail reaches the top of Cherry Knob (4,455 ft.) at 2.1 mi., where Paw Paw Ridge adjoins it from the west-southwest.

At 2.5 mi. the old unmaintained Haw Gap Branch Trail runs to the right; 0.1 mi. beyond on a flat part of the ridge there is the site of an old cabin. After more climbing, the trail arrives at Haw Gap back-country campsite at 3.4 mi. It has no facilities except wood, and water from a spring located 400 ft. farther on the trail past the gap.

At about 3.8 mi. there is a view of the new shelter on the west end of Spence Field. The trail then begins a wide swing around the headwaters of Gunna Creek, a branch of Eagle Creek. From then on the grade is easy, generally following the contours of the ridge. At 4.2 mi. the trail crosses a branch; at 4.4 mi. it crosses a stream. At 5.8 mi. it reaches a junction with the trail running to the old Spence Field A.T. Shelter. From the junction there is an excellent view south down the Eagle Creek basin. There is a Jenkins Ridge Trail sign 100 ft. beyond, and soon the trail terminates in the eastern end of Spence Field at the A.T. The Bote Mtn. Trail may be reached by following the A.T. for 0.3 mi. to the left (W) (see p. 279). The terminus of the Eagle Creek Trail is located 400 ft. farther west; there is a new shelter about 0.2 mi. down that trail (see p. 207).

(61) BONE VALLEY 1.7 mi.

Gated jeep trail / Max. elev. gain 100
Start: Bone Valley campsite on Hazel Creek Trail,
    2,380 ft.
End: Hall Cabin, ruins of old Kress building, 2,480 ft.
USGS quads: Thunderhead Mtn., N.C.
Trail connections: Hazel Creek

The Bone Valley Trail runs north from Hazel Creek to a
dead end at the Hall Cabin, a 12-ft.-square log structure
once used by herdsmen and now classified as an historical
building. The ruins of the Kress place are located adjacent
to the cabin. It was the private recreation and social club of
the Kress family and burned to the ground in 1960. Beyond
it, a fisherman's trail continues along Bone Valley Creek.

Trailhead: The trail starts at 5.6 mi. on the Hazel Creek
Trail across the bridge from the Bone Valley campsite.

Trail Details: At 0.4 mi. the trail fords Bone Valley Creek,
and the old Hall homesite is located immediately beyond
where a small clump of pawpaw bushes grow on the left.
The trail fords the main creek again at 0.7 and 1.1 mi., and
then the smaller Mill Branch. It makes one final ford of the
main creek at 1.5 mi. and ends at the Hall Cabin. At the
north side of the cabin there is a small side trail which leads
0.25 mi. to the Hall Cemetery. At the north end of the
area, where the trail terminates, Big Flats Branch flows into
Bone Valley Creek.

If you wish to continue up Bone Valley, look for an
obscure foot trail leading left at a point where the Bone
Valley Trail runs close to Big Flats Branch. Ford Big Flats
Branch on the unmaintained trail and keep to the left
around the point of the ridge.

Twentymile and
Eagle Creeks Section

Introduction

The Twentymile and Eagle Creek valleys are situated in the
remote southwestern corner of the park. Both basins are
roadless, and the only access to Eagle Creek is on foot or by
boat across Fontana Lake. Eagle Creek was never heavily
settled like nearby Hazel Creek, but a famous moonshiner,
Quill Rose, did live up the hollow along Eagle Creek. His
homesite may still be found today near the trail.

Ekaneetlee Creek is a major tributary to Eagle Creek. The
name is Cherokee for "by the water," and an ancient war-
path apparently ran along the creek. Today this area offers
good native trout fishing for those who wish to rough it.

Copper mines were once located in the lower section of
Eagle Creek basin where a mining company owned some
45,000 acres. Most of that land was purchased by the TVA
when Fontana Dam was constructed. Later, the Park Service received the land. Yet today the North Carolina Exploration Company still has a 1,920-acre inholding on Ecoah
Creek.

Fontana Dam was constructed during World War II in
order to provide power for Oak Ridge, where enriched
uranium was produced. The rising water of the lake cut off
Eagle Creek from easy land access, thus helping maintain its
primitive condition.

The nearest developed camping is located at the Forest
Service Cable Cove area on the south shore of Fontana
Lake near Tuskeegee, North Carolina. Back-country campsites are located along Eagle Creek, Lost Cove Creek, Twentymile Creek and up along the Wolf Ridge Trail below

Parson Falls. The Appalachian Trail shelter at Birch Springs will be useful to hikers in this section. The views from Shuckstack Firetower are superior, and the flame azalea display on Gregory and Parson Bald is world famous.

Hikers should note the Wolf Ridge Trail, which leads from Twentymile Creek to Parson Bald and on to the Sheep Pen Gap near Gregory Bald. Detailed information on the trail was not available, but it is well maintained and is suggested for a scenic loop through the Twentymile area.

The ranger station at Twentymile Creek is the major starting point for hikes in the area. It is located immediately north of N.C. 28, west of Fontana Village and east of the U.S. 129 intersection. The Appalachian Trail may be intercepted in this section by driving north on a county road as it leaves N.C. 28 about 2 miles east of Fontana Village. After crossing the dam, the road will dead end where the Appalachian Trail begins.

---

(62) PINNACLE CREEK 3.5 mi.

Horse trail / Max. elev. gain 1,164
Start: Eagle Creek, 1,800 ft.
End: Pickens Gap, Jenkins Ridge, 2,964 ft.
USGS quads: Fontana Dam, Thunderhead, N.C.
Trail connections: Eagle Creek, Jenkins Ridge, Sugar
    Fork

This trail provides lateral access from Eagle Creek to Jenkins Ridge and Hazel Creek. It follows a road built by the U.S. Army Corps of Engineers sometime during the early years of World War II. The Smokies were a good place for them to practice mountain road building. Additionally, the road led to the vicinity of an old copper mine, whose ore might become valuable to the war effort. But the road was never used much, the former residents of the coves having already moved away.

Today the once-good roadway makes a good trail, especially its culverts for most of the creek crossings. It follows along Pinnacle Creek, which is the park boundary. The land to the southeast of the creek is an inholding still owned by a copper mining company.

Note: there is a new back-country campsite, Pinnacle Creek campsite, located at approximately 1.7 mi. on the Pinnacle Creek Trail.

Trailhead: The trail starts at a sign at 1.0 mi. on the right of the Eagle Creek Trail.

Trail Details: The trail fords Eagle Creek and ascends in a northeasterly direction along Pinnacle Creek. Soon the World War II road becomes evident. At 2.8 mi. the trail leaves Pinnacle Creek and climbs eastward somewhat steeply to end at 3.5 mi. at Pickens Gap and a trail junction. The Jenkins Ridge Trail starts there and runs 5.9 mi. to the left (W) to Spence Field on the A.T. (see p. 203). Straight ahead (E) is the terminus of the Sugar Fork Trail, which has climbed 2.4 mi. from the Hazel Creek Trail (see p. 202).

---

(63) **EAGLE CREEK** 9.1 mi.

Foot trail / Max. elev. gain 3,170
Start: Fontana Lake and Lost Cove Creek, 1,720 ft.
End: A.T. at Spence Field, 4,890 ft.
USGS quads: Fontana Dam, Thunderhead, N.C.; Cades Cove, Tenn.
Trail connections: Lost Cove, Pinnacle Creek, A.T., Bote Mtn., Jenkins Ridge

---

This pleasant trail offers good trout fishing, especially up the side creeks. The trail crosses Eagle Creek many times with no footbridges, but the fords are generally easy. The deepest ford is the first one, where beaver dams sometimes cause the water to be over a hiker's knees. The grade is very gentle for the first 6.0 mi.; the last mile is quite steep.

Note: there is a new back-country campsite, Lower Ekaneetlee campsite, located at 2.0 mi. on the trail.

Trailhead: The trail starts at the Lost Cove Creek back-country campsite where that creek enters Fontana Lake. There is a trail register. The Lost Cove Trail also starts there (see p. 210).

Trail Details: The trail heads east along the lake shore and within 0.2 mi. begins to follow Eagle Creek. At 0.5 mi. the trail begins a long curve around Horseshoe Bend. Signs of beavers will become evident in this area. At 1.0 mi. the Pinnacle Creek Trail begins on the right and follows Pinnacle Creek up to Pickens Gap. The trail continues along Eagle Creek, crossing the main stream several times. At 2.0 mi. it crosses Ekaneetlee Creek; the Ekaneetlee Manway goes up that stream. Fishermen keep the manway fairly open near the stream, but it becomes rough before it reaches Ekaneetlee Gap on the Smokies Crest.

Following Eagle Creek, the Eagle Creek Trail reaches the Eagle Creek Island back-country campsite at 3.4 mi. There are no facilities there and you must get water from the creek. This campsite is the former Camp 10 logging camp, located near the mouth of Camp Ten Branch. The island was created when a sluice was built from the main creek.

Past the campsite and still following the main stream, the trail passes a pleasant pool. At 4.1 mi. a side branch crosses the trail. To the left up the branch in some white pines are the foundations of a block stillhouse. There the famous moonshiner, Quill Rose, once made his product. At 5.0 mi. the trail passes the site of old Camp 11, where Tub

Mill Branch enters the main stream. This area is known also as The Big Walnuts and is a good potential camping spot.

Continuing along Eagle Creek, at 5.9 mi. the trail reaches the confluence of Paw Paw Creek and Gunna Creek and follows the latter to the left. After about 0.7 mi. Fodderstack Rock is located on the right of the trail. It is a 15- to 20-foot-high rock shaped like a corn shuck. Camping may be possible there; check with the Park Service.

The trail begins to climb and at 6.8 mi. goes through a sharp curve to the right. The grade becomes steeper and finally ascends very steeply up Spence Cabin Branch for the last mile. At 8.9 mi. the trail passes a good spring and then reaches the new Spence Field Shelter. The trail terminates at the A.T. at 9.1 mi. The Bote Mtn. Trail terminates 400 ft. to the right on the A.T., having climbed 6.6 mi. from Cades Cove Road in Tennessee (see p. 279). Three-tenths of a mile beyond that junction is the terminus of the Jenkins Ridge Trail. It leads 5.9 mi. to Pickens Gap on Jenkins Ridge (see p. 203).

---

(64) LOST COVE 3.1 mi.

Foot trail / Max. elev. gain 1,930
Start: Fontana Lake and Lost Cove Creek, 1,720 ft.
End: Sassafras Gap on the A.T., 3,650 ft.
USGS quads: Fontana Dam, N.C.
Trail connections: Eagle Creek, A.T., Twentymile

This trail is a lateral connector between Eagle and Twentymile Creek basins. Although it is not maintained, the Park Service uses it on its patrols, and in the near future it will be placed on the maintenance schedule. Until then you should be careful because it may be grown over partially. Check with the Park Service about the status of the trail.

The lower half of the trail follows an old railroad grade and has a gentle ascent. Ginseng, a rare mountain herb, can still be found growing in this remote cove. Water is abundant along the trail.

Note: there is a new back-country campsite, Upper Lost Cove campsite, at about 1.5 mi. on the trail.

Trailhead: The trail starts at the Lost Cove Creek back-country campsite on Fontana Lake. Facilities are water and wood. The Eagle Creek Trail also begins there (see p. 207).

Trail Details: Leaving the campsite, the trail goes northwest, climbing slightly along Lost Cove Creek. Soon it becomes nearly level, and you must ford the creek several times. At 1.0 mi. an obscure side trail goes right to Ekaneetlee Creek. The Lost Cove Trail continues straight to 1.1 mi. where the trail curves left (SW) to cross Coldspring Branch. Then it crosses a flat area and regains Lost Cove Creek, which it again follows closely.

At 2.4 mi. the trail goes right (N) and leaves the stream. It immediately begins to climb steeply through a series of switchbacks to end at Sassafras Gap at 3.1 mi. There the A.T. goes left (S) 0.4 mi. to Shuckstack Fire Tower, from which there is an excellent view. The A.T. goes right (N) 1.0 mi. to Birch Spring Gap Shelter. Straight ahead (W) is the terminus of the Twentymile Creek Trail, having climbed 5.3 mi. from the Twentymile Ranger Station on N.C. 28. To the left (S) it is 3.7 mi. on the A.T. to a road 0.6 mi. north of Fontana Dam.

65 TWENTYMILE CREEK (Shuckstack) 5.3 mi.

Gated jeep trail / Max. elev. gain 2,355
Start: Twentymile Ranger Station on N.C. 28, 1,295 ft.
End: Sassafras Gap on the A.T., 3,650 ft.
USGS quads: Tapoco, Fontana, N.C.
Trail connections: Wolf Ridge, Long Hungry Ridge, A.T., Lost Cove

This trail provides a good route from the south to Shuckstack Fire Tower. Many hikers will prefer it because it has a more gentle grade than the A.T. (which also leads to the tower) and it leaves from the ranger's cabin, where they can obtain camping permits. Additionally, the trail gives access to the Wolf Ridge and Long Hungry Ridge trails. It follows a well-used maintenance road. The Twentymile back-country campsite is located along this trail.

Trailhead: Drive on N.C. 28 for 6.2 mi. west of Fontana Village or for 2.8 mi. east of the junction with U.S. 129. Park near the Twentymile Ranger Station. The trail begins up the road 200 yds. on the other side of a gate.

Trail Details: The trail passes a barn at 0.2 mi. It crosses a bridge at 0.6 mi. There the Wolf Ridge Trail goes left to climb up to Gregory Bald. At 0.7 mi. the Twentymile Creek Trail passes cascades on Twentymile Creek. After crossing two additional bridges at 1.5 and 1.7 mi., look for yellow lady's-slipper and showy orchis on the right side of the trail. Twentymile Creek back-country campsite is located at 1.8 mi. by the next bridge. Facilities include one table, fireplace and pit toilet. Water is available from the creek.

At 2.3 mi. the trail crosses Turkey Gap Branch, and at 2.6 mi. it crosses the last bridge. It reaches Proctor Gap and a trail junction at 3.3 mi. There the Long Hungry Ridge Trail begins on the left and climbs 4.4 mi. to Rich Gap.

The Twentymile Creek Trail then climbs away from the main stream. An old telephone line to Shuckstack Fire Tower leaves the trailway at 3.7 mi. Soon the trail begins to climb more steeply, making four switchbacks and climbing 1,200 ft. in the final 1.5 mi. At the point of a ridge, near 4.1 mi., there is a good view of Shuckstack Fire Tower. At 5.3 mi. the trail ends at Sassafras Gap on the A.T. From there the A.T. goes right (S) 3.7 mi. to a road 0.6 mi. north of Fontana Dam. To the north on the A.T. it is 1.0 mi. to the Birch Spring Gap Shelter. Straight ahead (E) is the terminus of the Lost Cove Trail, which has climbed 3.1 mi. from its trailhead at Fontana Lake.

---

(66) LONG HUNGRY RIDGE 4.4 mi.

Horse trail / Max. elev. gain 2,240
Start: Proctor Gap, Twentymile Creek, 2,360 ft.
End: Rich Gap, 4,600 ft.
USGS quads: Fontana Dam, N.C.; Cades Cove, Tenn.
Trail connections: Twentymile Creek, Gregory Bald, Gregory Ridge

---

This is a somewhat popular trail leading to Gregory Bald, which is world-famous for its flame azalea display in June and its fine views. The trail also offers a good view from Rye Patch but the grade is fairly steep just before reaching that point. It ends at Rich Gap, which is also called Gant Lot. According to Horace Kephart, cattle were once kept there before going to market. They were intentionally made thin and bony, or "gaunted," so they would be nimble for the walk to town.

Note: there is a new back-country campsite, Upper Flats campsite, located at about 1.2 mi. on this trail.

Trailhead: The trail starts at Proctor Gap, at 3.3 mi. on the Twentymile Creek Trail.

Trail Details: The trail goes left (NE) and at 0.1 mi. crosses a small stream named Proctor Creek. At 0.5 mi. it begins to follow along the side of Twentymile Creek. At about 1.2 mi. it crosses two small tributaries that drain a flat area to the right, Upper Flats. The trail crosses Twentymile Creek at 1.3 mi. and begins to climb along Rye Patch Branch.

At 1.8 mi. the trail makes a sharp right and crosses Rye Patch Branch, the last sure source of water. The elevation there is 3,000 ft. The trail then goes through a series of turns while climbing the side of Long Hungry Ridge. It is steep in places. At 3.5 mi. it levels off at Rye Patch, 4,400 ft., from which there are good views because the vegetation is fairly low. At the patch the trail turns right (NE) to follow along the crest of Long Hungry Ridge. At 4.4 mi. the trail ends at Rich Gap on the Smokies Crest at a trail junction. The Gregory Bald Trail, following a path along the crest that was formerly the A.T., runs to the right (E) 2.0 mi. to end at the A.T. at Does Knob (see p. 292). One hundred yds. to the left (W) on the Gregory Bald Trail is a trail intersection: at that point a side trail leads left (S) 0.4 mi. to the Moore Spring and Shelter, while the Gregory Ridge Trail terminates on the right, having climbed 5.0 mi. from the turnaround on the Forge Creek Road in Tennessee (see p. 289). Continuing west and uphill, the Gregory Bald Trail after 0.7 mi. more leads to the crest of Gregory Bald. From there on clear days there are fine views of the western end of the park, the Unicoi Mtns. to the southwest and the Snowbird Mtns. far to the south.

Cosby Section
(Tennessee)

Introduction

Cosby Creek drains the northeastern corner of Great Smoky Mountains National Park. The creek flows through a small but wide basin bounded on the south and east by a curve in the Smokies Range. The basin is rich in the tradition of the moonshiner and blockader. Despite determined efforts by the authorities to prevent it, whiskey is still distilled in isolated hollows both inside and outside the park. Cosby boasts the nickname of "Moonshine Capital of the World."

There are two outstanding features to be seen in this area. One is the excellent 360° view of the eastern portion of the park from the fire tower on Mount Cammerer. The other is the Albright Grove on Indian Creek—a sample of the great virgin cove forests that once covered the southern Appalachians.

Most of the trails in the valley originate at the Park Service's Cosby Developed Campground (camping, picnicking, running water, toilets) and lead to the Smokies Crest or west to the Indian Creek watershed. During the winter of 1971-72, the campground was closed, so hikers had to walk an additional 1.5 miles to reach the trailheads. Alternatives to Cosby Campground are the back-country campsites located near Maddron Bald, on Mount Cammerer, and in Sugar Cove on Gabes Mountain.

The approaches to the Cosby section are as follows: From Newport, Tennessee, drive south on Tenn. 32 and go straight through the junction with Tenn. 73 at the Cosby

Post Office. The entrance to the park is located on the right
about one mile past the junction. Cosby Road, which is
paved, continues on to the Cosby Campground. From Interstate 40, take the Foothills Parkway west to the intersection with Tenn. 32, turn left (south) and follow Tenn. 32 as
above. From Gatlinburg, Tennessee, take Tenn. 73 east to
its junction with Tenn. 32 at the post office, turn right
(south) and proceed as above.

---

(67) **COSBY CREEK** (Low Gap) 2.5 mi.

Gated jeep trail / Max. elev. gain 1,800
Start: Cosby Campground, 2,450 ft.
End: Low Gap on the A.T., 4,240 ft.
USGS quads: Luftee Knob, N.C.
Trail connections: Lower Mt. Cammerer, A.T., Low
  Gap

The Cosby Creek Trail provides one of the shortest and
easiest hikes from any open road to the state line and
the A.T. The trail is an old one, parts of it dating back to
the earliest settlements in the mountains. Today Park Service jeeps use it to reach Mt. Cammerer Fire Lookout and
the Cosby Knob Shelter. The underfooting is rocky and
eroded. There is a good spring near the end of the trail.

Trailhead: The trail begins in the southeast corner of Cosby
Campground. Park your car at the amphitheatre and follow
the paved road uphill around the perimeter to the southeast
corner. The trail starts as a gated fire road at a sign reading
"Low Gap 2½ mi."

Trail Details: Follow the fire road through second-growth
poplars past the campground's concrete water reservoir and
a log cabin (or crib) built by the original settlers of the

cove. After about 0.5 mi. the road reaches a turnaround where there is a trail register on the right. Cosby Creek flows immediately beyond and is crossed on a log bridge.

On the other side of the creek, a horse trail enters on the left. At about 1.0 mi. the trail enters an area of nearly virgin poplar, hemlock and buckeye, with an understory of rhododendron. The trail gains elevation through a series of four switchbacks, passing into a thicket of beech and rhododendron. It continues upward, sometimes steeply, and crosses a branch (dry in late summer and fall). At about 2.0 mi. Low Gap is visible through the trees on the right. An excellent piped spring is located in a bend of the trail at 2.1 mi. The trail ends at Low Gap on the A.T. at 2.5 mi. This junction is also the terminus of the Low Gap Trail, which has come 2.3 mi. from Walnut Bottoms in the Big Creek section (see p. 74). To the left (E) on the A.T. it is 2.5 mi. to Mt. Cammerer, from which there is a 360° panoramic view of the eastern end of the Smokies. To the right (W) the A.T. leads 0.8 mi. to the Cosby Knob Shelter.

---

(68) **LOWER MOUNT CAMMERER** (Lower White-rock) 7.6 mi.

Horse trail / Max. elev. gain 1,300
Start: Cosby Campground, 2,300 ft.
End: A.T., 3,600 ft.
USGS quads: Hartford, Tenn.
Trail connections: Cosby Creek, A.T.

The Lower Mt. Cammerer Trail follows the contours around the northern slope of Mt. Cammerer and eventually arrives at the A.T. at a spot 2.9 mi. from the Mt. Cammerer Fire Tower. The fire tower offers one of the best views in the entire park.

There are no steep stretches on the trail, which provides a long gradual stroll through an area recovering from past settlement. The underfooting varies from gravel to eroded dirt and rock, or to soft pine needles. Water is frequently available along the route. In late spring wild iris bloom along nearly the entire trail; in the fall wild grapes are abundant. Mt. Cammerer is named for Arno B. Cammerer, a former director of the Park Service who worked tirelessly to bring about Great Smoky Mountains National Park.

Trailhead: The trail begins at a gated fire road on the upper east side of Cosby Campground. To reach it, park your car at the Cosby amphitheatre parking area and follow the paved perimeter road uphill a short distance before turning left onto the fire road. The Park Service sign at that point reads "A.T. 9.0 mi., Davenport Gap 11 mi., Sutton Ridge Overlook 1½ mi.," but the A.T. is actually only 7.6 mi. away.

Trail Details: The trail immediately crosses Cosby Creek on a foot log, passes through the horse concession area and continues on the fire road through second-growth poplars. At 0.7 mi. there is a rocked-off spring on the right. At 0.8 mi. the fire road ends. The trail crosses both Panther Branch of Toms Creek and Toms Creek proper before reaching the shoulder of Sutton Ridge at 1.5 mi. where a trail leads right 100 yds. up the ridge to an overlook. From the overlook, you can see good views of Cosby Creek Valley, Green Mtn. and Gabes Mtn., which are especially beautiful at sunset.

The trail continues around the contour of the ridge, passing just below a small cascade on the right of the trail at the back of the valley. Gilliland Creek campsite is located at 3.5 mi. There is level ground and a horse hitch rack (see pp. 48–49 for capacities).

About 6.0 mi. from Cosby Campground, the Ground

Hog Ridge Manway crosses the trail. This ma.
leads directly to the lookout tower on Mt. Camn.
maintained. It is steep, rough and obscure in
should not be attempted by inexperienced hikers.

At 7.6 mi. the Lower Mt. Cammerer Trail ends on a
shoulder of Mt. Cammerer at a junction with the A.T. From
the trail terminus, Davenport Gap is 2.8 mi. downhill to the
left (E) on the A.T. To the right on the A.T. it is 0.2 mi. to
a spring and 2.3 mi. to the Mt. Cammerer side trail, which
leads 0.6 mi. more to the lookout tower. The tower, no
longer manned, is a substantial stone and wood structure
located on an extremely exposed rocky point that drops off
steeply on three sides. A walkway around the outside of the
tower provides spectacular views: on a clear day you can
see Mt. Pisgah to the southeast; Mt. Sterling due south;
Inadu Knob, Old Black and Mt. Guyot to the southwest
along the Smokies Crest; and to the north, the lower valley
of the Pigeon River.

---

(69) SNAKE DEN MOUNTAIN 5.0 mi.

Gated jeep trail / Max. elev. gain 3,400
Start: Cosby Campground, 2,400 ft.
End: Inadu Knob on the A.T., 5,800 ft.
USGS quads: Luftee Knob, N.C.
Trail connections: Maddron Bald, A.T.

This trail climbs along Inadu Creek and Snake Den Mountain to reach the main crest of the Smokies. It is steep,
especially in the middle section. *Inadu* means "snake" in
the Cherokee language and pertains to the snake dens on
the mountainside. The Maddron Bald back-country campsite and spring are located high up along this trail.

Trailhead: The trail begins at the southwest corner of

Cosby Campground. Park at the amphitheatre parking area and follow the perimeter road around to the trailhead at the far corner. Look for the Park Service sign reading "Snake Den Trail to A.T. 5 mi." at a gated fire road.

Trail Details: Follow the gravel fire road through second-growth forest. At 0.2 mi. a horse trail enters from the left. The road passes a small cemetery on the right, which is still tended by former residents of the cove. At about 1.0 mi. it reaches the end of the fire road and a trail register. Continuing upward, it crosses Rock Creek on a log bridge and enters a grove of small hemlocks. It follows the bank above Inadu Creek for 0.2 mi. and then turns sharply back to the left, where it enters a beautiful open woods of large hemlock, buckeye, locust and poplar. After a sharp right turn, it climbs gradually up the left side of the cove, high above the creek. At about 2.0 mi. and 3,500 ft. elevation, it crosses Inadu Creek. This is the last water before 2.0 mi. of steep climbing.

The trail slabs up the side of Snake Den Mtn. through deep hemlock and rhododendron, and enters a series of switchbacks up a dry ridge where pine and laurel grow. At the third turn, on the right, there is an overlook of Cosby Cove. The trail drops off to the side of the ridge crest and enters a forest of hemlock, beech and locust. Then it switchbacks to the right and climbs steeply through deep woods. Tunneling through rhododendron and laurel, it emerges onto a small heath bald on the ridge line from which the entire state line from Inadu Knob to Mt. Cammerer is visible.

The trail continues upward with several small switchbacks. The character of the surroundings gradually becomes more Canadian, with spruce and fir. At 4.3 mi. the Maddron Bald Trail terminates on the right, down which it is 7.5 mi. to reach Tenn. 73 on Indian Creek. Straight ahead, 50 yds. past the junction on the Snake Den Mtn.

Trail, is the Maddron Bald back-country campsite, which has a spring and a picnic table.

The trail continues 0.7 mi. farther through balsam forest to terminate at the A.T. just below the peak of Inadu Knob. A few yards east or west of the junction, there are good views of the Balsam Range and the Big Creek Valley.

---

(70) GABES MOUNTAIN (Messer) 7.0 mi.

Gated jeep and foot trail / Max. elev. gain 1,300
Start: Cosby Campground Road, 2,000 ft.
End: Indian Camp Creek Trail, 2,300 ft.
USGS quads: Luftee Knob, N.C.; Hartford, Jones Cove, Mt. Guyot, Tenn.
Trail connections: Henwallow Falls, Indian Camp Creek

The Gabes Mtn. Trail is a midland trail and therefore requires only easy to moderate climbing. Connecting the Cosby and Indian Camp Creek valleys, it passes by the beautiful Henwallow Falls and, later, several groves of mature cove hardwoods. The first mile is on a gated jeep road and may be avoided by following instead the preferred Henwallow Falls Trail (see the end of this trail description).

Note: there is a new back-country campsite on the Gabes Mtn. Trail, at Sugar Cove (about 5.0 mi.)

Trailhead: The trail begins 1.3 mi. from Tenn. 32 on the road to Cosby Campground, where there is a gated fire road on the right (W) and a sign reading "Gabes Creek 4 mi., Indian Camp Trail 7 mi."

Trail Details: The trail goes past the gate and follows a jeep road through second-growth forest for 1.1 mi. It crosses two major branches of Crying Creek before reaching a turnaround at the junction with the Henwallow Falls Trail.

Gabes Mtn. Trail continues on from the back of the turnaround, climbing through open woods to a small gap. There, 10 yds. to the right of the trail, is the grave of Sally Sutton, one of the former residents of Cosby Cove. The trail continues through the gap, gradually gaining elevation, and reaches Messer Gap, which is marked by a Park Service sign. A short distance past the gap, it crosses a small branch with a falls. The trail slabs the side of Gabes Mtn. through an area of rocky bluffs and overhangs to reach a side trail at 2.2 mi. which leads down to the foot of Henwallow Falls. Before going to the foot of the falls, continue along Gabes Mtn. Trail to the top of the falls for a view of Big Ridge across Cosby Creek Valley and to note the narrowness of Henwallow Creek at the brink. Return to the side trail and, descending by switchbacks, proceed to the bottom of the falls. There you will see that, from a width of about 2 ft. at the top, the falls spreads out remarkably across the bare rock mountain face during its descent until it is about 20 ft. wide at the bottom.

From Henwallow Falls the Gabes Mtn. Trail continues along the side of the mountain for about 100 yds., then turns back and to the left, up the valley of Henwallow Creek. It crosses the creek just below a mossy cascade, only to switch back to the right to follow the creek again. There the creek has flattened out, flowing shallow and wide. The trail continues upward, leaving the creek, and passes through a small gap.

A half mile farther, the trail enters the groves of virgin poplar and hemlock that characterize the remainder of the trail. For a distance of about 2.5 mi. the trail is relatively level, dropping slightly to cross small branches of Gabes Creek and rising gently through small gaps. It crosses Greenbrier Creek in Sugar Cove, after which it begins to descend gradually until it reaches Cole Creek. It follows Cole Creek downhill, crossing and recrossing it several times, before leaving the stream and ending at the Indian Camp Creek

Trail. To the right about 1.2 mi. is the Laurel Springs Road. To the left the Indian Camp Creek Trail leads 1.1 mi. to a turnaround where the Maddron Bald and Albright Grove Nature trails begin.

HENWALLOW FALLS TRAIL provides pleasant walking and varied terrain and is therefore preferred to the initial fire-road section of the Gabes Mtn. Trail. It begins 1.9 mi. from Tenn. 32 on the road to Cosby Campground. The trailhead is located on the right just below a picnic area at a sign reading "Henwallow Falls 2 mi." The trail follows an eroded roadbed through second-growth timber above Rock Creek. At about 0.2 mi. it reaches a junction with a feeder trail from Cosby Campground. It continues to the right, passing a log bench on the left, and crosses Rock Creek on a log bridge. This is an area of large trees. Another log bench is provided for those who would like to sit and contemplate them—big hemlocks and poplars, with an understory of rhododendron. The trail crosses several small branches on more log bridges, passing through a grove of small holly trees before reaching Crying Creek. Just past the last log bridge, it merges with the Gabes Mountain Trail at the turnaround and follows it to the side trail that leads to the falls.

---

(71) INDIAN CAMP CREEK 2.3 mi.

Gated road / Max. elev. gain 900
Start: Near Tenn. 73 highway, 1,900 ft.
End: Road turnaround, 2,800 ft.
USGS quads: Jones Cove, Mt. Guyot, Tenn.
Trail connections: Gabes Mtn., Maddron Bald, Albright Grove

This trail is used primarily for access to the Albright Grove of virgin timber and the Gabes Mtn. and Maddron Bald trails. Its grade is gentle.

Trailhead: The most difficult part of the Indian Camp Creek Trail is finding where it starts. The trail begins at a gated fire road 0.2 mi. along the Laurel Springs Road from Tenn. 73. (The Laurel Springs Road leaves Tenn. 73 at a distance of 15.4 mi. east of the Gatlinburg Chamber of Commerce Building, or 2.9 mi. west of the Cosby Post Office.) The fire road is located next to the trout pond of the privately owned Safari Campground; the trail goes south beyond the gate.

Trail Details: The walking is easy, through rhododendron and second-growth forest. Much of the land along the trail is former farmland, with a 30-year growth of poplars rapidly reclaiming the countryside. Within 0.5 mi. the trail passes an old log cabin which has received some maintenance from the Park Service. The trail crosses Cole Creek and then follows alongside it. At about 1.2 mi. the Gabes Mtn. Trail terminates on the left, having come 7.0 mi. westward from the Cosby Campground Road. Indian Camp Creek Trail continues south and eventually parallels Indian Camp Creek. It ends at a car turnaround at 2.3 mi. The Maddron Bald Trail begins on the south side of the turnaround and runs 5.0 mi. to the Snake Den Mtn. Trail.

ALBRIGHT GROVE NATURE TRAIL is an outstanding remnant of virgin forest which is located at 0.7 mi. on the Maddron Bald Trail. Since most visitors to the grove will initially use the Indian Camp Creek Trail to reach the grove, the nature trail is described here.

At the turnaround on Indian Camp Creek Trail, go south on the Maddron Bald foot trail and ascend gently to cross Indian Camp Creek. The trail then climbs the side of a ravine and near the top, at 0.7 mi., the Albright Grove Nature Trail begins straight ahead, while the Maddron Bald Trail continues to the left. The grove trail makes a loop for

0.7 mi. and then rejoins the Maddron Bald Trail. From that junction go left and descend for 0.2 mi. to reach the start of the grove trail. Thus the entire circular route through the grove itself is about one mile. A round trip from the end of Indian Camp Creek Trail, through the grove and back, will add up to about 2.4 mi.

The Albright Grove of poplar and hemlock escaped the lumbermen's axes and today is one of the finest examples of virgin forest in the Smokies. It was named after Horace M. Albright, second director of the National Park Service, who played a significant role in the establishment of this park. He also was responsible for blocking a highway along the Smokies Crest where the A.T. now runs.

The grove is located between Dunn Creek and Indian Camp Creek. At a point just below the grove, these creeks are only a few hundred yards apart. Although these two creeks are so close at their headwaters, at the mouth they are 15 miles apart. Dunn Creek flows into the east fork of the Little Pigeon River, while Indian Camp Creek empties into Cosby Creek, a tributary of the Big Pigeon River.

Strolling through the Albright Grove, one experiences a feeling of peace and reverence. The grove must be visited to be appreciated. It is truly a deep green wood.

---

(72) MADDRON BALD 5.0 mi.

Foot trail / Max. elev. gain 2,600
Start: End of Indian Camp Creek Trail, 2,800 ft.
End: Snake Den Mountain Trail, 5,400 ft.
USGS quads: Luftee Knob, N.C.; Mt. Guyot, Tenn.
Trail connections: Indian Camp Creek, Albright Grove, Snake Den Mtn.

The Maddron Bald Trail is probably the most interesting

and spectacular of all the trails in the Cosby section. It passes through a virgin forest and a heath bald with excellent views. There is a back-country campsite (#29) at Otter Creek near 3.5 mi. This area is the location of an old CCC sub-camp that was used in the 1930s. Campsite capacity is 15 people.

Trailhead: The trail begins at the turnaround on, or terminus of, the Indian Camp Creek Trail, 2.3 mi. from the Laurel Springs Road.

Trail Details: The trail rises gently through hemlock and rhododendron for 0.2 mi. with the creek audible from below. It crosses Indian Camp Creek on a foot log at 0.5 mi.; a beautiful pool with twin falls running into it is located just above the creek crossing. The trail climbs the side of a ravine. Near the top at 0.7 mi., the Albright Grove Nature Trail begins and runs straight ahead, while the Maddron Bald Trail bears to the left. Huge hemlocks and poplars grow roundabout. The woodland appears much the same as it did when the first settlers arrived. A quarter of a mile after its departure, the nature trail rejoins the main trail from the right.

The Maddron Bald Trail continues upward and soon crosses Indian Camp Creek again. Although the creek is quite wide, there is no foot log, so use caution while crossing on the rocks. The trail next crosses Copperhead Branch, which is also difficult. The rocks below the actual trail offer the best chance of keeping your feet dry. Then there is another (easier) crossing of Indian Camp Creek, and the trail begins to loop back to the south. It crosses Indian Camp Creek again, curves to the east and crosses Copperhead Branch for the second and last time. It soon enters a small laurel slick, with an overlook at the point of the ridge to the left of the trail. Maddron Bald may be seen to the northeast, Pinnacle Lead and Snag Mtn. to the west, and the entire Cosby Valley to the north.

The trail slabs the side of the ridge, crossing a rock slide, a small branch and then Otter Branch (the last water for almost 2.0 mi.). It climbs the side of Maddron Bald and turns a sharp right up the ridge before breaking out into the open bald. This is a heath bald, covered primarily with mountain laurel and rocky outcroppings. There is almost a 360° panoramic view.

The trail crosses the bald and reenters the forest. It ends 1.0 mi. above the bald at the Snake Den Mtn. Trail (see p. 219). To the left the Snake Den Mtn. Trail has climbed 4.3 mi. from Cosby Campground. To the left on that trail, it is 0.6 mi. to the Snake Den Mountain backcountry campsite. To the right from the trail terminus, it is 0.7 mi. to the A.T.

Le Conte and
Greenbrier Section
(Tennessee)

Introduction

The Mount Le Conte and Greenbrier Cove areas adjoin each other and share some characteristics of primitive wilderness. Yet they differ in their degree of development and use. Mount Le Conte, one of the most distinctive features in the entire park, is almost draped with trails. Greenbrier Cove, on the other hand, has relatively few trails within its vast basin and is less often visited.

Mount Le Conte is a very impressive mass—a spur—situated about four miles north of the Smokies Crest. From the base of the mountain near Gatlinburg, its sides rise steeply for more than a mile to a height of 6,593 feet. It is the third highest mountain in the park. Extraordinary views can be seen from two vantage points on top: Myrtle Point, which is best at sunrise, and Cliff Top, which is best at sunset. The view is unobstructed from both places because they are covered only with small rhododendron and sand myrtle. The remainder of the mountain is covered with virgin spruce and fir.

Mount Le Conte has long been the focal point for trips in the Smokies. It is named for Professor Joseph Le Conte, a native of Georgia, who became a famous geologist at Harvard and later taught at the University of California. Le Conte never saw his namesake but spent much time hiking in the West with the Sierra Club. In 1924 two members of the important Southern Appalachian National Park Committee organized national support for a Smokies park after being shown the wilds of Mount Le Conte. In 1925 Paul Adams established a guest cabin on the mountaintop with the permission of the landowner, Champion Fibre Company. (Adams's pamphlet "Mt. Le Conte," which is available in the park, contains a fine account of the explorations on the mountain during the 1920s.) The guest cabin later became the Mount Le Conte Lodge and is now operated as a concession by agreement with the Park Service. The lodge can be used as a place for refreshment in the middle of a hiking trip. Reservations are necessary; contact Le Conte Lodge, Gatlinburg, Tennessee 37738.

Hiking on Le Conte is understandably very popular, even in the winter season. All of the trails leading to it are rewarding, but since horse travel on the Rainbow Falls Trail is popular, hikers may wish to avoid that one. An excellent two- or three-day loop is possible using the Alum Cave, Boulevard and Appalachian trails, but hundreds of other hikers will probably be encountered along the way. During the summer the mountaintop is crowded, so do not expect to find room in the 12-man Mount Le Conte Shelter. It is full nearly every night at this time and is frequently full on winter weekends.

Access to the Alum Cave and Boulevard trails is via the Newfound Gap Road, but the other trails originate from Cherokee Orchard, an area a few miles south of Gatlinburg. In 1920 several thousand apple trees were planted there on about 800 acres, causing it to become known as the Orchard. In 1931 the acreage was acquired by the state of Tennessee, which subsequently transferred it to the National Park Service, but commercial growing was phased out only after another 25 years. Now the forest has reclaimed much of the orchard, but the name lives on as the jumping-off point for the very popular trails serving the north face of Mount Le Conte.

Cherokee Orchard is located 3.4 miles by road from Gatlinburg. From Gatlinburg's main street, Parkway (also known as U.S. 441 and Tenn. 73), turn south onto Airport

Road. Pass the Municipal Auditorium and at 0.8 mile enter the park. At 2.6 miles this paved road passes the start of the Junglebrook Nature Trail, an excellent wildflower trail where more than 40 kinds of native trees grow. Just beyond Junglebrook the two-way road ends at a fork, which is the beginning and the end of a one-way loop. Take the right fork, the start of the loop, and continue to 3.4 miles where there is a parking area in the middle of Cherokee Orchard; the Rainbow Falls and Bullhead trails begin there. The one-way loop continues through the upper part of the orchard and arrives at a fork at 3.7 miles. The left fork is the remainder of the loop. It leads north back to Junglebrook.

The right fork becomes the Cherokee Orchard-Roaring Fork Motor Nature Road and leads 6.1 miles to Tenn. 73 just east of the center of Gatlinburg. It also is a one-way road, and it has a 10-mph speed limit. At 1.7 miles along it, you will come to the Grotto Falls parking area for the Trillium Gap Trail.

The road to Cherokee Orchard is open all year, except after heavy snow. The Cherokee Orchard-Roaring Fork Motor Nature Road is usually closed from late autumn to mid-spring, so those intending to hike the Trillium Gap Trail must plan on walking 1.7 miles before reaching the trailhead.

Greenbrier Cove is a comparatively primitive section of the park. The dark, cool forest with its understory of mosses, lichens, and fungi mixed with ferns, dog-hobble, viburnum and wild hydrangea possesses a unique, wild character. In keeping with the wilderness ethic, there are no developments other than trails. Those who love wilderness and are prepared for off-trail hiking will find no better area than Greenbrier Cove.

To get to Greenbrier Cove, drive east from Gatlinburg on Tenn. 73 for about 6 miles, until you see a sign on the right (just before the concrete bridge spanning the Middle Prong

of the Little Pigeon River) indicating the Greenbrier Road.
Turn right onto it. At 0.9 mile the road passes the
Greenbrier Ranger Station on the right. At 2.8 miles there
is a small primitive campground (note: area is now
permanently closed). Its 12 tent-sites are usually full, and no
overflow camping is allowed. If you do stop there, be sure
to boil any water you take from the creek. At 3.1 miles
there is a fork, marked by signs. The road straight ahead
(south) is the Porters Creek Road. It follows Porters Creek
and ends 0.9 mile farther at a gate and parking area. Trails
to Brushy Mountain and Porters Creek start there.

The road to the left (east) is the Ramsey Prong Road. It
ends 2.0 miles from the fork at a small parking area from
which trails lead to Greenbrier Pinnacle and Ramsey Cascade.

In 1976 the Ramsey Prong Road was blocked by the Park
Service at a gate 2.0 mi. from the fork, which adds 1.5
miles beforehand to the hikes along the Greenbrier Pinnacle
and Ramsey Cascade trails. But when there is snow on the
ground, vehicular access to all these trails may be barred by
a closed gate at the ranger station back near the beginning
of the Greenbrier Road.

---

(73) BOULEVARD 5.1 mi.

Foot trail / Max. elev. gain 1,080
Start: A.T. at Mt. Kephart, 6,034 ft.
End: Mt. Le Conte, 6,400 ft.
USGS quads: Mt. Le Conte, Tenn.
Trail connections: A.T., Trillium Gap, Alum Cave,
    Rainbow Falls, Bullhead

The Boulevard is a high spur ridge leading northwest from
the Smokies Crest to Mt. Le Conte. The Boulevard Trail
follows the narrow ridge top, which is frequently the only

level ground available. It is very popular because of its origin at the A.T. and because it involves the least climbing of all the trails to the summit of Mt. Le Conte. During early spring, persistent patches of ice and snow may cover the trail near Myrtle Point. There are a shelter and a spring on the summit of Le Conte. Near the trailhead there is one reliable source of drinking water.

Trailhead: The trail starts at Mt. Kephart on the A.T. To reach the trailhead, park at Newfound Gap and hike east on the A.T. for 2.5 mi. to a well-marked junction at 6,034 ft. on Mt. Kephart. The Boulevard goes left (N) while the A.T. bears right to Ice Water Spring Shelter. Most of the climbing on this route to Le Conte is done on the A.T. before reaching the Boulevard trailhead.

Trail Details: About 100 yds. after the junction, there is a sign marking an obscure trail that leads right (N) to the Jumpoff—cliffs on the side of Mt. Kephart. On clear days this 0.5-mi. side trip is well worthwhile, for there there will be exceptional views of Charlies Bunion on the A.T., and Lester Prong far below.

From the A.T. trail junction, the Boulevard Trail descends 500 ft. through spruce and fir forest to the low point on the Boulevard at 0.9 mi. During the descent the trail crosses the headwaters of Walker Camp Prong, the only reliable source of drinking water on the trail. The path follows the high ridges and is never far from the crest. Beech gaps are interspersed among the dominant conifers. There are several overlooks on both sides of the path, to the right (NE) Horseshoe Mtn. and several laurel slicks along the knife-edge ridges below are impressive.

At about 2.5 mi., at the second sharp right turn, Anakeesta Knob lies about 500 ft. away, directly to the left (S). *Anakeesta* is a Cherokee word meaning "balsam place," and indeed the balsams (Fraser fir) there make an inviting rest spot. Past Anakeesta the ridge is frequently only a few feet wide, with precipitous drops to Boulevard Prong on the right (NE) and to Huggins Hell, left. Clingmans Dome looms on the skyline to the left (SW).

As the trail begins to climb around the east flank of Mt. Le Conte, the cliffs below Myrtle Point come into view. In late summer the green and white flowers of grass-of-parnassus, red fruits of mountain ash (inedible), plus purple monkshood and gentians and yellow goldenrod bloom along the trail. At 4.5 mi. the headwaters of Cannon Creek drop steeply immediately below the trail as it swings left (W) around Myrtle Point to the north face of Le Conte. In a final short switchback, the trail reaches the summit ridge at a sign marking a trail running east to Myrtle Point. This rough manway leads 0.2 mi. to ledges of rock where sand myrtle blooms profusely among the rocky ledges in late spring, and purple rhododendron flowers in the second half of June. There are excellent panoramic views from the point; the Boulevard Ridge appears prominently.

The Boulevard Trail continues west from the junction for another 0.2 mi. At 4.8 mi. it passes over the highest point on Le Conte, High Top (6,593 ft.), and then descends to pass by the Mt. Le Conte Shelter. The shelter has wire bunks for 12 people. The Boulevard Trail descends to a saddle and then ends beside the Le Conte Lodge. Here the trail, continuing straight (NW), leads to the Alum Cave, Rainbow Falls and Bullhead trails. To the right, the Trillium Gap Trail descends to pass a good spring after 100 yds.

(74) **ALUM CAVE** 5.5 mi.

Foot trail / Max. elev. gain 2,560
Start: Grassy patch on Newfound Gap Road, 3,840
    ft.
End: Mt. Le Conte, 6,400 ft.
USGS quads: Mt. Le Conte, Tenn.
Trail connections: Bullhead, Rainbow Falls, Trillium
    Gap, Boulevard

Mt. Le Conte and other high peaks in the Smokies are
subject to extreme conditions of rain and temperature. The
annual precipitation is more than 90 inches, which qualifies
the summits as rain forests. And during the winter, the
temperature drops below zero. This combination of conditions causes rapid weathering on the mountainsides. To
see good examples of ancient rock weathering plus scars of
recent landslides, you should hike the Alum Cave Trail.
Probably no other trail of this length in the park leads past
as many attractive features—Arch Rock, Alum Cave and the
precipitous slopes of Le Conte. Additionally, access is easy,
so the trail is popular with both novice and experienced
hikers.

   Caution: during the winter some sections of Alum Cave
Trail beyond Arch Rock can be exceedingly dangerous
because great hummocks of ice can block the way. During
other seasons the trail, with several cables to hold onto
along the cliffs, is quite safe. Nevertheless, young children
should be kept within sight of adults in the party at all
times. It is advisable to carry water when hiking this trail.

Trailhead: The trail starts at the Newfound Gap Road 8.6
mi. south of the Sugarlands Visitor Center or 4.3 mi. north
of Newfound Gap. There is ample parking, and signs mark
the beginning of the trail.

Trail Details: After crossing Walker Camp Prong, the trail goes east for 1.0 mi. along Alum Cave Creek. The Park Service has installed several interpretive signs along the trail as far as Alum Cave; these add interest for the hiker. The trail bends to the north along Styx Branch and, after three crossings of that branch on foot logs, passes through Arch Rock at 1.5 mi. A wide crack in the rock provides a tunnel for the trail; it is the result of weathering of the slatey rock formation. About 200 yds. past Arch Rock, the trail crosses Styx Branch for the last time and leaves the valley to start climbing to Alum Cave.

At 2.0 mi. the footpath passes a fine overlook in a small heath bald. If you are sharp-eyed you will be able to see a hole through a knife-edge ridge just to the west of the overlook, where the weather is spectacularly and relentlessly attacking the mountain. At 2.3 mi. and 5,000 ft., the trail passes under Alum Cave bluff.

Alum Cave is not a cave at all but an overhanging bluff, about 100 ft. high. Ground water seeping through the rock has deposited minerals in the form of alum on the face of the bluff. The alum has undoubtedly given rise to greatly exaggerated accounts that have circulated in the past about valuable minerals being found there. Actually, the minerals have been more of geologic than economic interest, yet the stories of large deposits of saltpeter persist. Occasionally, extensive portions of the overhanging bluff crash down upon the rocks below. Rubble from a 1960s rockfall may be seen below the trail. Dust in the "cave" upon the trail itself is a good example of even further weathering—the conversion of rocks into soil.

About 0.2 mi. past Alum Cave, the trail bends sharply to the right around a spur on the ridge; just off the trail to the left (N) there is a small rocky overlook which affords magnificent vistas of the deep valley of Trout Branch and of the south face of Mt. Le Conte. The prominent rocky scars visible on the mountain resulted from a cloudburst on Labor Day weekend in 1951, when the deluge carried soil and vegetation far down the slopes and choked the streams with debris. The route ahead twice traverses one of these scars near a sharp switchback.

As the trail climbs below Cliff Top, the westernmost of the three highest peaks of Le Conte, there are places where cables have been installed to steady the hiker as he follows the narrow footway across the face of steep cliffs. These places are especially hazardous during the winter when ice frequently buries the cables. At 5.0 mi. the trail turns east around the flank of Cliff Top and soon joins the Bullhead Trail and the Rainbow Falls Trail (see p. 238). The three now form a common trail which goes 0.1 mi. along the top of the mountain to reach the Le Conte Lodge cabins and the end of the trail at a junction. Straight ahead, 0.2 mi. on the Boulevard Trail, is the Le Conte Shelter. To the left (NE) the Trillium Gap Trail descends to pass a good spring at 100 yds.

---

(75) BULLHEAD 7.1 mi.

Foot trail / Max. elev. gain 3,820
Start: Cherokee Orchard, 2,580 ft.
End: Mt. Le Conte, 6,400 ft.
USGS quads: Mt. Le Conte, Tenn.
Trail connections: Rainbow Falls, Alum Cave, Trillium Gap, Boulevard

---

Bullhead is a hump on the long ridge that leads westward from the summit of Mt. Le Conte. It includes Balsam Point and West Peak and is named for a fancied resemblance to the head of a bull. The Bullhead Trail climbs this western flank. It is a dry hike, so you should start out with a full canteen of water. (There is a reliable spring near the lodge on the top of Le Conte.)

Trailhead: The trail begins at 3.4 mi. on the Cherokee Orchard Road, where there is a parking area on the loop. The Rainbow Falls Trail also starts there. The Bullhead Trail leads to the right (W) on a jeep road.

Trail Details: The trail crosses Le Conte Creek. At 0.4 mi. it turns left (S), away from the road, and passes through second-growth forest. It soon traverses the steep sides of Bullhead while passing great, gray boulders of sandstone. It runs south of Bullhead and at about 2.5 mi. enters a slight sag to the east of the peak. From this spot there are excellent views of the valley of Le Conte Creek and Cherokee Orchard. About 0.5 mi. beyond is a small heath bald from which there are fine views of the length of Sugarland Mtn. to the southwest, of Blanket Mtn. to the west, and of Mt. Winnesoka and English Mtn. to the northeast. Then the trail enters a conifer forest. Red spruce becomes common on Le Conte at 4,000 to 5,000 ft., and you will see the first Fraser fir at about 5,000 ft. Both of these Canadian zone conifers grow profusely above these elevations in the central and eastern parts of the park.

The trail goes around the south end of Balsam Point and gains the ridge. Near the summit of West Peak, off-trail and uphill to the right (S), grows the largest Fraser fir in the park—about 2.5 ft. in diameter.

At 6.4 mi. the Rainbow Falls Trail runs in from the left (N) (see p. 238). Down it, it is 6.6 mi. to Cherokee Orchard. At 7.0 mi. the Alum Cave Trail enters from the right (W), having come 5.5 mi. from the Newfound Gap Road. Continue straight (SE) along the mountaintop and soon reach Le Conte Lodge and a trail junction. Trillium Gap Trail goes left, passes a spring and descends 6.5 mi. to the Roaring Fork Motor Nature Trail (see p. 240). Straight ahead 0.2 mi. is the Le Conte trail shelter on the Boulevard Trail.

---

(76) RAINBOW FALLS (Rocky Spur) 6.6 mi.

Horse trail / Max. elev. gain 3,820
Start: Cherokee Orchard, 2,580 ft.
End: Mt. Le Conte, 6,400 ft.
USGS quads: Mt. Le Conte, Tenn.
Trail connections: Bullhead, Alum Cave, Trillium
   Gap, Boulevard

This interesting trail follows the valley of Le Conte Creek
for about 4.0 mi., past Rainbow Falls, and then climbs
from the steepening valley to Rocky Spur, which it follows
to the summit of Mt. Le Conte. Many years ago this trail
used to follow Le Conte Creek all the way to the top of the
mountain, where a wooden tower was then in use. But the
old trail was too steep, so the route was changed. On the
Rainbow Falls Trail you may find yourself suddenly climbing in and out of banks of clouds which hover along the
steep side of the mountain.

The main trail is rocky and sometimes very muddy
because of heavy use by horses. An alternative trail, a
footpath, branches off of the main trail just beyond the
trailhead in Cherokee Orchard and crosses to the west bank
of Le Conte Creek. This footpath is rougher and a little
steeper than the main trail, but it is recommended for
people hiking only as far as Rainbow Falls. It joins the main
trail about 0.4 mi. below (before) the falls.

You should carry along a canteen of water on this trail,
for Le Conte Creek may be contaminated.

Trailhead: The trail begins at the parking area at 3.4 mi. on
the one-way loop of the Cherokee Orchard Road. The
Bullhead Trail also starts there. The Rainbow Falls Trail
leads directly south from the parking area.

Trail Details: The trail follows the left (E) bank of Le

Conte Creek. The alternative foot trail soon leaves on the right and crosses the creek to climb the right bank. At 0.1 mi. a horse side trail comes in from the left; the Rainbow Falls Trail continues straight up the creek. Then it climbs through a series of switchbacks. At about 2.0 mi. the alternative foot trail runs in from the right. At 2.4 mi. the trail reaches Rainbow Falls, which is beautifully scenic. The creek falls in a fine spray some 80 ft. over a series of exposed ledges where small plants manage to grow. During the winter sustained cold sometimes freezes the spray into a pinnacle of blue-white ice reaching clear up to the brink. In less severe weather, the afternoon sun on the spray creates the delicate colors of a rainbow.

About 0.5 mi. past the falls, the trail leaves Le Conte Creek and climbs up Rocky Spur via several switchbacks to magnificent overlooks at 5.0 mi. There, at 5,700 ft., the forest gives way to the characteristic growth of a heath bald, with sand myrtle, mountain laurel and purple rhododendron alternating with outcroppings of gray sandstone. The trail enters a rhododendron tunnel and then passes into the spruce-fir zone which encompasses the heights of Mt. Le Conte.

At 5.8 mi. the trail joins the Bullhead Trail, 6.4 mi. from its trailhead at Cherokee Orchard (see p. 236). Both routes then lead uphill (E) for another 0.6 mi., at which point the Alum Cave Trail runs in from the right, having run 5.5 mi. from the Newfound Gap Road (see p. 234). Continue straight for 0.1 mi. to a trail junction by the lodge. Here the Trillium Gap Trail runs in from the left; down it, it is 6.5 mi. to the Roaring Fork Motor Nature Road. (If you want drinking water, follow the Trillium Gap Trail for 100 yds. to a reliable spring.) From the junction the Boulevard Trail leads 5.1 mi. to its trailhead on the A.T. (see p. 231). Four hundred yds. along that trail you will arrive at the Le Conte Shelter.

---

77 **TRILLIUM GAP** 6.5 mi.

Horse trail / Max. elev. gain 3,300
Start: Roaring Fork Motor Nature Road, 3,100 ft.
End: Mt. Le Conte, 6,400 ft.
USGS quads: Mt. Le Conte, Tenn.
Trail connections: Brushy Mtn., Bullhead, Rainbow
    Falls, Alum Cave, Boulevard

This is the only Mt. Le Conte trail which has a connection
to the Greenbrier area. Climbing mostly in the Roaring
Fork watershed, it has the least elevation gain of the three
trails on the northwest side of the mountain. Additionally,
it provides a good opportunity to observe several transitions
from one type of conifer to another: pines near the trailhead, hemlock to Trillium Gap, then red spruce and finally
Fraser fir as the trail reaches the high ridges. There are good
sources of water near the beginning and end of the trail.

Trailhead: The trail starts at the east end of the Grotto
Falls parking area at 1.7 mi. on the Roaring Fork Motor
Nature Road.

Trail Details: Leaving the parking area, the trail passes by
almost virgin forest, including groves of very large hemlocks. The trail crosses several small streams which provide
good drinking water. At 1.5 mi. it arrives at lovely Grotto
Falls. There you can reach the opposite bank of Roaring
Fork by fording the stream or by walking behind and under
the falls.

Roaring Fork is the steepest long stream in the park and
possibly one of the steepest in the entire East. The source
of this beautiful tumbling creek is a small spring far above
that supplies water for the facilities on the summit of Mt.
Le Conte. In the course of its 6.5-mi. length from there to

its junction in Gatlinburg with the West Prong of the Little Pigeon River, the creek loses a full mile of elevation. The sound of the fork when it is running full readily accounts for its name.

From Grotto Falls the trail climbs through hemlocks to Trillium Gap (4,700 ft.) at 3.0 mi. where there is a trail intersection. The Brushy Mtn. Trail leads to the left (N) for 0.3 mi. to terminate at Brushy Mtn., and 5.3 mi. straight ahead to its trailhead at a gate at the end of Porters Creek Road. Trillium Gap Trail turns right (S) toward Mt. Le Conte.

From then on the trail follows contours along steep ridges, passing through red spruce and finally Fraser fir as it climbs even more. In a sharp switchback at 4.3 mi., it closely approaches one of Roaring Fork's steep tributaries which plunges down the mountain in a long cascade.

Near the mountaintop the trail crosses a trickle from the spring that is the source of Roaring Fork. A hydraulic ram uses the power of this tiny stream to pump a steady supply of water uphill to a storage tank to serve the Le Conte Lodge. About 100 yds. uphill from the spring, the trail reaches a junction beside the Le Conte Lodge. The trail to the right is the common terminus of the Alum Cave, Bullhead and Rainbow Falls trails. To the left, the Boulevard Trail goes 0.2 mi. to Le Conte Shelter and continues to the A.T.

---

(78) **BRUSHY MOUNTAIN** (Trillium Branch) 5.6 mi.

Horse trail / Max. elev. gain 3,010
Start: End of Porters Creek Road, 1,900 ft.
End: Brushy Mtn. near Trillium Gap, 4,910 ft.
USGS quads: Le Conte, Tenn.
Trail connections: Porters Creek, Trillium Gap

This trail is the only direct connection between Greenbrier Cove and the Mt. Le Conte trails. It climbs to a major trail intersection at Trillium Gap and then to the top of Brushy Mtn. From the gap you can follow the Trillium Gap Trail to Mt. Le Conte. The forest along the way alternates between mixed hardwoods of the coves, and oaks and pines of the dry ridges. Wildflowers are abundant along the trail, especially during the spring. There are several sources of water along the way.

Trailhead: The trail starts at the gate at the end of the Porters Creek Road, 4.0 mi. from Tenn. 73. There is ample parking on the left. This is also the trailhead of the Porters Creek Trail. Both trails begin together on the other side of the gate.

Trail Details: The combined trail follows a jeep road roughly parallelling Porters Creek. After an easy ford across Long Branch, the road ends in a small loop at 1.0 mi. The Smoky Mountains Hiking Club Cabin is located in an area to the right of the loop. The Porters Creek Trail leads upstream to the left. A trail sign on the south side of the loop indicates the route to Trillium Gap, which is the Brushy Mtn. Trail.

From the loop the Brushy Mtn. Trail climbs very gradually through Porters Flat. At 2.3 mi. an obscure trail on the left leads slightly downhill 100 ft. to Fittified Spring. This variable spring welling from sandstone seems to have recovered from its "spell," for recently its storied ebb and flow have not been apparent.

At 2.6 mi. the trail passes through the first of several abrupt changes in vegetation: within a distance of 100 ft., the mixed hardwood forest is left behind and the pine-oak-laurel type of vegetation found on many other south-facing slopes becomes dominant. Trailing arbutus grows prolifically along the ground and usually begins to flower in March. The trail slowly climbs back into a shady hardwood forest; this pattern will be repeated farther along the trail. At 3.3 mi. (3,450 ft.) the trail crosses a large sandstone boulder which provides a convenient overlook. Trillium Gap is situated due west, the peaks of Le Conte loom high above to the southwest and just below to the southeast is the confluence of Trillium Branch and Cannon Creek. Table Mountain pines, characterized by their plump, spiny cones, grow around this overlook.

At 3.7 mi. (3,750 ft.) the trail makes the first of two crossings of Trillium Branch, as it passes by very large hemlocks and tulip poplars. In a boulder field just beyond the branch a large Dutchman's-pipe vine is growing. Its flowers, which bloom in April, resemble the traditional Dutchman's pipe. At 4.6 mi. there is a large linden (basswood) tree with a typical clump of small trees and shoots growing from its base. The trail crosses Trillium Branch again at 5.0 mi.; this is a good source of water. Then the trail becomes grassy and at 5.3 mi. (4,700 ft.) enters Trillium Gap. The gap is a beautiful grassy spot, shaded by small beech, yellow birch and striped maple trees. During April and May, not only trilliums but also hundreds of spring beauties and trout lilies bloom there.

At the gap the Trillium Gap Trail leads left (S) 3.5 mi. to end at Mt. Le Conte, and straight ahead (W) 3.0 mi. to its trailhead at the Roaring Fork Motor Nature Road. The Brushy Mtn. Trail turns to the right (N) and runs for 0.3 mi. to terminate at the summit of Brushy Mtn. An overlook there provides tremendous views of Greenbrier Cove, Porters Creek Valley and the imposing bulk of Mt. Le Conte, nearly 2,000 ft. above.

> **(79) PORTERS CREEK** (Porters Gap) 3.7 mi.
>
> Gated jeep and foot trail manway / Max. elev. gain
>   3,476 if going off-trail to the A.T.
> Start: End of Porters Creek Road, 1,900 ft.
> End: Porters Flats campsite
> USGS quads: Mt. Le Conte, Mt. Guyot, Tenn.
> Trail connections: Brushy Mtn., A.T., Richland Mtn.

This trail consists of two sections which are very different in character. For 4.0 mi. it is an easy walking trail through an undisturbed forest. After that it turns into an unmaintained manway and becomes *very* steep, rising nearly 2,000 ft. in the last mile. This last section is for the *experienced* hiker only and even for him only one-way. Nobody should attempt to descend this trail from the A.T. The latter section is the most difficult and dangerous stretch of trail described in this entire guidebook. Don't do it!

The first 4.0 mi. of trail are suitable for a family hike. The path winds along Porters Creek through a mature forest of large oaks, maples, basswoods and tulip poplars. It is maintained and open with only a gradual climb. When the going becomes difficult, most hikers simply return via the same trail.

There is a back-country campsite at Lester Prong and water is available from the numerous creeks nearby.

Trailhead: The trail starts at a gate at the end of the Porters Creek Road, 4.0 mi. from Tenn. 73. There is ample parking on the left. This is also the trailhead of the Brushy Mtn. Trail. Both trails begin on the other side of the gate.

Trail Details: The combined trail follows a jeep road roughly paralleling Porters Creek. After an easy ford across Long Branch, the road ends in a small loop at 1.0 mi., where there are signs. The Brushy Mtn. Trail parts company from the Porters Creek Trail and runs from the south side of the loop to Trillium Gap. The Porters Creek Trail leaves the loop on the left. (Note: the Park Service sign calls this the Porters Gap Trail.) The Smoky Mountains Hiking Club Cabin is located to the right of the loop.

The Porters Creek Trail passes through a rich lowland called Porters Flat. At 1.5 mi. it crosses Porters Creek on a bridge which is in disrepair; use caution. About 500 yds. past the bridge there is a small waterfall to the left (E) of the trail. Many large trees grow roundabout in the rich cove hardwood forest. Because this trail is little used, its under-footing is soft and spongy. The trail gradually narrows and at about 3.7 mi. fords a good-size creek. This is the point at which most day hikers will wish to turn around.

The trail makes a series of creek fords which should be counted, for at the sixth ford Lester Prong joins Porters Creek. (There are no trail signs there.) Follow the footway toward the southeast and avoid the obscure trail running south along Lester Prong. (That trail leads about 0.2 mi. to an obscure campsite on Lester Prong's left bank.)

After another series of fords, the Porters Creek Trail stops crossing and runs mostly up the stream bed. The stream is small or nonexistent for about 500 yds. (except after heavy rains) but it reappears mysteriously at a higher elevation. Presumably, the explanation is that the valley floor is filled with rock fragments from the ridges above, so that the stream flows through the debris far below the surface. But higher up the valley where the slope is too steep for loose rocks to pile up, the stream reappears on the tilted ledges of the Anakeesta Formation.

The footway continues in or near the stream until at about 4,700 ft. there is a prominent fork. Follow the open, rocky chute to the right (SSW). After scrambling over loose rocks for about 50 yds., look carefully for the manway opening to the left, marked by a small rock cairn. After the opening the maintained footway begins to climb steeply along a very small branch. After some final zigzags, it ends at the A.T. in Dry Sluice Gap on the Tenn.-N.C. state line. Just a few yards to the left (E) along the A.T. is the terminus of the Richland Mtn. Trail, which, with connections, leads south toward Smokemont Campground (see p. 136). Despite an earlier trail sign, the Porters Creek Trail never approaches Porters Gap, which lies 1.0 mi. to the east of Dry Sluice Gap on the A.T.

---

(80) **RAMSEY CASCADE** 2.5 mi.

Foot trail / Max. elev. gain 1,660
Start: End of Ramsey Prong Road, 2,640 ft.
End: Ramsey Cascade, 4,300 ft.
USGS quads: Mt. Guyot, N.C.
Trail connections: Greenbrier Pinnacle

The Ramsey Cascade Trail is one of the most popular trails in the park because it is short enough for the beginner and rewarding for the experienced hiker. It provides an easy walk along clear Ramsey Prong which tumbles through a mature forest of big trees. Along the trail you will notice young yellow birch trees growing upon raised roots. These young trees began to grow on old logs which have since rotted away, leaving the birch roots exposed and supporting their trees in midair. Since the trail is heavily used, the soil is compacted underfoot. There is a source of water, near the end of the trail.

Several sources mention a manway and campsite upstream from Ramsey Cascade, but these are completely overgrown and should be considered off-trail hiking. There are no through connections between this trail and the surrounding ridges. Thus, it, along with the Greenbrier Pinnacle Trail, is one of the few dead-end trails in the park.

Trailhead: The trail starts at the end of the gravel Ramsey Prong Road, 6.6 mi. from Tenn. 73. There is ample parking, and there are pit toilets nearby. This is also the trailhead for the Greenbrier Pinnacle Trail. The Ramsey Cascade Trail runs southeast past a trail register with a sign and continues straight. (Note: due to a roadblock, add 1.5 mi. to this hike.)

Trail Details: The trail climbs gradually upstream along the north bank of Ramsey Prong. Just after it crosses the first foot log at 0.7 mi., there is a very large silverbell tree, 2.5 ft. in diameter, growing on the left. On the right is the largest sweet birch on record, 3.5 ft. in diameter. A little farther on is a grove of tulip poplars with diameters of 4 to 5 ft. Nearby is a specimen of the rare yellow cucumber tree, which exhibits its canary yellow flowers in May. After the trail crosses the second foot log at 1.4 mi., several large black cherry trees, 3 ft. in diameter, can be seen; their fruit falls to the ground in September.

The trail ends at 2.5 mi. at a third foot log at the bottom of 60-foot-high Ramsey Cascade. This is a large, beautiful falls located in a rich forested glen. By careful scrambling around the large sandstone boulders at the base of the falls, you may find a suitable lunch spot and photogenic view of the cascade. Caution: it is extremely dangerous to climb around or above the cascade itself because the soil and rocks are very slippery; many hikers have been seriously injured there by careless climbing. Return to the trailhead via the same trail, taking time to appreciate the many wildflowers growing along the trail from early spring through autumn.

The safest source of drinking water on this trail is a small side stream that crosses the trail about 100 yds. down the trail from the cascade.

81 **GREENBRIER PINNACLE** 3.5 mi.

Gated jeep trail / Max. elev. gain 1,960
Start: End of the Ramsey Prong Road, 2,640 ft.
End: Fire tower on Greenbrier Pinnacle, 4,600 ft.
USGS quads: Mt. Guyot, N.C.
Trail connections: Ramsey Cascade

Greenbrier Pinnacle is part of a long high ridge called
Pinnacle Lead which generally runs east-west and connects
with Old Black (6,370 ft.) on the Smokies Crest. There is a
fire lookout tower at the west end of the ridge on the
pinnacle. The ridge top is covered by almost impassable
heaths (laurel and rhododendron) so no trail exists there,
but there is a trail up the side of the pinnacle to the
tower—the Greenbrier Pinnacle Trail. It follows a seldom-
used jeep road which is not as rocky and bare as many
others. Water sources are not dependable along the trail,
but the most likely one is a piped spring on the left at
about 2.9 mi.

At first the trail passes through pine and oak forest. In
July you may see white rhododendron blooming along the
lower part of the trail. Near the ridge crest, the dense heath
crowds out much of the forest; the mountain laurel and
purple rhododendron are at their peak on the crest in June.
The dominant species of pine on the pinnacle is the Table
Mountain pine, which can be recognized by its well-
rounded cones armored with sharp spines.

Trailhead: The trail starts at the end of the Ramsey Prong
Road, 6.6 mi. from Tenn. 73. There is plenty of room to
park, and there are pit toilets nearby. This is also the
trailhead for the Ramsey Cascade Trail. The two trails start
together and at 0.1 mi. the Greenbrier Pinnacle Trail goes
left (NW). Note: due to a recent roadblock, add 1.5 mi. to
this hike.

Trail Details: At 0.3 mi. the trail crosses Ramsey Branch. It climbs steadily through a series of long switchbacks. At about 2.9 mi. there is a piped spring on the left, downhill. The trail curves to the right around the west end of the ridge, and at 3.1 mi. there is an excellent view, to the left, of Greenbrier Cove directly below. The trail then ascends gradually to end at the fire tower at 3.5 mi. A record-size Table Mountain pine grows by the trail about 100 yds. from the tower.

Fire protection practices in the area have changed in recent years. The towers are used only occasionally, so there is little chance of encountering a friendly towerman and being invited inside the lookout. Nevertheless, you can see fine views by climbing partway up the open tower stairway. Mt. Le Conte and Brushy Mtn. rise across the valley to the southwest; Mt. Guyot is to the east at the head of the Ramsey Prong watershed. Caution: in stormy or freezing weather, there is considerable risk in climbing the stairway.

Elkmont Section

(Tennessee)

Introduction

Most sections in this guidebook are delineated by ridge lines. The Elkmont section is an exception because its eastern boundary is the West Prong of the Little Pigeon River which parallels the Newfound Gap Road. Additionally, Elkmont is bounded on the south by the main crest of the Smokies Range, including Mount Collins, Clingmans Dome, Mount Buckley, Silers Bald and Cold Spring Knob, and on the west by the Dripping Spring Mountain-Miry Ridge system. The main areas within the Elkmont boundaries are Sugarland Mountain, which extends north-south to the west of the West Prong, and the upper valley of the Little River, which flows between Sugarland Mountain and the western ridge system.

The Little River Lumber Company established the first large logging operation anywhere in the Smokies in the Elkmont section in 1901. It erected mills at Townsend and Elkmont, and built a railroad up the gorge of the Little River. In 1926 Colonel W.E. Townsend, the head of the company, sold 76,000 acres of land in the Elkmont and Tremont sections to the government to become the first portion of the Great Smoky Mountains National Park. Meanwhile, the company continued logging. When it ceased operations in 1938, it had removed more than a half-billion board feet from Elkmont and Tremont.

Two trails in this section ascend to follow the ridges of Sugarland Mountain and Miry-Dripping Spring. Two lovely lowland trails, Meigs (pronounced "Megs") Mountain and Cucumber Gap, follow the old Oconaluftee Fault. The

Goshen Prong and Rough Creek trails at the head of the Little River are only partially maintained—that area is somewhat primitive. The Blanket Mountain Trail on the western ridge system makes a good day hike. Other popular day hikes include Cove Mountain to the northern boundary, and the Chimney Tops and Road Prong trails, which begin at the Chimney Tops parking area on the Newfound Gap Road. The Road Prong Trail provides one of the finest short hikes in the park.

The Elkmont Developed Campground, with 340 sites, is the park's largest campground, yet because of its popularity it is usually full. It is located in the general area of the old Elkmont logging camp. A colony of private summer cottages is situated nearby. The owners of the cottages were actively opposed to a national park during its creation; they have been granted leases to continue occupation of their enclave. Several new back-country campsites have been established in this section, so that ten sites are now designated there.

To reach the Elkmont section, start at Park Headquarters at Sugarlands and drive west on old Tenn. 73, which the Park Service now calls the Little River Road. At 4.9 miles a paved road leads left (southeast) for 1.5 miles to the Elkmont Campground. Immediately before the campground, a road on the left runs 0.6 mile to a road junction near the summer home colony. (Hikers take note: At this point this road has recently been permanently blocked.) Hiking along the road, at 3.0 miles the Cucumber Gap Trail begins on the right. At 3.3 miles on the other side of a small bridge, the Huskey Gap Trail starts on the left. The road ends at 4.2 miles, where the Rough Creek and Goshen Prong trails begin.

Back at the road junction in the cottage colony, the Jakes Creek Road (also gravel) goes to the right and passes several summer homes. At 0.4 mile there is a gate on the left. This gate is the trailhead of the Meigs Mountain Trail, the access point to the Blanket Mountain Trail, and the terminus of the Cucumber Gap Trail.

The road to the Elkmont Campground remains open throughout the winter season, but the gravel roads beyond it are closed.

---

(82) **CHIMNEY TOPS** 2.0 mi.

Foot trail / Max. elev. gain 1,350
Start: Chimney Tops parking area, 3,400 ft.
End: Chimney Tops, 4,750 ft.
USGS quads: Mt. Le Conte, Tenn.
Trail connections: Road Prong, manway to Sugarland
  Mtn.

The Chimneys, two steep-sided pinnacles, are a well-known landmark in the Smokies. They overlook the West Prong of the Little Pigeon River and the Newfound Gap Road in Tennessee. They are part of the Anakeesta Formation, a dark, silty-slatey metamorphic rock which formed such rough, steep areas as Peregrine Peak and Anakeesta Ridge. The Chimney Tops Trail is short but moderately steep. Because it is one of the more popular hikes in the park, it has recently been reconstructed and widened to accommodate heavy use.

Trailhead: The trail starts at the Chimney Tops parking area, on the right at 8.7 mi. south of Sugarlands on the Newfound Gap Road. There is plenty of parking space. This is also the trailhead of the Road Prong Trail. Both trails begin on a graded path leading downhill to a footbridge over the West Prong of the Little Pigeon River. Do *not* descend on the steep erosion gullies created by other hikers.

Trail Details: After crossing the river, the combined trail soon crosses Road Prong on a second footbridge. It continues to the base of a ridge and turns left (S) to ascend the side of the ridge. There are two more footbridges at 0.2 and 0.7 mi., as the trail passes through a beautiful cove called Beech Flats. Wildflowers bloom there in the spring.

On the other side of the fourth bridge, the Road Prong Trail turns left to follow Road Prong up to the Smokies Crest. The Chimney Tops Trail turns right and climbs steadily along the northeast side of Sugarland Mtn. At about 1.8 mi. an open trail begins on the left and climbs 0.4 mi. to the Sugarland Mtn. Trail. The Chimney Tops Trail reaches the twin pinnacles at 2.0 mi. From there you will see excellent views of the Sugarland Valley to the northwest, Mt. Le Conte to the northeast and Mt. Mingus to the southeast. Caution: do not enter the natural chimney in the rock summit.

---

(83) **ROAD PRONG** (Indian Gap) 3.3 mi.

Foot trail / Max. elev. gain 1,870
Start: Chimney Tops parking area, 3,400 ft.
End: Clingmans Dome Road, 5,270 ft.
USGS quads: Clingmans Dome, Mt. Le Conte, Tenn.
Trail connections: Chimney Tops, A.T.

This trail follows Road Prong from its mouth at the West Prong of the Little Pigeon River to its headwaters at Indian Gap. Although it is difficult to imagine that the trail was ever a road, it used to be part of the only wagon road that crossed the Smokies before construction of the modern highway. The nineteenth century wagon road was called the Oconalufty Turnpike.

At one time an old Indian foot trail wound from

Cherokee villages on the Oconaluftee and Tuckasegee rivers in what is now N.C. to the crest of the Smokies at Indian Gap. From there it descended along Road Prong and the Little Pigeon River into what is now Tenn. In 1831 white settlers started building the wagon road from the N.C. side, closely following the route of the old Indian trail. They never completed the road, but they did manage to construct a good road to the Smokies Crest. The route was later extended during the Civil War when Indian Confederate troops under the command of Col. William H. Thomas turned the trail down the Tenn. side into a crude road in order to haul munitions across the mountains. According to historian Horace Kephart, the road was so bad that the troops had to remove cannon from their carriages and drag them over bare rocks and clay.

Today the wagon road on the N.C. side is a modern highway, the Newfound Gap Road. On the Tenn. side, it has reverted to a fairly rough footpath, the Road Prong Trail. Many hikers prefer descending this trail to climbing it.

Trailhead: The trail starts at the Chimney Tops parking area, 8.7 mi. south of Sugarlands on the Newfound Gap Road. Ample parking is available. This is also the trailhead of the Chimney Tops Trail. Both trails begin on a graded path leading downhill to a footbridge crossing the West Prong of the Little Pigeon River. Do *not* descend on the steep erosion gullies created by previous hikers.

Trail Details: After crossing the river, the combined trail soon crosses Road Prong on a second footbridge. It continues to the base of a ridge and turns left (S) to ascend the side of the ridge. There are two more footbridges at 0.2 and 0.7 mi., as the trail passes through a beautiful cove called Beech Flats. Wildflowers bloom there in the spring. On the other side of the fourth bridge, the Chimney Tops Trail turns right, and the Road Prong Trail turns left, following Road Prong.

The trail climbs to a moderately difficult stream ford at 1.1 mi. where you must cross by hopping on rocks. This is the only crossing which might cause any problem. The trail continues to climb the narrow valley, always close to Road Prong. Fine examples of phacelia, squirrel corn and hobblebush grow along this section. At about 1.4 mi. the trail reaches Indian Grave Flats, where an unwilling Cherokee scout was shot and buried by Union troops in 1864. The trail then runs through a rich forest and makes several easy stream crossings before ending after 3.3 mi. at the Clingmans Dome Road in Indian Gap. From there Newfound Gap is 1.7 mi. to the left via the A.T., and Mt. Collins Shelter is about 3.0 mi. to the right on the A.T. Good views of Deep Creek Valley may be seen by crossing the Clingmans Dome Road. There is ample parking at the gap.

 84 CUCUMBER GAP (Little River Truck) 2.4 mi.

Horse trail / Max. elev. gain 320
Start: Little River Gravel Road, 2,600 ft.
End: Jakes Creek Road, 2,350 ft.
USGS quads: Gatlinburg, Tenn.
Trail connections; Huskey Gap, Blanket Mtn., Meigs Mtn.

This easy, pleasant trail is suitable for the entire family. It winds its way through laurel and second-growth hardwoods in the rich lowlands.

Trailhead: The trail starts on the right (W) at a point 3.0 mi. beyond the permanent barrier on the Little River Gravel Road above Elkmont Campground. While walking to the trailhead, notice the Huskey Branch waterfall to the right at 2.8 mi. There is a sign at the start of the trail.

Trail Details: The trail angles up an old logging grade, climbing gently. It crosses Huskey Branch on a flat foot log at 0.4 mi. and continues through deep young forest with a rich ground cover of ferns. At 1.1 mi. it reaches Cucumber Gap (2,840 ft.), which is a saddle located between Burnt Mtn. to the north and Bent Arm ridge to the southeast. Past the gap a manway leads left to climb Bent Arm and join Miry Ridge. That trail is heavily grown over.

The Cucumber Gap Trail begins a gentle descent and reaches Tulip Branch at 2.1 mi. There it is easy to cross the creek by stepping on stones. On the other side the trail immediately joins a jeep road, which is also the route of the Blanket Mtn. Trail (see p. 263). (The Meigs Mtn. Trail begins 0.1 mi. uphill to the left, see p. 267.) Follow the road downhill to the right for 0.3 mi., where it runs into Jakes Creek Road. The gate there is the terminus of the Cucumber Gap Trail and the trailhead of the Blanket Mtn. Trail. The gate is located 0.4 mi. from the summer colony junction.

---

(85) **HUSKEY GAP** 3.8 mi.

Horse trail / Max. elev. gain 500
Start: Little River Gravel Road, 2,600 ft.
End: Newfound Gap Road, 1,880 ft.
USGS quads: Gatlinburg, Tenn.
Trail connections: Sugarland Mtn., Cucumber Gap

From the Little River Valley, this trail crosses Sugarland Mtn. and descends to the Newfound Gap Road in the valley of the West Prong of the Little Pigeon River. It is a good, graded trail and is recommended for family hiking. Note: when hiked in the reverse direction, the climb is much greater (1,220 ft.).

Trailhead: The trail starts on the left (NE) 3.3 mi. along the Little River Gravel Road from the permanent barrier which recently blocked the road to auto traffic. Plan to add this mileage to your hike.

Trail Details: The trail runs for 0.5 mi. through the flat bottom land of the Little River. Then it turns north to ascend the ridge of Sugarland Mtn., crossing several small branches with no difficulty. The forest on either side is all second growth because the area was extensively logged by the Little River Lumber Co. in prepark days. At 2.0 mi. the trail enters Huskey Gap (3,100 ft.) and intersects the Sugarland Mtn. Trail. That trail begins 2.6 mi. to the left on the Little River Road (formerly Tenn. 73) and runs 8.9 mi. to the right to Mt. Collins and the Clingmans Dome Road (see p. 260).

The Huskey Gap Trail then runs downhill through a fine second-growth hardwood forest. It ends at 3.8 mi. at the Newfound Gap Road, 1.7 mi. southeast of the Sugarlands Visitor Center.

---

(86) ROUGH CREEK 3.4 mi.

Foot trail or manway / Max. elev. gain 1,530
Start: End of Little River Gravel Road, 2,730 ft.
End: Sugarland Mtn. Trail, 4,260 ft.
USGS quads: Silers Bald, Gatlinburg, Tenn. (trail not on Silers Bald map)
Trail connections: Goshen Prong, Sugarland Mtn.

Reports on the condition of this trail vary, so its status is uncertain. But it is probably a frequently used manway and kept well open. It could serve as a major connection between the lowlands and the Sugarland Mtn. Trail. There is a back-country campsite a short distance from the trailhead.

Trailhead: The trail starts 4.2 mi. beyond the new roadblock on the Little River Gravel Road. Plan to add this mileage to your hike. This spot is also the trailhead of the Goshen Prong Trail. The Rough Creek Trail starts to the southeast, past the gate.

Trail Details: The trail runs uphill, following the old Little River Road. At 0.5 mi. it arrives at the Rough Creek back-country campsite, which has room for about 14 people.

The trail continues up the road to 0.8 mi., where it turns left to ascend along Rough Creek. It crosses the creek three times before it begins a steep climb up the side of Sugarland Mtn. At 3.4 mi. it terminates at an unmarked junction with the Sugarland Mtn. Trail. That trail begins 6.3 mi. to the left on the Little River Road (formerly Tenn. 73) and runs 5.2 mi. more to the right to Mt. Collins and the Clingmans Dome Road (see p. 260).

 GOSHEN PRONG (Fish Camp Prong) 7.3 mi.

Foot trail or manway / Max. elev. gain 3,020
Start: End of Little River Gravel Road, 2,730 ft.
End: Near Double Springs Gap on the A.T., 5,750 ft.
USGS quads: Silers Bald, Tenn.
Trail connections: Rough Creek, A.T.

This trail follows an old jeep trail in its lower sections but becomes narrow and steep later on. The Park Service does not indicate regular maintenance, but several hikers report that it is quite passable. It begins in the lowlands and ends high on the Smokies Crest near the Double Springs Gap Shelter. There is plenty of water along the trail.

Note: there is a new back-country campsite located at about 2.1 mi. on the trail at Camp Rock.

Trailhead: The trail starts 2.1 mi. beyond the new roadblock on the Little River Gravel Road. Plan to add this mileage to your hike. This spot is also the trailhead of the Rough Creek Trail. The Goshen Prong Trail begins on the right side of the trail register.

Trail Details: The trail starts out on a nice, wide, abandoned roadway which leads to the Little River, where the bridge has been washed away. But a path leads left upstream 50 yds. to a point where you can cross the stream by rock hopping. Caution: the rocks can be very slippery. (This is the only difficult part of the trail.) On the other side a footpath leads back downstream 30 yds. to the main trail.

The trail runs up the very beautiful valley of Fish Camp Prong. This is a wonderful stream of changing complexion, from tumbling cascades and churning falls to placid, flat stretches flowing easily over deep pools. There are signs that the trail is following an old railroad bed; note the depressions where crossties rotted away many years ago. At 2.1 mi. on the left there is a rock ledge overhang which makes a suitable campsite. At 3.1 mi. the trail reaches a flat area at the confluence of Ash Camp Branch and Fish Camp Prong. There the trail turns southeast and soon follows Goshen Prong.

The trail becomes narrower and steeper as it begins to climb toward the Smokies Crest. At 4.3 mi. there is a small cave on the left. The last reliable source of water is crossed at 4.8 mi. The trail continues to ascend the ridge. At 7.3 mi. it ends at the A.T. From there the Double Springs Gap Shelter is 0.6 mi. to the right (W) on the A.T. It has built-in bunks to accommodate 12 people. To the left (W) the A.T. leads 2.3 mi. to the summit of Clingmans Dome.

> **(88) SUGARLAND MOUNTAIN** 11.5 mi.
>
> Horse trail / Max. elev. gain 3,700
> Start: Fighting Creek Gap on Little River Road,
>   2,300 ft.
> End: Clingmans Dome Road, 5,900 ft.
> USGS quads: Gatlinburg, Mt. Le Conte, Clingmans
>   Dome, Tenn.
> Trail connections: Cove Mtn., Huskey Gap, Rough
>   Creek, manway to Chimneys, A.T., Fork Ridge

This long trail begins in the lowlands on the Little River Road (formerly Tenn. 73) and follows the crest of Sugarland Mtn. all the way to Mt. Collins on the Smokies Crest. Along the way you can see excellent views of the Elkmont and Le Conte sections of the park. Near its terminus the trail passes by the Mt. Collins Shelter. Because there are few sources of water along this trail, you should carry a full canteen.

Note: there is a new back-country campsite, Medicine Branch Bluff campsite, located at about 3.5 mi. on the Sugarland Mtn. Trail.

Trailhead: The trail starts from a parking area at Fighting Creek Gap on the Little River Road, 3.8 mi. west of the Sugarlands Visitor Center. This spot is also the trailhead of the Cove Mtn. Trail. That trail runs north; the Sugarland Mtn. Trail runs south.

Trail Details: The trail starts on the left of the highway and climbs steeply to the southeast, gaining about 600 ft. in elevation within the first 0.6 mi. Then the grade becomes more gradual. At 1.0 mi. the trail arrives at an open area which gives spectacular views of the Sugarland Valley to the left (E), with Mt. Le Conte looming in the background. At 1.2 mi. at Mids Gap an old abandoned trail leaves on the

right (W) and goes down Mids Branch to Elkmont. The
Sugarland Mtn. Trail continues up the crest of the ridge. At
2.6 mi. it reaches Huskey Gap (3,100 ft.) and a trail
intersection. On the right the Huskey Gap Trail has come
2.0 mi. from its trailhead on the Little River Gravel Road.
On the left (E) it runs 1.8 mi. to the Newfound Gap Road
(see p. 256).

The Sugarland Mtn. Trail continues up the ridge to the
southeast. To the west you will be able to see Little River
Valley with Miry Ridge in the distance. At 6.3 mi. the
Rough Creek Trail terminates on the right, having come 3.4
mi. from the Little River Gravel Road (see p. 257). There is
no sign marking the junction.

The Sugarland Mtn. Trail continues to climb along the
ridge through rhododendron and hardwoods. At 7.9 mi. a
sign on a tree points left to a manway which leads 0.4 mi.
to the Chimney Tops Trail (see p. 252). The Sugarland Mtn.
Trail continues on, offering fine views of Mt. Mingus and
Mt. Le Conte to the left (E). At 10.7 mi. it reaches the Mt.
Collins Shelter, where there are wire bunks for 12 people, a
fireplace, a spring and pit toilets.

The trail continues through spruce forest until at 11.1
mi. it turns left (E) on the A.T. After 0.3 mi. a side trail
leads 0.1 mi. to the right to the Clingmans Dome Road.
This point on the road is 3.2 mi. west of Newfound Gap
and 450 ft. east of the parking area for the Spruce Fir
Nature Trail. Straight ahead, on the other side of the road,
a sign marks the terminus of the Fork Ridge Trail, which
has climbed 4.9 mi. from the Deep Creek Valley in N.C.
(see p. 171).

---

89 **COVE MOUNTAIN** 3.8 mi.

Foot, horse and gated jeep trail / Max. elev. gain
  1,780
Start: Fighting Creek Gap on Little River Road,
  2,300 ft.
End: Cove Mtn. Fire Tower, 4,080 ft.
USGS quads: Gatlinburg, Tenn.
Trail connections: Sugarland Mtn., Little Brier

This trail begins on the Little River Road (formerly Tenn.
73) and climbs to the fire tower on Cove Mtn. The first 1.3
mi. to Laurel Falls is a very popular (paved) foot trail. After
that the way turns into a horse trail and climbs through
rich, nearly virgin forest, which is very pleasant. No water is
available near the top of the mountain, so plan to carry
some.

Trailhead: The trail starts from a parking area at Fighting
Creek Gap on the Little River Road, 3.8 mi. west of the
Sugarlands Visitor Center. This spot is also the trailhead of
the Sugarland Mtn. Trail. That trail runs south; the Cove
Mtn. Trail runs north.

Trail Details: A paved trail starts on the right side of the
highway and goes west, then northwest, through a beautiful
second-growth forest of hardwoods and hemlock. This portion of the trail is very easy and has been traveled even by
babies pushed in strollers. At 1.3 mi. the trail arrives at
Laurel Falls, where the pavement ends.

Cross the stream below the falls. The trail, which is now
a horse trail, climbs through a rich, mature forest. At 2.7
mi. the Little Brier Trail leaves on the left and runs 3.7
mi. to Wear Cove Gap. The Cove Mtn. Trail goes to the
right (N) and climbs along Chinquapin Ridge. At 3.7 mi.
it reaches the ridge crest and a jeep trail. It turns left (W)

onto the jeep trail to reach the summit of C\
the Park Service lookout tower. Excellent 360°\
be seen from the tower. (Exercise caution while c\
the tower steps.) To the northwest Wear Cove lies be\
with the Chilhowee Mtn. Range rising far away in the\
distance. To the south the Smokies Range stretches from
east to west.

From Cove Mtn. the jeep trail leads east along the
northern boundary of the park for 9.0 mi. to Park Headquarters at Sugarlands. Along the way it passes by Phils
View, Mt. Harrison and Holy Butt.

---

(90) **BLANKET MOUNTAIN** (Jakes Creek) 4.0 mi.

Gated jeep trail / Max. elev. gain 2,260
Start: Gate on Jakes Creek Road, 2,350 ft.
End: Blanket Mtn., 4,610 ft.
USGS quads: Gatlinburg, Silers Bald, Tenn.
Trail connections: Cucumber Gap, Meigs Mtn., Miry
    Ridge, Panther Creek

This trail makes a good day hike and offers fine views of
the Smokies from near the summit of Blanket Mtn.

Blanket Mtn. acquired its name during an 1802 land
survey, when the Indian commissioner, Return Jonathan
Meigs, was retracing the Cherokee boundary line from an
old treaty. Meigs's survey lines were to run from the top of
Chilhowee Mtn. to the Smokies Crest, but several high,
rugged ridges intervened. In order to provide a definite
target for his compass, a bright-colored blanket was hung
from a high pole on what has since become Blanket Mtn.

Trailhead: The trail starts at a gate on the left of the Jakes
Creek Road, 0.4 mi. from the junction at the summer
colony. This spot is also the terminus of the Cucumber Gap

rail (see p. 255). Park alongside the road. There is a trail register.

Trail Details: Both trails begin as one, on the other side of the gate, and climb a jeep road. At 0.3 mi. the Cucumber Gap Trail parts company on the left and runs 2.1 mi. to the Little River Gravel Road. The Blanket Mtn. Trail continues along the old road to 0.4 mi., at which point the Meigs Mtn. Trail begins on the right and runs 8.7 mi. to Tremont (see p. 267).

At 1.5 mi., past Newt Prong, the road becomes rougher. It crosses Newt Prong (hop on the rocks) and continues up Jakes Creek. After several switchbacks and small stream crossings, it reaches Jakes Gap (4,055 ft.) and a trail intersection at 3.3 mi. The Miry Ridge Trail begins there and leads left (S) 5.0 mi. to the A.T. Straight ahead (W) the Panther Creek Trail runs 2.3 mi. to its trailhead on the Tremont Road (see p. 276).

The Blanket Mtn. Trail turns to the right and climbs the side of Blanket Mtn. It reaches the summit at 4.0 mi. Just before that there are excellent views from a rock outcrop. On the summit you will see a few remains of an old lookout tower and cabin that once stood there. This is a fine place for a picnic lunch.

(91) **MIRY RIDGE** (Dripping Spring Mountain) 5.0
  mi.

Horse trail / Max. elev. gain 900
Start: Jakes Gap, Blanket Mtn. Trail, 4,055 ft.
End: Buckeye Gap on the A.T., 4,960 ft.
USGS quads: Silers Bald, Tenn.
Trail connections: Blanket Mtn., Panther Creek, Lynn
  Camp Prong, A.T.

The Miry Ridge Trail provides access from either Tremont
or Elkmont to the A.T. on the Smokies Crest. The climb
along Miry Ridge is gentle in most places and provides the
hiker with good views of Clingmans Dome, Mt. Collins and
Sugarland Mtn. Water is plentiful near the beginning of the
trail, and there is a small spring toward the end. In 1965 the
last half of the trail was proposed as part of the route of a
new transmountain highway. Conservation groups strongly
opposed the project, which now seems to be dead.

   The last mile of the trail amounts to a dividing line
between two types of forest. East of there, Canadian-type
trees (red spruce and Fraser fir) cover the crests of the
Smokies. To the west of the ridge, there are no Canadian-
type trees. Hardwoods predominate. During early- and
mid-May an outstanding display of painted trillium and
creeping phlox blooms along the trail.

   Note: there are two new back-country campsites on the
Miry Ridge Trail—Jakes Gap campsite at 0.5 mi. and
Dripping Spring Mtn. campsite at 2.2 mi.

Trailhead: The trail starts at Jakes Gap, which is reached by
hiking 3.3 mi. on the Blanket Mtn. Trail or 2.3 mi. to the
end of the Panther Creek Trail (see p. 276). Miry Ridge
runs south from the trail intersection.

Trail Details: The trail bears southwest around the western end of Dripping Spring Mtn. There, ground water continually seeps from a long series of exposed slate ledges, making the entire mountainside appear to be a dripping spring. At about 1.6 mi. the trail arrives at a clear area from which you will see enjoyable views of the Tremont Valley to the west and the Smokies Crest to the south. Additionally, in early August a fine feast of blueberries may be found there.

The trail then tunnels through some dense rhododendron which is very pleasant and cool on hot days. At 2.2 mi. the Bent Arm Manway begins on the left (NE). At 2.4 mi. the Lynn Camp Prong Trail ends on the right, having climbed 3.3 mi. from its trailhead on the Greenbrier Ridge Trail.

The Miry Ridge Trail turns south along Miry Ridge. After a moderate ascent, it levels off and at 3.2 mi. passes an old abandoned overgrown trail which leads left to Ben Parton Lookout. For easier access to a fine view, continue along the Miry Ridge Trail 200 yds. as far as a large rock on the right. Leave the trail on the right and scramble up the ridge. You will top a rock summit from which you will be able to see the Tremont Valley to the northwest. (Trees limit the view in other directions.)

Past the large rock, the Miry Ridge Trail continues southwest up the ridge toward the Smokies Crest. At about 4.9 mi. it crosses a small spring. The trail terminates at the A.T. at 5.0 mi. From there Buckeye Gap is about 0.2 mi. to the left (E) on the A.T., and Derrick Knob and Shelter are located 2.7 mi. to the right (W).

⑨② MEIGS MOUNTAIN (Lumber Ridge) 8.7 mi.

Horse trail / Max. elev. gain 380
Start: Jakes Creek, Blanket Mtn. Trail, 2,500 ft.
End: Tremont Environmental Education Center,
    1,350 ft.
USGS quads: Gatlinburg, Wear Cove, Tenn.
Trail connections: Blanket Mtn., Cucumber Gap,
    Curry Gap, Buckhorn Gap

This is an east-west, lowlands trail which connects the
Elkmont section with the Tremont section of the park.

During the first half of its journey, it crosses several small
creeks, which are probably potable, and runs through what
used to be farmland. Many old homesites will be fairly
conspicuous to the observant hiker. A close look at these
places reveals foundations, wash tubs, broken glass and even
old beds. Many old road scars are also visible in the area.
This is an easy and enjoyable trail to walk at any season,
but it is a special pleasure in late April and early May when
patches of bright yellow jonquils bloom within what now
appears to be a full-grown forest.

During the entire course of its journey, the trail follows
the route of the old Oconaluftee Fault along the northern
base of Meigs Mtn., which is named for Return Jonathan Meigs (pronounced "Megs"), who became the U.S.
agent for the Cherokee Indians in 1801. For two decades he
tried to help them while he was supposed to be furthering
their removal—a frustrating position. Meigs's name has been
adopted, also, for a survey marker, Meigs Post, which he
placed on top of Mt. Collins.

Note: there are two new back-country campsites on this
trail—Kings Branch campsite at 1.6 mi. and Upper Henderson campsite at 3.7 mi.

Trailhead: The trail begins on the right at 0.4 mi. on the Blanket Mtn. Trail. (The Blanket Mtn. Trail begins at a gate on the left of the Jakes Creek Road, 0.4 mi. from the summer colony junction near Elkmont Campground: see p. 263. The gate also serves as the terminus of the Cucumber Gap Trail: see p. 255.)

Trail Details: The trail, following an old railroad grade, crosses Jakes Creek and enters an old pasture. There a side trail runs to the right to a farmstead. The Meigs Mtn. Trail continues west into a second-growth forest, ascending moderately. This is the area of former farmlands; many old homesites are evident. The trail has a gentle grade as it crosses through low gaps and descends into small coves. At about 3.2 mi. it reaches the Curry Gap Trail from Metcalf Bottoms (see p. 272). This jeep road is maintained to give access to a mountain community cemetery which you will pass a few hundred yards on the right.

Continuing through good second-growth forest, the Meigs Mtn. Trail hits unsettled territory as it reaches a spur ridge near Big Buckhorn Gap at about 4.2 mi. The marked trail you will see branching to the left there could give access to the Honey Cove Shelter but it is not maintained and is not recommended at this time. (The Park Service plans to open it in the future.) The Meigs Mtn. Trail leads right (N) and descends to Little Buckhorn Gap and a trail intersection at 5.1 mi. The Buckhorn Gap Trail terminates on the right (E), having climbed 3.3 mi. from The Sinks (see p. 273). The unmaintained Spruce Flats Trail runs to the left (W) down an old logging road to reach the maintenance road above Tremont near the Honey Cove Shelter.

The Meigs Mtn. Trail continues north and then west along Lumber Ridge, which it finally descends through several switchbacks. At 8.7 mi. the trail ends on the paved road at the Environmental Education Center in Tremont. (This location is called Camp Townsend on the USGS quadrangle map.)

Tremont Section
(Tennessee)

Introduction

The Tremont section consists principally of all the drainage of the Middle and West prongs of the Little River. This area is bounded on the east by the Dripping Spring Mountain— Miry Ridge system, and on the south by the Smokies Range, including Cold Spring Knob, Derrick Knob, Thunderhead Mountain and Spence Field. It is bounded on the west by Bote Mountain. The northern boundary is formed by the Little River Road (formerly Tenn. 73) running west from Elkmont as far as the Townsend "Y," and by the Cades Cove Road, which begins at the "Y" and runs southwest to Cades Cove.

Walker Valley on the Middle Prong of the Little River has a history of settlement predating logging operations by several decades. There "Black John" Walker, son of early pioneers, cleared some land and established a colony over which he reigned. Walker acquired several wives and established each one in a house on her own plot of land in Walker Valley. Other buildings included a schoolhouse and a church. The colony was self-sustaining and had little contact with the outside world. With the aging of the patriarch and the arrival of loggers, the colony eventually dispersed, leaving behind a legend actually not uncommon in America's frontier history.

The Tremont section was thoroughly logged in conjunction with the Elkmont section. During that period the Little River Lumber Company established a girl scout camp at the site of Black John's colony. The camp operated until the late 1950s. Then the Park Service removed the scout facilities and established instead a primitive campground, which was later closed down. In 1966 the U.S. government built a Job Corps Camp on the same site. In 1969 that project was abandoned, and Maryville College in cooperation with the National Park Service began operating an Environmental Education Center there. During the school year, students are trained to become elementary education teachers; during the summer, various college-level and adult-education programs are carried on there. For instance, a Youth Conservation Corps encampment held there in 1971 and 1972 will become an annual event.

In the northern part of the Tremont section, trails originate at both the Little River and Cades Cove roads. Several trails lead away from the Tremont Road as it parallels Middle Prong, the major basin. These run east to Elkmont, south to higher elevations on the Miry Ridge and Smokies Crest, and west toward Cades Cove. The final trail link to Cades Cove Campground was scheduled for completion in 1972. Additionally, the Park Service is considering the possibility of clearing and opening a number of neglected trails in this area, such as the Defeat Ridge Trail, which would provide access to the very remote center of the Tremont region.

There are no developed campgrounds in the Tremont section. The primitive campground previously maintained at Camp Townsend has been closed. But there are several back-country camps: West Prong campsite on the West Prong Trail, Laurel Creek campsite on the Turkey Pen Ridge Trail, Marks Cove campsite on the Lynn Camp Prong Trail and Bee Cove campsite. Unfortunately, no trails lead to the last one. To reach it, follow the Bote Mountain Road for one mile, drop down to the left to the West Prong River and hike upstream for four miles to the junction of Bee Cove Creek and the West Prong.

There is an overnight shelter located in Honey Cove. To

reach the shelter, drive to the Environmental Education Center and start hiking to the south by the sign at the water tank. Follow a foot trail generally upstream for 0.7 mile and cross Spruce Flats Branch. Then climb a graded narrow trail as it switchbacks up a steep slope for about 0.2 mile until it reaches a railroad grade. Turn left on the grade; this is the unmaintained Spruce Flats Branch Trail, which leads 2 miles to Little Buckhorn Gap. After 30 yds. on that trail, turn right onto a well-used side trail (also making use of an old railroad grade) and follow it about 1 mile to the shelter. The shelter, in a very peaceful setting on the site of an old mountain farm, was built by Youth Conservation Corpsmen in 1971. It has bunk space for 12, a fireplace and a pit toilet. There is a fine spring nearby. Additional access to the shelter may soon be provided via a connecting path from Big (Upper) Buckhorn Gap.

Road access to the area is as follows: starting from Sugarlands, the Little River Road at 5 miles arrives at the Elkmont Road, at 9.8 miles at Metcalf Bottoms (trailhead of the Curry Gap Trail), at 12 miles at The Sinks (trailhead of the Buckhorn Gap Trail) and at 18 miles at the Townsend "Y." At the "Y" the road to the right (Tenn. 73) runs out of the park to Townsend and Kinzel Springs.

The road straight ahead is the Cades Cove Road, which is known also as the Laurel Creek Road. Starting at the "Y," the Cades Cove Road passes at 0.2 mile on the left the Tremont Road, at 3.8 miles on the left the Bote Mountain Trail, and at 3.9 miles, on the right, the Schoolhouse Gap Trail. At 6 miles it reaches Sugar Cove (also called Big Spring Cove), where the Lead Cove and Finley Cove trails run to the left and the Turkey Pen Ridge Trail runs to the right.

Back at 0.2 mile on the Cades Cove Road, the Tremont Road leads south and at 0.5 mile passes the Tremont Ranger Station on the right. At 2 miles the pavement ends at the Environmental Education Center. There the West Prong Trail goes west, the Meigs Mountain-Lumber Ridge Trail goes east and the Honey Cove Shelter side trail goes south. In severe weather the Tremont Road may be gated there (first gate). The road continues south alongside the Middle Prong. At 3.5 miles it passes the trailhead of the unmaintained Spruce Flats Trail; at 5.4 miles it reaches the site of the old Tremont logging camp. At this point there is a second gate which has recently been permanently closed. Near the gate, the old unmaintained Defeat Ridge Trail leads to the right up Thunderhead Prong. At 2.5 miles beyond the permanent gate, the Panther Creek Trail goes left. At 3.1 miles there is a third and final gate, at the site of an old CCC camp. The Greenbrier Ridge Trail begins there.

---

93 CURRY GAP (Metcalf Bottoms) 3.0 mi.

Gated jeep trail / Max. elev. gain 1,100
Start: Metcalf Bottoms, 1,700 ft.
End: Meigs Mtn. Trail, 2,800 ft.
USGS quads: Wear Cove, Tenn.
Trail connections: Meigs Mtn.

This trail follows an old road to a community cemetery, traveling near Curry He and Curry She Mtns. Although there are no scenic views to be seen from the trail, it is nevertheless a pleasant hike through second-growth forest.

"Curry He" is the white man's corruption of the Cherokee *Gura-hi* which means "Gura is there"—gura being a plant much used by the Indians as a spring salad. Apparently some Indian once pointed out the mountain as a good source of the vegetable, and the name stuck. A companion knob nearby was later named Curry She.

Trailhead: Park at the Metcalf Bottoms picnic area, 9.8 mi. west of Sugarlands on the Little River Road (old Tenn. 73). Walk east on the highway, back toward Sugarlands, for about 1,000 ft. The trailhead is located on the right (SW) side of the highway.

Trail Details: The trail crosses a grassy area, where it is sometimes obscure because of high weeds, and enters a forest. Within the forest the path becomes a wide jeep road. At 0.6 mi. it crosses a small stream named Breakfast Branch. The trail leads around the northeast slope of Curry He Mtn. and at 2.0 mi. reaches Curry Gap.

From Curry Gap the trail climbs the eastern slope of Curry She Mtn. At 3.0 mi. it ends at the Meigs Mtn. Trail. On the left (E) the Meigs Mtn. Trail has climbed 3.2 mi. from near the Jakes Creek Road in the Elkmont section (see p. 267). On the right (W) it leads a few hundred yards to the old mountain cemetery, 1.0 mi. to Big Buckhorn Gap and 5.5 mi. to the Environmental Education Center in Tremont.

---

(94) BUCKHORN GAP (Meigs Creek) 3.3 mi.

Foot trail / Max. elev. gain 840
Start: The Sinks, 1,560 ft.
End: Little Buckhorn Gap, 2,400 ft.
USGS quads: Wear Cove, Tenn.
Trail connections: Meigs Mtn.

The Sinks is a favorite swimming place for many local people. But you should swim there only if you are very careful because several people have drowned in The Sinks. At this spot the Little River has cut through the neck of an old stream meander, thereby acquiring a steep gradient and a treacherous undertow in the pool.

The Buckhorn Gap Trail climbs from The Sinks, along Meigs Creek, to Little Buckhorn Gap. At present it is suitable for hiking. Nevertheless, maintenance may change, so it would be wise to check with the Park Service before starting out.

Trailhead: The trail begins at 12.0 mi. west of Sugarlands on the Little River Road (old Tenn. 73) at The Sinks. There is a parking area on the left (E) side of the highway just before the bridge. The trailhead is at the east end of the parking area.

Trail Details: The trail runs through the abandoned meander and climbs the steep side of the Little River Gorge. At 0.8 mi. it cuts sharply to the left and continues on to Meigs Creek at 1.3 mi. It ascends alongside Meigs Creek and fords Curry Prong at 2.1 mi. Ascend alongside a small creek to reach Little Buckhorn Gap and a trail junction at 3.3 mi. On the left (S) the Meigs Mtn. Trail has come 5.1 mi. from its trailhead in the Elkmont section (see p. 267). To the right (N) it runs 3.6 mi. to the Tremont Environmental Education Center (called Camp Townsend on the USGS quadrangle). The trail straight ahead is the abandoned Spruce Flats Trail, which descends Spruce Flats Branch to the Tremont Road. When opened up, this trail will provide access to the Honey Cove Shelter.

---

95 **WEST PRONG** (Fodderstack) and **FINLEY
COVE** 2.8 mi. and 2.8 mi.

Horse trail / Max. elev. gain 650
Start: Tremont Environmental Education Center,
1,350 ft.
End: Near Crib Gap on Cades Cove Road, 1,800 ft.
USGS quads: Wear Cove, Thunderhead, Tenn. (Finley
Cove Trail not on Thunderhead map)
Trail connections: Meigs Mtn., Bote Mtn., Lead Cove,
Turkey Pen Ridge

These two trails are part of a connector planned to provide
trail access between the Tremont and Cades Cove sections
of the park. The final stretch, between Sugar Cove and
Cades Cove, was constructed late in 1972. Additionally,
the West Prong Trail provides a convenient route from the
Tremont area to the Bote Mtn. Road, which goes to the
A.T. at Spence Field. The Thunderhead quadrangle uses the
name "Big Spring Cove" for Sugar Cove, and "Laurel Creek
Road" for Cades Cove Road.

Note: there is a new back-country campsite, West Prong
campsite, located at 1.7 mi. on the West Prong Trail.

Trailhead: The trail starts at the Tremont Environmental
Education Center, just behind the mobile homes. The center
also is the terminus of the Meigs Mtn. Trail (see p. 267).

Trail Details: The trail leads left and climbs the side of
Fodderstack Mtn. It traverses the mountain through some
fine second-growth tulip poplars. Then it runs downhill into
the valley of the West Prong and crosses the prong at about
1.7 mi. You may have to wade there. The trail then climbs
a ridge and ends at the Bote Mtn. Road at 2.8 mi. (see p.
279). The Bote Mtn. Road on the right has come 1.1 mi.

from its trailhead on the Cades Cove Road. On the left it leads 5.5 mi. to Spence Field at the A.T.

To continue on toward Cades Cove, go left up the Bote Mtn. Road for 0.4 mi. and exit right onto the beginning of the Finley Cove Trail. This trail runs west with little elevation change along the northern base of Bote Mtn. It crosses several small creeks. At 2.8 mi. it ends in Sugar Cove, east of Crib Gap, on the Cades Cove Road. To the right across the road is the trailhead of the Turkey Pen Ridge Trail, which leads north 3.6 mi. to the Schoolhouse Gap Road in Dorsey Gap. To the left is the beginning of the Lead Cove Trail, an alternative route to the Bote Mtn. Trail.

---

96 **PANTHER CREEK** (Catamount, Blanket Mountain) 2.3 mi.

Horse trail / Max. elev. gain 1,460
Start: Greenbrier Ridge Trail, 2,600 ft.
End: Jakes Gap, 4,060 ft.
USGS quads: Thunderhead, Silers Bald, Tenn.
Trail connections: Blanket Mtn., Miry Ridge

This is a pleasant trail for a day hike to Blanket Mtn. It also may be used as part of a loop with the Miry Ridge, Lynn Camp Prong and Greenbrier Ridge trails; plus 0.7 mi. on the Tremont Road to return to your starting point.

Panthers of course once roamed these mountains and were called painters or catamounts by the mountaineers.

Trailhead: The trail begins at 2.5 mi. on the Greenbrier Ridge Trail. This area is near the site of the old Tremont logging camp. Look carefully for a trail marker on the left of the road.

Trail Details: The trail immediately crosses Lynn Camp Prong; you must cross on the rocks. The trail then begins

climbing gently. At 0.2 mi. it makes the first of several
crossings over Panther Creek. The trail follows along that
creek for about 1.0 mi. and then starts to climb the slope of
Timber Ridge. At 2.3 mi. it ends at Jakes Gap and a trail
intersection. The Miry Ridge Trail begins there and leads
right (S) 5.0 mi. to the A.T. (see p. 265). Straight ahead the
Blanket Mtn. Trail has come 3.3 mi. from Jakes Creek Road
in the Elkmont section. To the left the Blanket Mtn. Trail
runs 0.7 mi. more to the summit of Blanket Mtn. (see p.
263).

 GREENBRIER RIDGE (Davis Ridge, Sams Gap,
Indian Flats) 8.4 mi.

Gated jeep trail / Max. elev. gain 2,864
Start: Tremont Road, 1,926
End: Sams Gap on the A.T., 4,780 ft.
USGS quads: Thunderhead, Tenn.
Trail connections: Lynn Camp Prong, A.T.

The Greenbrier Ridge and the Bote Mtn. Road are the only
two trails beginning in Tremont that terminate on the A.T.
The Greenbrier Ridge Trail follows a jeep road which is
used for the maintenance of the Derrick Knob Shelter. It is
eroded in several places but there are some nice mountain
vistas from the crest of the ridge. A back-country campsite
is located 1.5 mi. down a connecting trail. There is a spring
near the end of the trail.

The entire watershed having been logged, the present
forest demonstrates several stages of recovery (called "suc-
cessional patterns") which vary according to location. At
the lower elevations, there is a great deal of fire cherry still
standing, but it is being replaced by birch, hemlocks and
maples. At the higher elevations, the oaks (chestnut and

white) and hickories are taking over. Beautiful stands of rhododendron and mountain laurel grow along the trail.

Trailhead: The trail begins at the permanent gate on the Tremont Road.

Trail Details: The trail runs southeasterly along the gated jeep road for 3.3 mi. to a final gate. From there, following an old railroad grade, it climbs to a marked junction at 4.3 mi. There the Lynn Camp Prong Trail begins at a sharp left and leads 1.5 mi. to Marks Cove back-country campsite and 3.3 mi. to Miry Ridge.

The Greenbrier Ridge Trail continues straight south up Indian Flats Prong, which it crosses at about 4.7 mi. Then it curves to the northwest, climbs more steeply, and at 5.9 mi. tops out on a point of Greenbrier Ridge. The trail climbs the side of the ridge as far as a sharp left at 6.9 mi.; after that the trail is nearly level. It continues on around the west slope of Mt. Davis (the highest point of the ridge), passing a spring on the way. At 8.4 mi. it ends at the A.T. in Sams Gap. The Derrick Knob Shelter is located about 0.4 mi. to the right (W). This is one of the new shelters, with double-decker bunks, bear-proofing and an inside fireplace. It is located where a herder's cabin used to stand, in what was once an open field.

---

98 LYNN CAMP PRONG 3.3 mi.

Gated jeep and horse trail / Max. elev. gain 1,200
Start: Indian Flats Prong, Greenbrier Ridge Trail, 3,200 ft.
End: Miry Ridge, 4,400 ft.
USGS quads: Thunderhead, Silers Bald, Tenn.
Trail connections: Greenbrier Ridge, Miry Ridge

This trail climbs through the Lynn Camp Prong Valley to reach Miry Ridge. In late April and early May the valley displays one of the best blooms of the carpet-forming white fringed phacelia to be found anywhere. Large colonies of creeping phlox may be seen then, also. The Marks Cove back-country campsite is located about halfway up the trail.

Trailhead: The trail begins at 1.0 mi. on the Greenbrier Ridge Trail. The junction is marked by a sign. The Lynn Camp Prong Trail goes sharp left (NE).

Trail Details: The trail climbs gently on an old railroad grade which climbs the side of Mellinger Death Ridge. At about 1.5 mi. the railroad bed ends at the Marks Cove back-country campsite, where there are a table, fireplace and tent sites.

The trail continues through a cove environment where very large fire cherries remain dominant in the midst of a rapidly recovering cove hardwood forest. The trail ascends gently out of the valley to end at the Miry Ridge Trail at 3.3 mi. (see p. 265). On the left the Miry Ridge Trail has come 2.4 mi. from its trailhead on the Blanket Mtn. Trail in Jakes Gap. On the right it runs 2.6 mi. to terminate in Buckeye Gap at the A.T.

---

(99) BOTE MOUNTAIN ROAD 6.6 mi.

Gated road and jeep trail / Max. elev. gain 3,290
Start: Cades Cove Road, 1,600 ft.
End: A.T. at Spence Field, 4,890 ft.
USGS quads: Thunderhead, Wear Cove, Tenn.
Trail connections: West Prong, Finley Cove, Lead Cove, Anthony Creek, A.T., Eagle Creek, Jenkins Ridge

---

The Bote Mtn. Road is a part of a toll-road project undertaken in the mid-1830s to connect the Little Tennessee Valley of N.C. with the market of the Knoxville area. Dr.

Isaac Anderson, first president of Maryville College, was in charge of construction on the Tenn. portion of the road. The road was to extend from Happy Valley, through Schoolhouse Gap, across the Laurel Creek Valley, over the crest and down Hazel Creek to its mouth at the Little Tennessee River, where copper mines were developing. The exact route was determined by a vote among the builders—a Cherokee Indian labor force. Because there is no "v" sound in their language, the Cherokees indicated their vote by saying "Bote." The ridge they chose in this area became known as Bote Mtn., and the ridge which they did not pick became known as Defeat Ridge.

Dr. Anderson and the Cherokees finished the Tenn. section as far as the state line at Spence Field, but the N.C. section was never finished. Thereafter, cattle drivers herded their animals up Bote Mtn. Road to Spence Field, and in the twentieth century, Jim Martin, who operated a sawmill on the south slope of Spence Field, used the road to get his lumber down to market. During the 1930s the Park Service and the CCC improved the road as far as a turnaround located 1.5 mi. from the crest in order to provide access for maintenance and fire control. Today, only short-wheelbase jeeps can continue beyond the turnaround onto the unimproved original roadbed.

The Park Service opens the Bote Mtn. Road to a motor caravan about twice a week during the summer. A park naturalist accompanies the group on a short hike to Spence Field.

As a walking trail, the Bote Mtn. Road is monotonous, except for an occasional vista of the mountain crests to the east. A shorter and more pleasant way to climb Bote Mtn. uses the Lead Cove Trail, which starts about 1.0 mi. east of Crib Gap at Sugar Cove on the Cades Cove Road and runs 1.7 mi. to intersect the Bote Mtn. Trail at the 3.9-mi. point.

Bote Mtn. is a dry ridge trail, except near the top, so carry a well-filled canteen, especially during the summer.

Trailhead: The trail starts at a gate on the left (E) side of the Cades Cove Road, 3.8 mi. from the Townsend "Y." A sign marks the spot.

Trail Details: The improved road leads southeast and ascends along a small stream. At 1.1 mi. the West Prong Trail ends on the left, having come 2.1 mi. from the Tremont Environmental Education Center (see p. 275). To reach Bee Cove back-country campsite, descend to West Prong and go four rough miles upstream. The road climbs gradually to 1.5 mi., where the Finley Cove Trail begins on the right and runs 2.2 mi. to a point east of Crib Gap on the Cades Cove Road (see p. 275).

The Bote Mtn. Road is now following the ridge. At 3.9 mi. in Sandy Gap the Lead Cove Trail terminates on the right. Near this junction there is a very rough access, to the left, to the Bee Cove campsite. The road continues to climb along the ridge. At 5.0 mi. the Anthony Creek Trail ends on the right, having come 3.4 mi. from the Cades Cove picnic area (see p. 286). (There is water 600 ft. down that trail.) The improved road ends at 5.3 mi.

The unimproved road continues and ends at the A.T. at 6.6 mi. in Spence Field. About 400 ft. to the right, the Eagle Creek Trail also terminates at the A.T., having run 9.1 mi. up the N.C. side of the crest from Fontana Lake (see p. 207). There is a new shelter about 0.2 mi. down that trail. To the left 0.3 mi., the Jenkins Ridge Trail also terminates at the A.T., having climbed 5.9 mi. from Pickens Gap in the Hazel Creek section in N.C. (see p. 203). Down it at 0.1 mi. there is a side trail to the old Spence Field Shelter.

Cades Cove Section
(Tennessee)

Introduction

The Cades Cove section includes all of the national park
north of the Smokies Crest from Spence Field west to
Gregory Bald. It is bounded on the east by Bote Mountain,
on the north by a series of mountains which separate it
from Tuckaleechee Cove, and on the west by Hannah
Mountain. Abrams Creek drains the entire cove and is one
of the largest streams in the park. It is known as a good
trout stream. Another major stream is Hesse Creek, which
drains the extreme northwestern corner of the park—an
area known as the Hurricane.

Cades Cove was part of the territory once ruled by Old
Abram of Chilhowee, a famous Cherokee chief. Both Abrams Creek and Abrams Falls are named after him. Further-
more, tradition holds that the cove itself is named after Old
Abram's wife, Kate.

According to tradition, the first white settler, John Oliver, entered the cove in 1818, one year before the Indian
Treaty of 1819 ceded these lands away from the Cherokees.
William Tipton arrived in 1821. The ancestors of Randolph
Shields, who contributed the Cades Cove material to this
guidebook, moved from Virginia to Sevier County, Tennessee, in 1780 and then settled in Cades Cove in 1828. These
three families, along with the Lawsons, Cables and Greg-
orys, became the dominant names in the history of the
cove. Because the soil of the valley was rich, a thriving
agricultural community soon developed, complete with three
schools and several churches.

The Parson's Branch Road, along which traffic is permitted today only in one direction, was one of the early access routes to the cove. It was built to haul corn from the Little Tennessee Valley to Cades Cove, where a very large licensed and bonded distillery was operated by Julius Gregg. The distillery was the principal industry of the region until Tennessee outlawed such endeavors in 1886, or there-abouts. Close observation along the Parson's Branch Road will disclose several early homesites and fairly large agricul-tural areas now well along in succession toward a climax forest.

On the east of Cades Cove, the area came to be dominat-ed after the turn of the century by the Little River Lumber Company's extensive logging operations. There, as in Tre-mont and Elkmont, the logging railroads reached up all the major streams. Today many miles of park trails and jeep and truck roads used for park maintenance and fire control follow the old railroad beds. With the exception of a few places in the western section, the forests traversed by these trails are in various stages of succession following the heavy logging.

In the prepark days of the early 1920s, Cades Cove supported between 90 and 100 families, numbering 500 to 700 people. Today the area is still farmed by descendants of the original cove families, who lease the land from the Park Service. The Park Service's goal is to preserve the cove in order to maintain a living mountain culture. Additionally, a grist mill and several old cabins have been restored for the benefit of visitors.

Geologically, this area is part of the Smoky Mountain overthrust, with the valleys (or coves), floored with Ordovi-cian limestone, appearing as windows through the overlying Precambrian rocks. In addition to the Cades Cove window, there are others at Tuckaleechee and Wear coves, outside the park. These may be seen from high viewpoints on ridge-crest trails along the park boundary. As would be expected with limestone, the drainage of some of this area is underground, and there are caves along the contact (or fault) line between the limestone and overlying Precambrian layer. (One may visit the park's caves only by special permission from the superintendent.) Another result of the limestone substrate is a very rich flora. The "Rich" used in the names of local topographic features applies to the luxuriance of growth that is often associated with limestone soils.

Virginia white-tailed deer are often seen along the Cades Cove trails. The presence of wild hogs is indicated almost everywhere by their rootings along the trails, over the forest floor (especially in oak and beech stands) and along small streams. They themselves are seen rarely, however, because they are essentially nocturnal. The black bear is uncommon.

All of the trails in the Cades Cove area except those associated with the Boundary Trail are described in this section of the book. Four trails lead to the Smokies Crest; loop trips may easily be fashioned for day or overnight hikes. Caution: be careful when planning to use the Parson's Branch Road in conjunction with a hike. Traffic is permitted on it going one-way only, to the southwest. Use of this road results in a very long circuitous auto trip around the western end of the park in order to return to Cades Cove. Also, the road is closed at night and during the winter season.

Two trails make especially nice day hikes. The Abrams Falls Trail offers an easy, pleasant trip down a beautiful trout stream to a 20-foot falls with a large, clear plunge pool. The Rich Mountain Loop climbs along the ridge on the northern border of Cades Cove. At the top the fire tower provides an outstanding view of rich, verdant green coves below and the massive mountain system which surrounds them.

As for camping, the developed campground at Cades Cove has 224 campsites and a picnic area adjacent to it. The

Look Rock Developed Campground on the Foothills Parkway west of the park has 92 sites. The Moore Spring Shelter on the Gregory Ridge Trail is a good accommodation while visiting the Gregory-Parson Bald area, and there is a new shelter at Scott Gap on the Rabbit Creek Trail. Additionally, there is a primitive campground near the Abrams Creek Ranger Station, and there are many back-country campsites.

A single two-way paved road, Cades Cove Road, runs both into and out of Cades Cove; two additional one-way dirt roads lead only out. The Cades Cove Road, running southwest from the Townsend "Y" intersection, leads to the developed campground.

From a point straight beyond the campground turn, the Cades Cove Loop Road runs for 11 miles around the periphery of the cove. Numerous roads and trailheads occur along the way. At the gate to the loop, the Rich Mountain Loop Trail exits on the right. After 3 miles, at the Baptist Church, the one-way Rich Mountain Road goes to the right 6 miles to Rich Mountain Gap (where the Ace Gap and Rich Mountain trails adjoin) and out of the park to Tuckaleechee Cove. Continuing on the loop, at 4.3 miles the Cooper Road (no autos) leaves on the right. At 4.9 miles the loop crosses the Abrams Creek bridge. A short distance beyond the bridge, a side road goes right 0.5 mile to the Abrams Falls parking area where the Rabbit Creek and Abrams Falls trails begin. The loop road continues to 5.6 miles, where it arrives at an intersection. To the right is the Cable Mill area which is well worth visiting. Straight ahead the Forge Creek Road runs for 2.3 miles to the Big Poplar Turnaround where the Gregory Ridge Trail begins. About 0.1 mile before the turnaround, the one-way Parson's Branch Road exits to the right and leads 3.3 miles to Sams Gap, where the Hannah Mountain Trail ends and the Gregory Bald Trail begins.

From the crossroads back at 5.6 miles, the loop continues to the left, heading eastward around the cove. On the way it passes the Pine Oak Nature Trail and some good examples of Cades Cove homesteads before arriving back at the developed campground. Note: the Cades Cove Road and Cades Cove Loop Road are generally kept open during the winter season, but the other side roads are closed.

The Foothills Parkway and Tenn. 73 provide access to the Abrams Creek Ranger Station area in the extreme western part of the park. Approaching from the east on Tenn. 73, drive past Townsend and Kinzel Springs to Walland. From Walland take the Foothills Parkway southwest along the crest of Chilhowee Mountain. After 11 miles you will pass the Park Service Look Rock Developed Campground. Continue until the end of the parkway at about 18 miles and turn left onto U.S. 129, which follows the north bank of the Little Tennessee River. After going a short distance on it, turn left onto the Happy Valley Road. Drive north about 7 miles to the Abrams Creek Ranger Station and Primitive Campground.

---

(100) **ANTHONY CREEK** 3.4 mi.

Gated jeep and horse trail / Max. elev. gain 1,860
Start: Cades Cove picnic area, 1,940 ft.
End: Bote Mtn. Road, 3,800 ft.
USGS quads: Cades Cove, Thunderhead, Tenn.
Trail connections: Russell Field, Bote Mtn.

This trail provides the only access from the Cades Cove Campground toward Spence Field and Russell Field on the crest of the Smokies. Spence Field is a large open grassy bald which is a popular destination for hikers. In the lowlands there are some large hemlocks along the trail; at several elevations trilliums in season are abundant. There is drinking water near the end of the trail.

Note: there is a new back-country campsite, Anthony Creek campsite, located at about 2.8 mi. along the trail.

Trailhead: The trail starts at the east end of the Cades Cove picnic area, adjacent to the developed campground. It is recommended that cars be parked near the ranger station about 0.5 mi. from the trailhead.

Trail Details: The trail goes southeast on a gated jeep road, running through old fields and then past the water supply for the campground. At about 0.5 mi. a side road leads right but you should continue straight ahead. The trail, now heading south, climbs gradually to a junction at 1.5 mi. The Russell Field Trail begins there and leads right 3.5 mi. to Russell Field.

Anthony Creek Trail goes left (E) as a horse trail. It crosses Anthony Creek at 2.0 mi. and ascends moderately alongside the creek. At 2.8 mi. it leaves the creek to climb, somewhat steeply, the side of Bote Mtn. About 600 ft. from the top, the trail crosses a small stream, and then at 3.4 mi. it runs into the Bote Mtn. Road at an acute angle. The trail sign is sometimes missing there. To the right it is 1.6 mi. to the A.T. and Spence Field. To the left it is 5.0 mi. to the beginning of the Bote Mtn. Road at the Cades Cove Road (see p. 279).

---

(101) RUSSELL FIELD (Leadbetter Ridge) 3.5 mi.

Horse trail / Max. elev. gain 1,860
Start: Anthony Creek Trail, 2,500 ft.
End: A.T. at Russell Field, 4,360 ft.
USGS quads: Cades Cove, Tenn.
Trail connections: Anthony Creek, A.T.

This is a rewarding trail which leads through a rich, mature cove hardwood forest and ends in an old field that was once the farm of Russell Sparks. As many mountaineers did, Sparks cleared the area and grazed cattle there. Since there is no more grazing, the field is going through natural succession to a heath community. There are a spring and shelter at the end of the trail.

Note: there is a new back-country campsite, Leadbetter Ridge campsite, located approximately at 0.8 mi. along the Russell Field Trail.

Trailhead: The trail starts at 1.5 mi. on the Anthony Creek Trail and leads right (S), while the Anthony Creek Trail goes left (E).

Trail Details: The trail crosses a small brook and passes through a homesite into a virgin forest of hemlocks, magnolias, sugar maples and northern red oaks. It crosses two more small streams as it runs through the rich cove forest. Some very large American holly trees grow along the trail.

After about 1.0 mi., the trail leaves the moist valley and climbs along a southeast slope to the crest of Leadbetter Ridge. There it runs almost level for about 1.0 mi. along this dry ridge crest. Roundabout is a dense growth of mountain laurel, which in June, when in full bloom, is a lovely sight. Additionally, you can see the Thunderhead Mtn. complex to the east and Cades Cove to the northwest. After a short steep stretch, the trail reaches the edge of Russell Field at about 3.0 mi. Little of the field is still open because it is now growing in so rapidly. In mid-June there is a beautiful display of mountain laurel there. The trail soon passes a spring which once supplied water for Russell Sparks's homestead. Just beyond is the A.T. and the Russell Field Shelter. The shelter has room for 14 people, and an inside fireplace. Spence Field is located about 2.5 mi. to the left (E) on the A.T.; Mollies Ridge is about the same distance to the right (W).

---

(102) **GREGORY RIDGE** 5.0 mi.

Foot trail / Max. elev. gain 2,660
Start: Turnaround on Forge Creek Road, 1,940 ft.
End: Rich Gap on Smokies Crest, 4,600 ft.
USGS quads: Cades Cove, Tenn.
Trail connections: Gregory Bald, Long Hungry Ridge

This popular trail ascends to the Smokies Crest through an outstanding virgin hardwood forest, passing the Big (tulip) Poplar. This patriarch of the forest is showing signs of old age but is still quite a sight. The route is frequently used to reach Gregory Bald, especially during mid-June when the flame azaleas are blooming. It becomes a dry trail shortly after leaving the valley, so summer hikers will get a bit thirsty before reaching Moore Spring and Shelter on the crest unless they carry some water along.

Two new back-country campsites have been established, Forge Creek (for groups only) at the trailhead and Eka-neetlee, located on the Ekaneetlee Manway, 0.5 mi. from the Big Poplar.

Trailhead: The trail begins at the Big Poplar Turnaround, 2.3 mi. on the Forge Creek Road from the Cades Cove Loop Road. During the winter season the Forge Creek Road is usually gated, which adds 2.3 mi. beforehand to a hike on the Gregory Ridge Trail.

Trail Details: The first 100 yds. of this trail lead around a ridge point on a steep slope just above Forge Creek. The trail then leaves the ridge for the bottom land along the stream. This is an abandoned farm field, last cultivated during the early twenties. As the path approaches the stream, a road scar can be seen on the right; the path joins the old road at this point. After a few yards, Bower Creek, which drains a large area between Pine and Gregory ridges, flows into Forge Creek from the right. To Cades Cove natives, this is the point of origin of Forge Creek. (They call the main stream above this point Marion Creek, after Marion Burchfield who lived in a cove farther up the valley.)

The trail crosses the main creek, ascends slightly and crosses the road scar to enter a second abandoned field. The old road branching to the right after about 200 yds. used to be the Fork Ridge Trail before the establishment of the national park. It gave access to Tipton's Sugar Cove, another high cove where people once lived. The old Fork Ridge Trail followed closely along the crest line up to about 3,000 ft. in elevation, where the present trail tops and joins it.

Past the second field the trail enters a nearly virgin forest which was once dominated by very large American chestnuts. Chestnut logs can be seen on the ground. Still growing at this site are very large white oaks, Canada hemlocks and white pines which used to share this stand with the chestnuts. For about 1.5 mi. the trail traverses this mixed mesophytic forest of hemlock, tulip poplar, northern red oak, silverbell, Fraser's magnolia, cucumber magnolia, basswood, beech and sugar maple. Then as the trail ascends the ridge slope, avoiding the creek fords, it penetrates a drier forest where many old boles are partially standing or prostrate. There the chestnut oak is dominant. Then the trail passes the Big Poplar. It is not the biggest tulip poplar in the Smokies, but it does stand within sight of some very massive hemlocks and other huge tulips. An unmarked manway (not recommended) leading from behind the large poplar goes to Ekaneetlee Gap.

Past the Big Poplar, the Gregory Ridge Trail crosses the main stream twice at about 2.0 mi., and then a small spring branch enters from the left. This is the last sure source of water until Moore Spring beyond the crest. The trail starts the climb to Gregory Ridge, an ascent which will not slacken much for the next 3.0 mi. After reaching the ridge crest, the trail continues to ascend while going southwest along the ridge. At about 3.4 mi. (3,100 ft. elev.) an obscure trail leads right 200 ft. to a spring; look closely because you could easily miss it.

This ridge forest was never logged but was grazed by cattle and was burned quite a bit, especially the south slopes. Evidence of the once-extensive chestnut forest is plentiful on the more northerly exposed slopes. The trail reaches the Smokies Crest at Rich Gap, which the natives call the Gant Lot. It was there that a large fenced area was maintained by cattle herders to assemble and sort their herds in the autumn after they had grazed during the summer on the grassy mountaintops, or balds, and in the surrounding forests.

At Rich Gap the Gregory Ridge Trail ends at the Gregory Bald Trail, which used to be the A.T. To the left (E) the Gregory Bald Trail leads 2.0 mi. to the A.T. at Doe Knob. About 100 yds. along the way, the Long Hungry Ridge Trail terminates on the right, having climbed 4.4 mi. from Twentymile Creek in N.C. (see p. 213). To the right (W) the Gregory Bald Trail runs 0.7 mi. to the crest of Gregory Bald. Straight ahead, at about 0.4 mi. on a side trail, are the Moore Spring and Shelter. The shelter is one of the older types, with bunk space for six. It has not been bear-proofed as the other shelters in the park have, but Moore Spring is one of the finest in the Smokies. From the shelter the side trail curves back to the crest and rejoins the Gregory Bald Trail after 0.5 mi.

---

(103) GREGORY BALD (Hannah Mountain) 6.9 mi.

Horse trail / Max. elev. gain 2,170
Start: Parson's Branch Road, 2,780 ft.
End: Doe Knob on the A.T., 4,520 ft.
USGS quads: Cades Cove, Calderwood, Tenn.
Trail connections: Hannah Mtn., Wolf Ridge, Gregory
    Ridge, Long Hungry Ridge, A.T.

Gregory Bald is one of the outstanding grassy balds in the
southern Appalachians. In the last half of June its display
of flame azalea is world famous. Many people hike in to see
its beautiful flowers, ranging from yellow to pink, orange
and red, as well as the excellent vistas. This dome-shaped
bald is named for the Gregory family who farmed the area
during the 1800s. In the Civil War one of that family,
Russell Gregory, was killed by a band of N.C. Confederates
on a raid through Cades Cove. Dr. Randolph Shields, who
was raised in Cades Cove and contributed most of the Cades
Cove material to this book, recalls herding sheep and cattle
on Gregory Bald as a youth. He has noticed a considerable
decrease in the size of the open bald since grazing stopped
in the early 1930s.

Once you commit your car to the Parson's Branch Road,
you cannot return to Cades Cove without a *long*, circuitous
route. There is camping at Sheep Pen Gap (see below) but the
shelter at Moore Springs is now closed. There are a few
seasonable streams halfway along the trail, and a fine spring
at the shelter. The second half of the trail (from Sheep Pen
Gap to Doe Knob) was formerly part of the A.T., which has
been relocated to leave the Smokies Crest about 2.0 mi. to
the east and run south to cross the Little Tennessee River at
Fontana Dam.

Note: there is a new back-country campsite, Sheep Pen
Gap campsite, at 3.5 mi. on the trail. (Water at 3.4 mi.)

Trailhead: The trail begins in Sams Gap, 3.3 mi. on the Parson's Branch Road from its beginning off the Forge Creek Road. The road is closed at night. This spot is also the terminus of the Hannah Mtn. Trail. From the parking area, go south across the road to find the trail (on the southeast side). There is a trail sign there.

Trail Details: The trail climbs gradually through pine along the south side of Hannah Mtn. Then it becomes somewhat steeper and ascends to Panther Gap at 2.7 mi., where it turns south to climb through a mature hardwood forest. At about 3.2 mi. it crosses several seasonable streams which are the only source of water until the Moore Spring. At 3.5 mi. it arrives on the Smokies Crest at Sheep Pen Gap. There the Wolf Ridge Trail leads right (W) 0.8 mi. on the old A.T. to Parson Bald and then south to Twentymile Creek Ranger Station. (West of Parson Bald, the old A.T. is no longer maintained and is difficult to hike.)

The Gregory Bald Trail climbs east along the main ridge and at 3.9 mi. reaches Gregory Bald (4,950 ft.). On clear days there are fine views of the western end of the park, the Unicoi Mtns. to the southwest, and the Snowbird Mtns. far to the south beyond Santeetlah Lake. Parson Bald can be seen only about 1.0 mi. to the west. The trail continues through the bald and runs downhill. On the right a side trail goes to the Moore Spring Shelter, which has been recently closed to overnight camping. However, the coolwater is still one of the finest springs in the Smokies. The side trail rejoins the main trail at Rich Gap at 4.6 mi. There the Gregory Ridge Trail leads left (N) 5.0 mi. to the Forge Creek Road. One hundred yds. farther, the Long Hungry Ridge Trail terminates on the right, having climbed 4.4 mi. from the Twentymile Creek Trail in N.C. (see p. 213).

The Gregory Bald Trail continues east along the ridge crest of the Smokies to end on Doe Knob at 6.9 mi. There the A.T. goes right (S) to Shuckstack and straight ahead to Mollies Ridge Shelter.

HANNAH MOUNTAIN 7.5 mi.

Horse trail / Max. elev. gain 1,160
Start: Scott Gap on Rabbit Creek Trail, 1,800 ft.
End: Sams Gap on Parson's Branch Road, 2,780 ft.
USGS quads: Calderwood, Tenn.
Trail connections: Rabbit Creek, Abrams Falls,
    Gregory Bald

This trail connects the Abrams Creek area with the high-country trails. The grade is moderate to easy in most places and water is available along the first half. There is drinking water also from creeks on Hannah Mtn. A new overnight shelter is located on the Rabbit Creek Trail just below Scott Gap, at the trailhead.

The trail, running mostly on or close to ridge crests, passes through a relatively mature, dry type forest which varies from oak and hickory on the north exposure to pine and oak on the south. Although this forest has never been logged, there are no very large trees in it because the area has been affected by grazing and burning. For instance, the pine stands, as elsewhere in these Smoky foothills, have been maintained for centuries by fire. Now, with protection, succession toward a hardwood association is taking place. This is good deer country; you are very likely to see them on the trail.

Note: there is a new back-country campsite at 3.1 mi. at Flint Gap.

Trailhead: This trail starts at Scott Gap on the Rabbit Creek Trail, 2.3 mi. southeast of the Abrams Creek Ranger Station. At the gap a 1.5-mi. connecting trail goes left (NE) to the Abrams Falls Trail (see p. 296). It necessitates a ford through Abrams Creek, which may be a problem during high water, so before using it, check with the Park Service. The Hannah Mtn. Trail goes right (SW) from this gap.

Trail Details: The trail begins a long gradual ascent along the slope of Polecat Ridge. It then descends slightly, crosses a small spring branch and reaches a sharp left turn at 1.8 mi. It rounds the northern point of Deadrick Ridge and runs nearly level to Flint Gap at 3.1 mi. From this gap it climbs the slope of Hannah Mtn., while crossing several small creeks—the last sure source of water. At 4.2 mi. it gains the crest and continues along the mountain ridge with only moderate to gentle grades. At 6.5 mi. the trail reaches its highest elevation of 2,960 ft. After that it descends gently to Sams Gap, where it ends at 7.5 mi. on the one-way Parson's Branch Road. On the opposite side of the road, the Gregory Bald Trail begins and runs for 6.9 mi. to Doe Knob on the A.T. There is a parking area at Sams Gap.

---

(105)   **RABBIT CREEK** 7.0 mi.

Gated jeep trail / Max. elev. gain 1,240
Start: Abrams Creek Ranger Station, 1,100 ft.
End: Abrams Falls parking area, Cades Cove, 1,810 ft.
USGS quads: Calderwood, Tenn.
Trail connections: Hannah Mtn., Abrams Falls

The Rabbit Creek Trail is a lowland trail connecting the Abrams Creek Primitive Campground (near Happy Valley) with Cades Cove. It also serves as an access route to the Hannah Mtn. Trail. It follows an old, little-used jeep road. There is a new shelter along the trail at Scott Gap.

Trailhead: The trail begins at the Abrams Creek Ranger Station, 7.0 mi. north of U.S. 129 on the Happy Valley Road. There is room to park at the ranger station.

Trail Details: Hike downstream to cross Abrams Creek on a footbridge at 0.2 mi. The trail then starts to climb up Pine Mtn. Descending on the other side, at 2.3 mi. it reaches

Scott Gap and a trail intersection. There the Hannah Mtn. Trail begins and runs to the right (SW) 7.5 mi. to Sams Gap. On the left a connecting trail leads northeast 1.5 mi. to the Abrams Falls Trail. Check with the Park Service before proceeding as there is a deep, possibly dangerous ford in Abrams Creek. The Scott Gap Shelter is located below the Rabbit Creek Trail, just beyond the gap. From the gap the Rabbit Creek Trail runs straight ahead and descends moderately to ford Rabbit Creek and reach a back-country campsite.

The trail, continuing east, then climbs to reach its highest elevation (2,340 ft.) at 5.0 mi. on Andy McCully Ridge. It runs across a flat area which was once farmed by a man named Andy McCully. Then it starts to run gradually downhill. It ends at 7.0 mi. at Forge Creek. You must wade the stream to reach the Abrams Falls parking area on the opposite side.

 (106) ABRAMS FALLS (Hatcher Mountain) 6.9 mi.

Foot and horse trail / Max. elev. gain 190
Start: Abrams Falls parking area, 1,710 ft.
End: Cooper Road, 1,900 ft.
USGS quads: Cades Cove, Calderwood, Blockhouse, Tenn.
Trail connections: Hannah Mtn., Little Bottoms Manway, Cooper Road, Beard Cane Creek

Abrams Creek, the only stream draining Cades Cove, carries a large volume of water and is known for its good trout fishing. This popular foot trail follows the creek to Abrams Falls and then continues as a horse trail to the Cooper Road. It is the key to hiking west of Cades Cove because it has connections with all the maintained trails in the area. Toward the end of the trail a fine stream provides a water source.

Old Abram was the Cherokee chief of Chilhowee Village on the Little Tennessee River, near the mouth of what is now called Abrams Creek. While under a flag of truce, Abram was murdered by men working for John Sevier, a pioneer and a military leader in Tennessee. The Cherokee leaders, including Abram, had assembled in their community lodge and were guarded by some of Sevier's men while Sevier himself went to another settlement. During his absence some of the whites talked a 17-year-old boy into killing Abram and the other chiefs in revenge for the massacre of his family—by Creeks, not Cherokees. The Cherokees sat with bowed heads while the lad split open their skulls with an axe .... John Sevier later became governor of Tennessee.

Trailhead: The trail starts at the Abrams Falls parking area at the end of a 0.5-mi. side road running west from the Cades Cove Loop just after the Abrams Creek bridge. You can take two other trails from the parking area: the Rabbit Creek Trail on the left (S) and an unnamed trail that goes right (NE) upstream 0.5 mi. to the Elijah Oliver Place, an interesting restored homesite. The Abrams Falls Trail goes slightly right (NW) and crosses Abrams Creek on a footbridge.

Trail Details: The foot trail, after passing a register box, leads downstream. At 1.0 mi. it crosses Arbutus Ridge to cut off the Big Horseshoe of Abrams Creek. Looking back and ahead from the gap where the trail crosses the ridge, you will see good views of the stream 200 ft. below, which travels about 1.0 mi. through an almost complete loop. At this point you are standing in the narrow neck of the loop.

The trail descends from the gap to continue down Abrams Creek. Occasionally it climbs over a low piney ridge where good views can be seen. At 2.5 mi. just past the mouth of Wilson Creek, a short side trail goes left to Abrams Falls. The stream is quite wide there; a large

volume of water drops about 20 ft. to a dark plunge pool
below.

The main trail past the falls turnoff is suitable for horses
and is sometimes called the Hatcher Mtn. Trail. It continues
downstream, rising well above the river in a place or two to
give good views. At 4.0 mi. a connecting trail leads left,
fords the river and runs 1.5 mi. to Scott Gap where the
Hannah Mtn. Trail begins (see p. 294). The connector is
difficult to spot and may not be well maintained, but
should be open and marked by 1973.

The Abrams Falls Trail then slabs north up a mountainside and passes on the left at 4.2 mi. the Little Bottoms
Trail, which runs west to the Cooper Road near the Abrams
Creek Ranger Station. Down it about 1.0 mi. there is a
back-country campsite. The Abrams Falls Trail continues to
climb and soon rounds the end of Hatcher Mtn., where
there is a good view down the valley of Abrams Creek
with the Chilhowee Mtns. in the background. About 1.0 mi.
later the trail reaches Oak Flats Branch, a good place to
sit awhile. There is plenty of clean water to drink, a serene
hemlock forest with a dense rhododendron understory, and
the music of a mountain stream.

After climbing gently along the crest of Hatcher Mtn., at
6.9 mi. the trail ends at the Cooper Road. Straight ahead
the Beard Cane Creek Trail runs 4.3 mi. to Ace Gap at the
park boundary (see p. 305).

The Cooper Road (see p. 303) is the major Park Service
link between the Abrams Creek Campground and Cades
Cove. It is gated at either end. To the right it winds 6.5 mi.
to the Cades Cove Loop Road at 4.3 mi. on the loop road,
or about 1.0 mi. away from the Abrams Falls parking area.
To the left the road leads 4.7 mi. to the Abrams Creek
Primitive Campground.

---

107 **RICH MOUNTAIN LOOP** 7.4 mi.

Horse and gated jeep trail / Max. elev. gain 1,740
Start: Gate for Cades Cove Loop Road, 1,920 ft.
End: Gate for Cades Cove Loop Road, 1,920 ft.
USGS quads: Cades Cove, Kinzel Springs, Tenn.
Trail connections: Boundary Trail, Indian Grave Gap

This trail forms a loop which climbs to the Rich Mtn. Fire Tower and offers some fine overlooks of Cades Cove and the surrounding mountains. While traveling along the ridge crest, it coincides with the Boundary Trail. This makes an especially nice walk in spring and early summer when many wildflowers are in bloom, and in late autumn when leaf color is at its height. The trail receives moderate use from the horse concession at Cades Cove. There is a back-country campsite halfway along the trail.

Trailhead: Park at the display by the gate to the Cades Cove Loop Road. Walk west on the road past the gate. The horse trail that begins immediately on the right is the Rich Mtn. Loop.

Trail Details: Hike along an old roadbed for 0.3 mi. and cross Crooked Arm Branch. To begin the loop, turn right just on the other side of the stream, where there is usually a trail marker, and proceed along a valley. After a few switchbacks, the trail crests out at about 1.9 mi. on Crooked Arm Lead just before a power line. This is the location of the Turkey Pen Ridge back-country campsite. At the power line the trail joins the Indian Grave Gap jeep road and follows it to the left to the fire tower on Rich Mtn. at 3.5 mi.

A little past the tower, the Boundary Trail (see p. 308) goes to the right (N) while the Rich Mtn. Loop Trail continues left (SW) on the jeep road along the crest of Cades Cove Mtn. At 4.4 mi. the jeep road and the horse trail part company: the road runs straight for 1.0 mi. more along Cades Cove Mtn. to end at the Rich Mtn. Road, while the horse trail (Rich Mtn. Loop) goes downhill to the left.

At 4.8 mi. the horse trail passes an overlook and then descends to the floor of the cove via Martha's Branch. There it passes close by the John Oliver cabin, a restored pioneer homeplace. About 1.0 mi. past the cabin, it completes its loop by returning to the first part of the trail at Crooked Arm Branch.

Boundary Trail Section
(Tennessee)

Introduction

A series of trails extends along the entire northwestern boundary of Great Smoky Mountains National Park from the Abrams Creek Ranger Station to Sugarlands. Sections of this route are given different names, but taken together this series totals a through-route of about 45 miles.

Unfortunately, several sections of the Boundary Trail are now not maintained. For instance, the Round Top Trail between the Townsend "Y" and Wear Cove Gap is separated from the rest of the Boundary Trail by a deep and dangerous ford through the Little River. The Park Service once had a swinging bridge there, but frequent raging floods of the river made it expensive to maintain, so it was removed. East of the ford, the trail is a manway as far as Little Round Top. The loss of this trail has cut off the Cove Mountain-Little Brier trails bounding the Elkmont section. Elsewhere, around the northwestern corner, the Hurricane Mountain Trail is now only a manway and is not recommended. But the Beard Cane Creek Trail offers an excellent substitute, connecting to the Cooper Road, which leads back near the boundary and on to the Abrams Creek Primitive Campground.

From west to east, the following sectional trails are open and form a continuous 25.7-mile-long route between Abrams Creek Primitive Campground and the Townsend "Y": Cooper Road, Beard Cane Creek Trail, Ace Gap Trail, Rich Mountain Trail, Scott Mountain Trail and Chestnut Top Lead Trail. The route begins by following several small streams through the western lowlands. A portion of the route follows the old Cooper Road, one of the first roadways into Cades Cove. After climbing to a point near Ace Gap, the route turns southeast along a series of ridges forming the boundary between Tuckaleechee and Cades coves. There it runs frequently near the Great Smokies Fault, which brought older Precambrian sedimentary rock over the Ordovician limestone. In some places erosion has destroyed the Precambrian overburden and exposed the younger limestone, forming "windows," as at Tuckaleechee Cove and Cades Cove. The trail in this section alternates between these two rock types, and the vegetation growing there changes correspondingly because of differences in soil fertility and pH.

Some variations in route are possible. For instance, in order to avoid the Cooper Road, from Abrams Creek Campground you could use the Rabbit Creek Trail, the Hannah Mountain Trail connector and the Abrams Falls Trail to reach the Beard Cane Creek Trail. This variation would also allow the use of the Scott Gap Shelter, but it would require a ford of Abrams Creek. Later on both the Rich Mountain Road and the Rich Mountain Loop Trail give access to the Boundary Trail from Cades Cove. Finally, there is a good link between the Boundary Trail and the A.T. via the following combination: Schoolhouse Gap Road, Turkey Pen Ridge Trail, Lead Cove Trail and the Bote Mountain Road. (This combination is briefly described at the end of the Rich and Scott mountains trail description.)

Camping places along the Boundary Trail are now abundant. New back-country campsites have been recently established at the Cooper Road, Hesse Creek, Kelly Gap and Crooked Arm Lead. The Little Bottoms Manway has been opened and a back-country campsite established on it within one mile of the Abrams Falls Trail. There is another campsite now along the Turkey Pen Ridge Trail; it could

be used when hiking from Schoolhouse Gap to the A.T.
Finally, a new shelter was built in 1972 by the Youth Conservation Corps near the Rich Mountain Fire Tower.

Except for the section passing the Rich Mountain Fire
Tower, the components of the Boundary Trail are generally
only lightly used and therefore may be a bit overgrown. But
they offer a fine chance to avoid the increasing hiking
traffic on the Smokies Crest.

---

(108) **COOPER ROAD** 4.7 mi.

Gated roadway / Max. elev. gain 800
Start: East end of Abrams Creek, 1,100 ft.
End: Hatcher Mtn., 1,900 ft.
USGS quads: Calderwood, Blockhouse, Tenn.
Trail connections: Little Bottoms Manway, Cane
    Creek, Beard Cane Creek, Abrams Falls

The Cooper Road is the access route between the Abrams
Creek Primitive Campground and Cades Cove. It is used by
Park Service vehicles but is closed to regular auto traffic.
Additionally, it provides the easiest and most direct access
to the Beard Cane Creek Trail.

The Cooper Road was one of the earlier roads into Cades
Cove. It ran entirely through the property of one David
Foute, which extended from the Chilhowees all the way to
the crest of the Smokies. Financed mostly by Foute, the
road was built by a man whose last name was Cooper.
Another old road, the Gold Mine Road, started at Montvale
Springs (also owned by Foute), ascended the valley slope of
the Chilhowees, crossed The Flats and joined the Cooper
Road at Gold Mine Gap. The Top of the World resort
development now has obliterated most of the Gold Mine
Road across the flats.

Note: it is possible to camp at a new back-country campsite on the Cooper Road near 1.0 mi.

Trailhead: The road begins at the Abrams Creek Primitive Campground, which is located about 0.5 mi. beyond the ranger station. (Note: if you camp there, boil your water.) The trailhead is a gate at the back of the campground.

Trail Details: The road follows Abrams Creek for a short distance until it leaves the main stream. At about 1.0 mi. the Little Bottoms Trail exits on the right. Down it there are two backcountry sites, Cooper Road at 0.1 mi. and Little Bottoms at about one mile. At. 2.5 mi. the old Gold Mine Road exits on the left toward The Flats. (It arrives at a dead end after 0.3 mi.) At about 3.1 mi. the Cane Creek (jeep) Trail leads left toward Miller Cove, while the Cooper Road turns right and heads southeast. At 4.7 mi., on the crest of Hatcher Mtn., it reaches a trail intersection. The Boundary Trail route goes left (NE), using the Beard Cane Creek Trail. On the right the Abrams Falls Trail has come 6.9 mi. from Cades Cove or 2.9 mi. from the Hannah Mtn. Trail connector. The Cooper Road continues straight ahead for 5.7 mi. more, generally in a southeasterly direction. It crosses three streams and ridges and finally connects with the Cades Cove Loop Road at 4.3 mi. on the loop road.

109 **BEARD CANE CREEK** 4.3 mi.

Horse trail / Max. elev. gain 400
Start: Cooper Road, 1,900 ft.
End: Ace Gap, 1,650 ft.
USGS quads: Kinzel Springs, Blockhouse, Tenn.
Trail connections: Cooper Road, Abrams Falls, Ace
   Gap

This trail, in the northwestern corner of the park, goes
through an area known as the Hurricane. The origin of the
name is obscure but is believed to have originated in the
early days of settlement when a terrific storm caused an
extensive blow-down of the forest. Such storms still hit the
area occasionally; they are usually local in nature.

The Hurricane is a deltoid drainage bounded on the
south by Cades Cove Mtn., on the northeast by Rich and
Hurricane mtns. and on the northwest by Hatcher Mtn. The
trail follows Beard Cane Creek as it flows between Hatcher
Mtn. and the parallel Beard Cane Mtn. to empty into Hesse
Creek. There is a good spring on the other side of the creek.

This entire drainage was logged early in the twentieth
century by the Little River Lumber Co. via a railway
running through Ace Gap. A logging camp was maintained
in the flat area near the mouth of Beard Cane Creek, and
rail spurs extended up almost every stream branch. After
the logging ceased, only a few families settled in the area.
Now, it is considered to be "wild."

The word "Cane" in Beard Cane Mtn. and Creek comes
from the native bamboo, *Arundinaria tecta*, known locally
as cane. It is a species of the grass family growing widely
throughout the Southeast. It is woody and a source of cane
fishing poles. Several small stands can be seen along the
Beard Cane Creek Trail and elsewhere in the Hurricane.

Note: there is a new back-country campsite, Hesse Creek campsite, at 3.0 mi. on the Beard Cane Creek Trail.

Trailhead: The trail begins on the left at 4.7 mi. on the Cooper Road from Abrams Creek Campground. The Abrams Falls Trail terminates on the right at the same spot, having run 6.9 mi. from the Abrams Falls parking area (see p. 296).

Trail Details: The trail ascends gently along the south slope of Hatcher Mtn. to Beard Cane Gap. From there it descends to follow an old railroad bed downstream along Beard Cane Creek, maintaining a very straight northeasterly course for a most pleasant 3.0 mi. The grade is gentle, with only a 600-foot descent. The trail crosses the stream several times. During the spring the whole valley is a flower garden. In early May it is one of the very few spots in the park where you can see the beautiful gay wings (*Polygala paucifolia*) blooming. The forest on either side is a fairly young second growth of mixed hardwoods. At 3.0 mi. the trail reaches Hesse Creek, the major stream in the Hurricane. It can usually be crossed by rock hopping, but in early spring when the water is high, you may have to wade.

The trail passes a nice spring and begins a short, straight climb to reach the park boundary at Blair Gap at 3.5 mi. There the trail makes a sharp right and continues eastward along the crest of the mountain to end at Ace Gap at 4.3 mi. At Ace Gap the Boundary Trail, using the Ace Gap Trail, continues southeast 4.2 mi. to Rich Mtn. Gap.

From Blair Gap the Hurricane Mtn. Trail, a section of the original Boundary Trail, leads left (W) to Cane Creek and the west end of Miller Cove. But it is now only a manway and is not recommended except in an emergency.

---

110   **ACE GAP** 5.8 mi.

Horse trail / Max. elev. gain 440
Start: Ace Gap, 1,650 ft.
End: Rich Mtn. Gap, 1,920 ft.
USGS quads: Kinzel Springs, Tenn.
Trail connections: Beard Cane Creek, Rich Mtn.

The Ace Gap Trail travels southeast from Ace Gap to Rich
Mtn. Gap. To the southwest lies the large drainage area of
Hesse Creek, known to the natives as the Hurricane. The
forest along the way is second-growth oak and hickory,
with pines dominating the drier south slopes. The trail
receives irregular maintenance and may be somewhat overgrown. There is a back-country campsite about halfway
along it. Camping may also be possible, by permission, at
Ace Gap, where there also is a spring.

Trailhead: The trail begins at Ace Gap, 4.3 mi. on the Beard
Cane Creek Trail from the Cooper Road. An alternative
route to Ace Gap is the Davis Branch Trail through private
land.

Trail Details: At the gap there is a fine spring which usually
needs cleaning out. This makes a good place for overnight
camping, but permission must be requested ahead of time
from the landowner, Mr. Willis Wright, Townsend, Tenn.
No one may camp there without his permission.

The trail leads south from the gap and then continues
generally on the crest or along the southwest slope of Rich
Mtn. You will see good views of Tuckaleechee Cove from
the crest. At 2.2 mi. the trail passes the Kelly Gap back-
country campsite. The trail parallels the park boundary in a
southeasterly direction. Just before reaching Rich Mtn.
Gap, it skirts around the edge of the Bull Cave depression:
what appears to be a valley on the right is actually a giant

sinkhole with the entrance to the remarkable Bull Cave at the bottom. This cave has never been explored, although a few unsuccessful attempts have been made by experts. Note: the Park Service forbids unauthorized exploration of this or any other cave in the park.

The trail arrives at 5.8 mi. at Rich Mtn. Gap. There the Boundary Trail crosses the Rich Mtn. Road (connecting Cades Cove and Tuckaleechee Cove) and, as the Rich Mtn. Trail, continues straight ahead to the Rich Mtn. Fire Tower.

---

(111) **RICH MOUNTAIN AND SCOTT MOUNTAIN**
     4.2 mi. and 3.8 mi.

Horse, gated jeep and foot trail / Max. elev. gain
  1,580
Start: Rich Mtn. Gap, 1,920 ft.
End: Schoolhouse Gap, 2,080 ft.
USGS quads: Kinzel Springs, Cades Cove, Tenn.
Trail connections: Ace Gap, Indian Grave Gap, Rich
  Mtn. Loop, Schoolhouse Gap Road, Chestnut Top
  Lead

This section of the Boundary Trail offers a variety of features and conditions. At first it is frequently used—the view from the Rich Mtn. Fire Tower shows almost the entire route of the Boundary Trail. But the latter Scott Mtn. portion receives only slight maintenance and use.

The trail at first travels along a portion of Rich Mtn. which is supported by Ordovician limestone. Where there is limestone there may be caves; to the west below the Ace Gap Trail is the site of the remarkable Bull Cave. A marker at the trailhead warns everyone not to enter the caves without permission. The Park Service forbids unauthorized exploration of any cave in the park.

Camping is possible at the new Rich Mtn. Shelter and at the Turkey Pen Ridge back-country campsite at the end of the Rich Mtn. Trail.

Trailhead: The trail begins at Rich Mtn. Gap. It may be reached by hiking 4.2 mi. on the Ace Gap Trail or by either of two auto routes.

To reach the gap from Cades Cove, turn right from the Cades Cove Loop Road at about 3.0 mi. (next to the Baptist Church) onto the one-way Rich Mtn. Road. This gravel road passes the exit of the Indian Grave Gap jeep road at 2.8 mi. and reaches the park boundary in Rich Mtn. Gap at about 6.0 mi. (The road continues as a two-way road to Townsend, Tenn.)

To reach the gap from outside the park, drive to Townsend in Tuckaleechee Cove. From the west end of town, by the Campground Methodist Church, follow a road that runs to the south. At the Tuckaleechee Chapel, go left (S) toward the base of Rich Mtn. Bear straight ahead at the first junction and proceed about 1.1 mi. to the next junction. There make a left (right-angle) turn and proceed up the mountain. (Another road to the left at this junction exits at a really sharp acute angle; that is the wrong road.) Past the junction the road is a poorly maintained section of the old Cades Cove Road that crossed the mountains in the mid-1920s. There are several hairpin switchbacks, but also some nice views of Dry Valley and Tuckaleechee Cove.

A parking area is provided at the park boundary in Rich Mtn. Gap. The trail begins inside the park about 100 yds. from the parking area, on the east side of the road. A trail sign usually marks the spot.

Trail Details: The first hundred yards run through an old field in the process of becoming a forest. Then the trail follows what was obviously an old roadbed to the crest of the ridge. On the way, to the right of the trail, several large shag-bark hickories can be seen. This is one of only two sites in the park where this tree grows. On the crest the trail turns sharply left; the roadbed goes straight. Built in the 1820s, this was the first of three roads crossing these mountains into Cades Cove. A small sinkhole just to the left of the trail is an indication of the limestone substrate.

After about 100 yds. the trail swings away from the crest onto the south slope of Rich Mtn. At this point the substrate shifts from the lower Ordovician limestone to the Precambrian shale and sandstone of the overthrust. The vegetation changes accordingly—woody plants like red-bud grow right up to the edge of the limestone but not on the shales. The change is most noticeable during the summer, in the herbaceous plants.

The trail alternates on southerly and northerly exposed slopes, at or near the park boundary line, and gives good samples of vegetation patterns of both exposures. During the winter you can see some good views of Dry Valley from the ridge crest. Near the top of the mountain the trail enters a dense stand of rhododendron to emerge along the headwaters of Hesse Creek into an open stand of beautiful mixed mesophytic forest. Although most of the Hesse Creek watershed was logged in the early part of this century, this stand somehow escaped the loggers' axes. The Rich Mtn. Shelter was built there by the Youth Conservation Corps during the summer of 1972. The trail swings around this little cove through what was once a chestnut-dominated forest to a gap and an intersection at 2.3 mi. There the Indian Grave Gap jeep road runs 0.4 mi. to the left to the Rich Mtn. Fire Tower.

This portion of the trail is a very popular hike for many local groups the year round. The tower, at 3,680 ft., offers a 360° vista, including the whole northwestern area of the park, Tuckaleechee and Wear coves north of the park, and the Smokies Crest in the south. It is a good place to learn

the topography of these S
peak, Rich Mtn. ties into th
west to Ace Gap and cont
Mtn. Directly to the west
tower, and swinging northe
the Boundary Trail runs.

The path to the tower r
the crest. This portion of
views of the Cades Cove
rounding it on the south an
jeep road for another 1.5 mi. to the power line on Crooked
Arm Lead, which supplies electricity and telephone service
to the Cades Cove recreational complex. The jeep road ends
there, at 4.2 mi. Following the power line straight ahead
will lead you to the Rich Mtn. Loop Trail from Cades Cove
(see p. 299). You will have to look closely for the Scott Mtn.
Trail, which begins at the power line and runs to the left.
Turkey Pen Ridge backcountry campsite is located about
100 yards down that trail, with camping on the left and a
spring on the right.

The Scott Mtn. Trail winds around the south slope
through a nice stand of white oaks to the north slope,
where the forest changes abruptly to cover hardwoods—
basswood, northern red oak, tulip, silverbell and some hickory. From early- to mid-May, this slope has the best show
of trilliums flowering in the Smokies. There are acres of
them. As they mature they show all stages from pure white
to deep red. Squirrel corn and Dutchman's-breeches are
plentiful at the same time.

The trail descends along the southeast slope of Scott
Mtn. to crest out on the park boundary at the contact line
of the Precambrian and Ordovician layers, and again the
change in vegetation is dramatic. To the right of the trail is
a great sinkhole area—the Whiteoak Sink. The basin of this
sink is quite flat and at one time supported some good
farmland. One of the caves in the basin is known as the

se of the strong air current blowing out of
Written permission from the Park Service is
fore entering any caves.

il swings around the point of Scott Mtn. to end at
in Schoolhouse Gap. From there a road scar can be
descending along a spring branch into the Whiteoak
k; this is the route of the old Bote Mtn. Road from Dry
Valley. A residence at the gap takes its water from the
spring. The trail runs outside the park for a very short
distance. Go through the gate and walk the road about 0.2
mi. back into the park to the crest of the ridge at
Schoolhouse Gap. The Chestnut Top Lead Trail begins
there and runs to the left.

Straight ahead the Schoolhouse Gap Road runs 2.0 mi.
to end at a gate on the Cades Cove Road (3.9 mi. west of
the Townsend "Y"). About 300 yds. left (NE) on the
highway, the Bote Mtn. Road Trail begins and goes 6.6 mi.
to the A.T. An alternate, shorter route from Schoolhouse
Gap to the A.T. would use side trails and thus avoid the
monotony of road hiking. Hike 0.9 mi. southeast on the
Schoolhouse Gap Road to Dorsey Gap and a trail junction.
There go right on the Turkey Pen Ridge Trail (also called
the Pink Root Trail) and continue generally south 3.6 mi.
to the Cades Cove Road. (Along the way there is a closed
back-country campsite, Laurel Creek campsite.) Cross the
road and continue straight up (S) on the Lead Cove Trail,
which goes uphill (note: the Finley Cove Trail goes left and
downhill from the Cades Cove Road). Continue on Lead
Cove Trail, climbing 1.7 mi. to reach the Bote Mtn. Road
Trail only 2.7 mi. from Spence Field on the A.T.

(112) CHESTNUT TOP LEAD 4.5 mi.

Foot trail / Max. elev. gain 200
Start: Schoolhouse Gap, 2,080 ft.
End: Townsend "Y," 1,120 ft.
USGS quads: Wear Cove, Tenn.
Trail connections: Schoolhouse Gap Road, Scott Mtn.

The Chestnut Top Lead Trail is the last open section of the
Boundary Trail. It follows a ridge crest for most of its
distance, skirting the southeast side of Tuckaleechee Cove.
There are some nice views of that cove and, to the south,
the Smokies Crest, notably Thunderhead Mtn. Along the
way the forest type changes from pines on the south slopes
to hardwoods (oak and hickory) on the northern exposures.
During May the last mile of the trail offers the wildflower
enthusiast a fine show. There, at first there is a southwestern exposure with a fine display of birdfoot violets, and
then later a northeastern exposure with a wide variety of
other spring flora. Many hikers may choose to start at the
Townsend "Y" and hike the trail in the opposite direction.

Trailhead: The trail begins at Schoolhouse Gap. You can
reach it by hiking the Scott Mtn. Trail from the Rich Mtn.
Fire Tower, or by hiking 2.0 mi. on the gated Schoolhouse
Gap Road, which runs to the right from the Cades Cove
Road at 3.8 mi. past the Townsend "Y." An alternative
route, which is 2.0 mi. longer but more pleasant, follows
the Turkey Pen Ridge Trail, which starts to the right at
about 6.0 mi. on the Cades Cove Road and reaches the
Schoolhouse Gap Road 0.9 mi. before the gap. The Chestnut Top Lead Trail begins on the right (N) at the high point
on the Schoolhouse Gap Road. This spot is about 0.2 mi.
before the park boundary and gate; there is usually a sign
marking the trailhead.

Details: The trail, which is wide, runs near the crest of ...estnut Top. It runs in a northeasterly direction. After 2.0 mi. it narrows somewhat and descends along the crest of Chestnut Top Lead. At about 3.5 mi. it makes a long loop northward to descend the steep sides of the Little River Gorge. During the spring fine wildflowers grow along this section of the trail. At 4.5 mi. the trail ends at the Townsend Road (Tenn. 73), about 1,000 ft. northwest of the Townsend "Y."

Appalachian Trail in Great Smoky Mountains National Park

Introduction

The marvelous trail system that runs more than 2,000 miles from Maine to Georgia—the Appalachian Trail—was the idea of one inspired man, Benton MacKaye. In 1921 MacKaye proposed a supertrail to run along the crest of the mountain ranges which constitute the Appalachian Mountain System.

The trail movement began with the incorporation of, and improvements to, four already-existing trail systems in New England and New York. There, local clubs banded together to form a federation that is now called the Appalachian Trail Conference. Over the years the trail was gradually pushed southward, with the assistance of newly formed southern trail clubs, the Forest Service and the Park Service, until it traversed 14 states. Today, the trail is protected under the National Trails System Act of 1968, but its maintenance remains essentially the responsibility of the various member trail clubs. It is truly a monument to the spirit of volunteer effort—the longest continually marked trail in the world.

Within the Smokies the Appalachian Trail is extremely popular—so much so that it is being "loved to death" by the large number of wilderness hikers who walk it each year. This book is intended to guide you to the many other worthwhile trails in and near Great Smoky Mountains National Park. Thus, the treatment of the Appalachian Trail here is short. (If you wish a more detailed description of the Appalachian Trail you should refer to the *Guide to the Appalachian Trail in Tennessee and North Carolina: Chero-*

kee, Pisgah and Great Smokies (1971), published by the Appalachian Trail Conference, Inc., Box 236, Harpers Ferry, West Virginia 25425.)

The Appalachian Trail runs along the crest of the Smokies almost their entire length. For descriptive purposes, the trail within the park has been divided here into an eastern section (from Davenport Gap, Tennessee, to Newfound Gap) and a western section (from Fontana Dam, North Carolina, to Newfound Gap). In the eastern section, the trail traverses many peaks over 6,000 feet high. You can see spectacular views from the summits of Mount Cammerer and Charlies Bunion. The massive bulk of Mount Guyot is also impressive; at 6,621 feet it is the third highest peak in the eastern United States. The forest of spruce and fir is much like the Maine woods. The trail in the eastern section is a well-graded, four-foot-wide footpath which can be easily followed.

The western section of the Appalachian Trail traverses Clingmans Dome (6,642 feet) and its surrounding high country with conifer forest, but beyond there most of the trail runs at lower elevations. Grassy and heath balds dominate, interspersed with hardwoods such as white oak, maple and beech. The balds offer wonderful 360° views of the southern Appalachians. During late May and June they are a blaze of color with the blooms of mountain laurel, rhododendron and flame azalea. The trail is not graded west of Clingmans Dome. It is marked by white painted blazes on trees and, where there are no trees, as through some of the balds, by a mowed path.

There are 18 trail shelters on the Appalachian Trail inside the park, spaced at intervals of one easy day's travel. In an attempt to limit the overuse (and abuse) of the trail, the Park Service as of June, 1972, requires hikers to obtain permits to camp overnight in the shelters. The stay at any one shelter is strictly limited to one night, and camping at unauthorized places along the trail is forbidden. Permits will only be issued until the shelter bunks are full for the night. No camping is allowed adjacent to the shelters. Fire wood is practically nonexistent around most of the shelters, so carry a stove. Do *not* cut green, live wood for fires; it won't burn well, anyway. The Park Service has now filled in all garbage pits, so you *must pack out* all your nonburnable refuse. All of the shelters are bear-proof, for their high concentration of people and food attracts "nuisance" animals. Mice can also be a nuisance; they are permanent residents in most shelters and are particularly adept at climbing, and gnawing into packs and food containers.

APPALACHIAN TRAIL EAST

Miles	Elev.	Description
0.0	1975	Davenport Gap.
0.9	2200	Davenport Gap Shelter, 12-man, spring.
2.8	3500	Lower Mt. Cammerer Trail goes right (N) 7.6 mi. to Cosby Campground.
4.7		Seepage spring to right of trail.
5.1		Side trail goes right 0.6 mi. to Mt. Cammerer (5025 ft.) and excellent views.
7.1	4240	Low Gap. Low Gap Trail goes left (S) 2.3 mi. to Walnut Bottoms; Cosby Creek Trail goes right (N) 2.5 mi. to Cosby Campground.
7.9	4800	Cosby Shelter, 12-man, spring. Enter a burned-over section for 4.0 mi.
9.5	4700	Camel Gap. Yellow Creek Trail goes left (S) 5.2 mi. to Walnut Bottoms.
11.7	5800	Maddron Bald Trail angles right and leads to Snake Den Mtn. and Indian Camp Creek trails. Back-country campsite located 0.7 mi. from A.T.

12.7	6020	Deer Creek Gap. Good views of Mt. Guyot, Luftee Knob, Mt. Sterling, Big Creek area. Enter virgin spruce and fir forest.
13.4	6180	Unnamed gap between Old Black and Mt. Guyot. Obscure and rough trail climbs left (S) up slope to top of Mt. Guyot (6621 ft.); some views available.
13.5	6240	Guyot Spring.
15.4	5960	Tricorner Knob. Balsam Mtn. Trail goes left 5.8 mi. to Laurel Gap Shelter. Short connection to Hyatt Ridge Trail.
15.5	5920	Tricorner Knob Shelters (2): new 12-man, with spring.
		Descend to Big Cove Gap, then ascend Mt. Chapman.
16.5	6220	Highest point of A.T. on Mt. Chapman. Obscure side trail leads right to summit and fine views.
		Descend through mature spruce and fir forest.
17.8	5980	Mt. Sequoyah summit, so-named in honor of the Cherokee who developed the Cherokee alphabet.
20.5	5850	Hughes Ridge Trail leaves from Pecks Corner and goes left (S) 11.8 mi. to Smokemont. Hughes Ridge Shelter is 0.5 mi. on that trail: 12-man, with spring.
		Fine views left (S) into Bradley Fork watershed.
22.9	5800	Side trail leads left 100 yds. to Lover's View and vistas of Mt. Le Conte, Mt. Kephart, Bradley Fork.

24.3   5230   False Gap. Shelter now closed.

25.4   5400   Porters Gap.
                The Sawteeth section with jagged ridge
                    crest. Great fire of 1925 destroyed
                    forest in this area, and recovery has
                    been slow. Excellent views available.
26.4   5380   Dry Sluice Gap. Richland Mtn. Trail leads
                    left (S) with connections to Bradley
                    Fork and Kephart Prong.
26.8   5400   Charlies Bunion. Probably most spectacular
                    view in park. Almost-sheer cliffs
                    drop more than 1000 ft. into Green-
                    brier section. Outstanding view of
                    Mt. Le Conte to west. Denudation
                    of area was probably result of 1925
                    fire. Side trail here is narrow, and
                    extremely dangerous in icy weather.
                Return to dense forest and ascend steeply.
27.8   5900   Ice Water Spring and old 6-man shelter. New
                    12-man shelter is just beyond, with
                    good view in front.
                Note: general area from Charlies Bunion to
                    Newfound Gap receives *very heavy*
                    day and overnight use. Shelters there
                    are nearly always overflowing.
28.1   6030   Boulevard Trail leads right to Mt. Le Conte.
                    About 100 yds. down that trail, side
                    trail leads right 0.6 mi. to excellent
                    views at The Jumpoff.
                Descend gradually down ridge of Mt. Kep-
                    hart.
29.1   5830   Sweat Heifer Trail goes left 3.6 mi. to Kep-
                    hart Prong Shelter.
                Continue descending through rich forest.

30.8	5040	Newfound Gap. Newfound Gap Road (formerly U.S. 441), parking lot, toilet facilities.

APPALACHIAN TRAIL WEST

0.0	1900	Paved road, 0.6 mi. north of Fontana Dam.
2.3	3800	Near Little Shuckstack, variable water on the right.
3.4		Jeep road leads right 0.1 mi. to Shuckstack Tower (4020 ft.). Excellent views, especially of Hangover Mtn. to the southwest.
3.7	3650	Sassafras Gap. Lost Cove Trail goes east to Eagle Creek; Twentymile Creek Trail goes west 5.3 mi. to ranger station.
4.7	3830	Birch Spring Gap. 12-man shelter with spring to the left.
6.7	4500	Doe Knob. To left (N) Gregory Bald Trail goes west 2.5 mi. to Moore Spring. Descend, ascend over Powell Knob, then descend.
8.1	3850	Ekaneetlee Gap. Water 100 yds. to the left. Ascend steeply, then gradually.
9.1	4600	Mollies Ridge Shelter, 14-man, spring. Cross Devils Tater Patch and descend steeply into Big Abrams Gap (4100 ft.).
11.2	4400	Russell Field Shelter, 14-man, spring. Russell Field Trail goes left (N) 3.5 mi. toward Cades Cove Picnic Area. Descend into McCampbell Gap and then climb steeply.
12.5	5040	Mt. Squires (Little Bald). Good views on the N.C. side. Note Hangover Mtn. to the southwest.

Descend gently through a beech stand to enter the grassy Spence Field area. Excellent views.

13.5   4890   Eagle Creek Trail exits right in Spence Field, leading to Fontana Lake. New 12-man Spence Field Shelter, with spring, is about 0.2 mi. down this trail.

13.5   4890   Bote Mtn. Road leads 6.6 mi. left (N) to Cades Cove Road; spring 0.1 mi.

Continue through grassy fields.

13.9   4960   Side trail leads right 0.1 mi. to spring. Connection with Jenkins Ridge Trail leading south.

Ascend 0.2 mi. through grassy area and turn sharp left at a small peak.

Descend and ascend steeply.

14.7   5440   Summit of Rocky Top. Views of Fontana Lake.

Cross small knobs and ascend gradually.

15.4   5530   Thunderhead Mtn. Rhododendron.

Descend on newly improved trail.

15.9   4840   Beechnut Gap.

16.9   Pass ledge with views south into Bone Valley area on Hazel Creek, N.C.

Go along south slope of Brier Knob (5100 ft.) and begin a very steep descent to

17.8   4530   Starky Gap.

Ascend gradually and then descend steeply into Sugar Tree Gap.

Generally ascend to cross Chestnut Bald.

19.6   4880   Descend slightly to Derrick Knob. 12-man shelter with spring. Keep left there.

19.9   4840   Descend steeply to Sams Gap where A.T. goes right and Greenbrier Ridge

		Trail goes left (N) 5.1 mi. to Tremont Road.

Trail goes left (N) 5.1 mi. to Tremont Road.

Go along south slope of Mt. Davis (Greenbrier Knob).

Continue along crest and then ascend steeply to

21.9   5240   Cold Spring Knob.

22.2   Descend to pass Miry Ridge Trail, which exits left (N) toward Elkmont.

22.4   4820   Descend to Buckeye Gap where faint trail crosses crest; water about 0.1 mi. to right.

Ascend along crest through beech.

25.0   5440   Silers Bald. Two shelters (6-man, 12-man) with spring.

Pass over crest of Silers Bald. Note Mt. Le Conte (NE) and High Rocks (SSE). Excellent views.

25.4   Welch Ridge Trail exits right (S) to High Rocks Fire Tower with connections to Hazel Creek trails.

Continue, passing The Narrows and then some grassy meadows.

26.2   While approaching Jenkins Knob (somewhat overgrown) keep to left.

26.7   5590   Descend into Double Springs Gap. 12-man shelter with variable springs on either side of trail; best one is to right.

Ascend gradually 0.6 mi. to reach Goshen Prong Trail which exits left (N), 7.3 mi. to Little River Gravel Road.

Forest becomes dominated by spruce and fir.

29.0	6580	Reach Mt. Buckley after ascending through burned section.
29.1		Pass Forney Ridge Trail, which exits right and leads to Clingmans Dome Road.
29.5	6643	Clingmans Dome, highest point on entire A.T.; side trail right 50 yds. to tower with excellent views; that path continues to parking lot.
		Descend steeply, then ascend Mt. Love.
30.6		Old campsite with water is 100 yds. right.
		Steep descents and ascents to reach
32.4	6190	Mt. Collins summit.
		Descend 0.2 mi. to trail junction. Sugarland Mtn. Trail goes left (N). 12-man Mt. Collins Shelter, with spring, is 0.5 mi. down this trail.
33.0		Connector trail goes right to Clingmans Dome Road.
35.3		Indian Gap. Road Prong Trail goes left 3.3 mi. to Chimney Tops parking area. A.T. bears slightly left and follows crest.
		Continue near crest, then parallel highway.
37.0	5040	Newfound Gap. Newfound Gap Road and parking lot. Toilet facilities. Car tourists gawk at hiking tourists.

Joyce Kilmer
Memorial Forest and
Slickrock Creek

Introduction

Joyce Kilmer Memorial Forest and Slickrock Creek form the only hiking area covered by this guidebook which is located outside Great Smoky Mountains National Park. The two basins of Joyce Kilmer and Slickrock, which are adjacent to one another but separated by a common ridge, lie southwest of the park in Tennessee and North Carolina. Conservationists have repeatedly suggested that the two basins would make an excellent 15,000-acre addition to the U.S. Wilderness System, which so far in the southern Appalachians consists only of two small areas—Linville Gorge and Shining Rock in North Carolina.

Unfortunately, there is a federal highway battle taking place today in this lovely area. The route selected by the Bureau of Public Roads for a scenic highway connecting Robbinsville, North Carolina, with Tellico Plains, Tennessee, would run right along the ridge between the two basins. If the road were built there, it would destroy the wilderness qualities of both. Conservationists are doing their best to try to preserve the Kilmer-Slickrock area intact. But more help is needed, in the form of overwhelming public support. A letter of concern addressed to the Chief of the Forest Service, South Building, 12th Street, Washington, D.C. 20250, would be appropriate. Enough letters like yours might reroute the highway someplace else.

Slickrock is the larger of the two basins—10,700 acres. It is an elongated, north-south basin bounded by the Unicoi Mountain Range on the west (which is part of the western rim of the Blue Ridge Mountains) and Hangover Lead on the east. Slickrock Creek drains north into the Little Tennessee River. It is ideal as a get-away-from-it-all place because it is easily accessible but little used. Camping is permitted at any established location. Simply set up a base camp and then poke around at your leisure. Slickrock Creek, a beautiful mountain stream with two waterfalls and many cascades, is reported to be one of the best brown trout streams in eastern North America. Both fishing and hunting are strictly regulated.

The Slickrock trail system extends around almost the entire perimeter of the basin, permitting an extended 22-mile hike. Four trails connect the perimeter trails with the interior trails along the creek. The less frequently used trails are likely to be somewhat overgrown because the trails in this section have been maintained only at three-year intervals. Note: the mileages on signs are generally inaccurate, so rely on this guidebook for distances.

The Joyce Kilmer Memorial Forest in the Little Santeetlah Creek watershed measures only 3,800 acres. Its oval-shaped basin orients toward the southeast, where the creek flows into Santeetlah Creek. No camping is permitted anywhere within the basin except on the ridge tops—Horse Cove Ridge on the southwest, and Haoe Lead to the northeast. The Forest Service has a campground near the entrance to Joyce Kilmer at Horse Cove (called White Pines picnic area on old maps). It has 19 family units, with tables, drinking water and toilets. It is popular, so may be crowded. The next nearest established campground is located at Cheoah Point, about five miles north of Robbinsville on U.S. 129.

There are many hiking trails in Joyce Kilmer. One climbs along Little Santeetlah Creek, straight up the center of the valley. Others follow the boundary ridges—Horse Cove Ridge and Haoe Lead. For an excellent but strenuous day

hike, go up the Haoe Trail to visit Hangover Mountain and
then return the same way. If you can handle a longer (by
1.5 miles) hike, go from Hangover Mountain to Naked
Ground and return on the Little Santeetlah Creek Trail.
This loop also makes an excellent overnight trip, with
camping at Naked Ground and a side trip to Stratton
Meadows. The mileages on signs are likely to be incorrect;
follow this book instead.

Like the national park, this land belonged to the
Cherokees until President Andrew Jackson arranged their
removal in 1836. Robbinsville, the county seat, used to be
called Fort Montgomery. The fort was built to house the
troops who supervised the removal of the Indians. The first
white settlers moved into what is now called Graham
County in 1840. From the time that they arrived, logging
has been a primary industry. The first big timber company
in the area, the Kanoah Hardwood Company, built a
railroad to Robbinsville and logged around Little Snowbird
Mountain. The railroad was later finished by the Bemis
Lumber Company, which is still active there today. In 1890
the Belton Lumber Company started lumbering up Little
Santeetlah Creek. It had plans to cut the entire creek
drainage, and had begun building the necessary splash dams
for the purpose, when it went bankrupt. This providential
development halted the cutting before it reached the trees
now known as the Joyce Kilmer Memorial Forest.

The memorial forest was established in 1936 in honor of
Joyce Kilmer, author of "Trees." This accomplished poet
and writer worked for the *New York Times* from 1913 to
1918, enlisted in the army during World War I and was
killed in the Battle of the Ovreq while on a volunteer
assignment. Later the Bosemain Bulges Post Number 1995
of the Veterans of Foreign Wars requested that some natural area of the United States be set aside in his honor. After
a nationwide search, the secretary of agriculture decided on

the Little Santeetlah Creek watershed as the best place for the memorial because of its completely virgin forest. The trees, primarily tulip poplar, are immense.

The Slickrock Creek watershed was logged from 1915 to 1922 by the Babcock Lumber Company of Pittsburgh, Pennsylvania. More than 70 percent of the watershed was cut; only the crests of the highest ridges were left untouched. A 1918 photo of the logging operation shows one tulip poplar tree that contained 20,165 board feet in four huge logs. The lumbering was finally stopped when rail access was cut off by the rising waters of Lake Calderwood. The U.S. Forest Service purchased the Slickrock Creek area from Babcock in 1936, and the basin has been healing well since then. But in 1967 the Forest Service built a timber road to Big Fat Gap—the first road access ever into the Slickrock watershed. And in 1969 it advertised for bids for cutting more than 400 acres of Slickrock timber. Loud protests from conservationists have managed to postpone the sale.

Hikers should take note of the fact that Kilmer-Slickrock is a high rainfall area, sometimes up to 80 inches a year. You can expect thunder showers every day during the summer. Rain gear and tents are necessary. Although wood is abundant, it is generally wet, so carry a stove. It is safe to drink the water from small streams unless there are signs of local contamination. You should inspect springs for recent signs of hogs (boars); water from hog wallows is not suitable for drinking. Slickrock Creek flash floods after heavy showers but usually does not overflow its banks except where they are lower than three feet. A more pleasant result of the high rainfall is the magnificent trees and the rich and varied plant life. The forest is mostly hardwoods, with some hemlocks and other conifers and a dense rhododendron undergrowth. The rhododendron makes off-trail hiking extremely difficult, especially when carrying a

backpack. It can become dangerous in the uplands be
the very steep terrain there is an additional complica
And you should not attempt it at all during the hun
season for boars (October-November) and deer (Novem
December), except on Sundays when hunting is alwa
prohibited.

Where did the boars come from? They are the net resu
of a scheme originated by a man named George Moore, who
moved to Graham County, North Carolina, during the
1880s with the intention of starting a game reserve. Moore
settled on Hooper Bald, south of Santeetlah Creek. There he
tried to establish buffalo, elk, bear and European wild boar.
Today, only the boars remain in sufficient numbers to hunt
(bears being protected by law) and they are thriving. They
have spread into Great Smoky Mountains National Park,
where their rooting causes some ecological problems. Boars
are frequently heard and seen, particularly in the Slickrock
Creek area. They are very large—three feet to the shoulder
and weighing as much as 300 pounds—and can be dangerous
if cornered. During October and November, hunters arrive
from all over the Southeast to take advantage of the boar
season.

Four USGS-TVA topographic quadrangles cover the entire Kilmer-Slickrock area. These 7½ minute maps are (1)
Tapoco, North Carolina, (2) Santeetlah Creek, North Carolina, (3) Big Junction, Tennessee and (4) Whiteoak Flats,
Tennessee. A fifth topo map, the Robbinsville, North Carolina, quadrangle, may be of some use in locating the access
roads. But many of the trails described in this guidebook do
not appear on the quadrangles because these maps are so
outdated.

Following are descriptions of three routes of road access
to the Kilmer-Slickrock area from Robbinsville, North
Carolina.

To Joyce Kilmer via Santeetlah Gap: From the north

end of Robbinsville, take U.S. 129 to the Joyce Kilmer sign 1 mile out of town. Turn left on County Road (CR) 1116. Pass the Santeetlah Ranger Station at 1.1 miles from U.S. 129 and continue to a stop sign at 3.5 miles. Turn right on CR 1127 and cross Snowbird Creek at 4.9 miles. Take the right fork (still CR 1127) at 5.7 miles. You will reach Santeetlah Gap at 10.5 miles (2,660 feet). There a gravel side road to the left goes 12 miles to Stratton Meadows and Beech Gap Road, where trails begin to Bob Bald and Cherry Log Gap.

Descending on CR 1127, pass the Big Santeetlah Fish and Wildlife Checking Station at 12.5 miles and cross Big Santeetlah Creek at 12.6 miles. Cross Little Santeetlah Creek at 12.9 miles and reach an intersection. The road on the left is Forest Service (FS) 305, which leads 0.6 mile to the Joyce Kilmer parking lot. The road straight ahead is the beginning of the controversial highway which is supposed to follow the ridge between Kilmer and Slickrock; conservationists have halted the road 5.7 miles from the intersection. There are good views of Lake Santeetlah from that road. The road on the right is FS 416, which leads 0.2 mile to the Forest Service's Horse Cove Campground and then continues, as a dirt road, for 6 miles to U.S. 129 (next access route described).

To Joyce Kilmer via the north shore of Lake Santeetlah: Take U.S. 129 north from Robbinsville. Pass the first Joyce Kilmer sign and drive 6.8 mi. on U.S. 129 to the second Kilmer sign. Turn left there and continue, soon to go right on a bridge over a dry riverbed. Turn left on a gravel road at 0.6 mile from U.S. 129. Pass the Goldmine Road on the right at 1.6 miles. You will reach Horse Cove Campground at 6 miles and a road intersection at 6.2 miles. The road left leads to Santeetlah Gap (first access route described). The road right is the controversial ridge road. Straight ahead at 0.6 mile more is the Joyce Kilmer parking lot.

To Slickrock via Big Fat Gap and Slickrock Road: Take U.S. 129 north from Robbinsville. Pass the first Kilmer sign and continue north on U.S. 129 for 13 more miles. Turn left on Slickrock Road across a bridge. (At this point, Tapoco is 1.5 miles farther on U.S. 129.) At 0.2 mile from U.S. 129, the road forks. The road to the left leads up Deep Creek to a shelter (1.6 miles) and eventually becomes the Deep Creek Trail, which goes to Saddle Tree Gap near Haoe Mountain. The Slickrock Road goes right as FS 62. You will pass the beginning of the Grassy Branch Trail at 3.6 miles and arrive at Big Fat Gap at 7.2 miles. The Slickrock Road continues for 0.7 mile more and then comes to a dead end. Two springs may be found on the right of the road; the best one is located about 0.4 mile north of Big Fat Gap. Slickrock Road is entirely a gravel, all-weather road, but the first 2.5 miles are in worse condition than the rest.

 LITTLE SANTEETLAH CREEK (Middle) 4.6 mi.

Foot trail / Max. elev. gain 2,645
Start: Joyce Kilmer parking lot, 2,200 ft.
End: Naked Ground, 4,845 ft.
USGS quads: Santeetlah Creek, Tapoco, N.C.
Trail connections: Stratton Bald, Plaque Loop, Haoe, Naked Ground

---

This trail follows Little Santeetlah Creek up through the center of Joyce Kilmer Memorial Forest to the top of the ridge at Naked Ground. It can also be used as part of a loop trail in connection with either the Haoe Trail or the Stratton Bald Trail. The last mile of this trail, although graded, is steep and slow going and can be slippery when wet. *Note*: no camping is allowed in Joyce Kilmer Memorial Forest, but it is possible at the end of the trail.

If you want an easy, pleasant day hike, go 0.6 mi. on the Little Santeetlah Trail and then left on a side loop. This side trail passes through a magnificent virgin grove where good wildflowers grow. It soon returns to the Little Santeetlah Trail where a right turn goes 1.4 mi. back to the parking lot, for a total hike of about 3.0 mi.

Trailhead: The trail begins at the Joyce Kilmer Memorial Forest parking lot. There are ample parking and toilet facilities. Look for the map sign at the upper end of the parking lot. The Stratton Bald Trail also begins there (see p. 339).

Trail Details: At the map sign, turn right, ascend about 50 ft. to the main trail, then climb to the left. You will immediately see the poem "Trees" carved in a wooden sign. The Plaque Loop Trail goes straight ahead; the Little Santeetlah Creek Trail goes to the right and ascends a fairly steep grade. At 0.1 mi. it reaches a trail junction with signs. The Haoe Trail goes to the right (see p. 335). The Little Santeetlah Trail bears left, maintained and graded.

At 0.6 mi. an unmarked trail exits to the left. This is the loop that goes through a beautiful virgin grove on the west side of the stream and rejoins the main trail at 1.4 mi. It requires little extra time and is recommended. The main trail crosses a spring branch on a foot log at 1.0 mi., and crosses Indian Spring Branch at 1.2 mi. on a foot log over a sliding rock. It runs downhill and follows alongside Little Santeetlah Creek. At 1.4 mi. the loop trail enters from the left, unmarked except for a large downed tree crossing the main trail.

The Little Santeetlah Creek Trail next passes through a forest of enormous mixed hemlocks and poplars, crossing several small streams on foot logs. At 2.7 mi. it crosses a spring branch next to four big poplars. After crossing a large stream at 3.5 mi., it enters a forest where oaks and maples grow among the poplars and hemlocks.

At 3.8 mi. the trail begins a steep climb on graded switchbacks. It is a good idea to fill canteens before starting this climb. At 4.3 mi. the trail cuts sharp right about 50 ft. from a small stream. The water that may be heard gurgling through the rocks nearby is the last source of water on the trail. There is a good view of the valley from this spot. The trail switchbacks steeply to terminate at the ridge crest at Naked Ground. The signposts there are inaccurate. To the left the Naked Ground Trail leads to Stratton Bald. To the right (E) that trail leads along the crest 1.0 mi. to its trailhead at Haoe Mtn. (see p. 337). Despite the name, Naked Ground is no longer open, but is in young forest. Water is available from Naked Ground Branch, about 300 ft. north behind the signpost. Caution: this water may be fouled by wild boar. There is ample room for camping on the back side of the ridge.

---

(114) PLAQUE LOOP 1.0 mi.

Foot trail   Max. elev. gain 400
Start: Joyce Kilmer parking lot, 2,200 ft.
End: Joyce Kilmer parking lot, 2,200 ft.
USGS quads: Santeetlah Creek, N.C.
Trail connections: Haoe, Little Santeetlah Creek, Stratton Bald

---

This delightful trail is a must for all visitors to the Kilmer Forest. It passes through a truly magnificent grove of virgin poplars and hemlocks, probably the best example of primeval forest in the southern Appalachians. Although larger single trees may be found growing elsewhere, the charm of the Kilmer Forest is the cathedral effect created by its abundance of large, healthy trees. Wildflowers are good in the spring, but animal life is not abundant. Birds are frequently too high up in the hundred-foot canopy to be easily observed.

No camping is allowed and the disturbance of any plant, living or dead, is strictly forbidden. Please do not wander off the trails or leave any litter behind. This area is heavily used—yet it will retain its beauty if we take care of it.

Trailhead: The trail begins at the Joyce Kilmer parking lot, slightly to the right of the shelter. There is plenty of room to park, and there are toilet facilities.

Trail Details: The trail goes about 150 ft. uphill to the poem "Trees" carved in a wooden sign. At a trail junction there, the common beginning of the Little Santeetlah Creek and Haoe trails goes to the right. The Plaque Loop Trail goes left and descends slightly to cross Little Santeetlah Creek via a large foot log. Note the rich moss on the rocks and thick rhododendron along the stream banks. A log bench is provided at 0.2 mi. for your comfort. The trail climbs gradually along the side of a ravine and passes several large fallen chestnut trees, reminders of the 1925 blight. A huge stump is reached on the right at 0.4 mi. After crossing Poplar Cove Branch the trail ascends gently and at 0.5 mi. reaches the Memorial Plaque, set on a large rock in the midst of a grove of very large poplars and hemlocks.

The Poplar Cove Loop Trail begins behind and to the left of the plaque. That loop extends for 0.4 mi. through an outstanding grove of huge tulip poplars. The first part of the loop is lined with hepatica (liverleaf), which flower in early- and mid-April. Twin poplars are passed at 0.2 mi., and then the trail curves right to rejoin eventually the Plaque Trail.

Continuing past the plaque, the Plaque Loop Trail crosses a stream bed on a log at 0.5 mi. and Wild Boar Branch at 0.6 mi. There is a bench at 0.7 mi. where the trail crosses a small ravine on a log. At 0.9 mi. there is a register box and a trail junction. The Stratton Bald Trail goes right to Stratton Bald (see p. 339). The Plaque Trail goes downhill to the left and crosses Little Santeetlah Creek on a foot log. This signals the approach to the parking lot, which is reached at 1.0 mi.

---

115 **HAOE** (Jenkins Meadow) 3.9 mi.

Foot trail / Max. elev. gain 3,049
Start: Joyce Kilmer parking lot, 2,200 ft.
End: Haoe Mtn., 5,249 ft.
USGS quads: Santeetlah Creek, Tapoco, N.C.
Trail connections: Stratton Bald, Plaque Loop, Little
    Santeetlah Creek, Naked Ground, Deep Creek,
    Hangover Lead

The Haoe Trail climbs steeply and steadily to some very fine views from Haoe Mtn. Additionally, it is linked to the Hangover Lead Trail via a short connector, and thus provides the only direct access into the Slickrock Creek basin from Joyce Kilmer. Because it ascends along the side of a south-facing ridge which receives much direct, drying sunlight, the vegetation is less rich than in the cove below. There is no water near the top, so take some along with you.

Trailhead: The trail begins at the Joyce Kilmer parking lot, slightly to the right of the shelter. Ample parking and toilet facilities are available at the parking area. The Stratton Bald Trail also begins there (see p. 339).

Trail Details: The trail goes about 150 ft. uphill to the poem "Trees" carved in a wooden sign. At the trail junction there, the Plaque Loop Trail goes straight ahead. The common path of the Haoe and Little Santeetlah Creek trails goes right. Soon a second fork is reached. The Little Santeetlah Creek Trail goes left (see p. 331). The Haoe Trail goes right and climbs steeply to pass a rock outcrop at 0.3 mi. It reaches a Haoe Lead spur at 0.6 mi. and ascends the ridge to an overlook of Horse Cove Brook on the right at 0.8 mi. Climbing becomes difficult from 0.9 mi. until the trail reaches the ridge top at 1.1 mi.

After following the ridge crest, the trail slabs left and then returns to the ridge at 1.4 mi. During the winter you can see Santeetlah Lake to the east. The trail passes large boulders on the left and reaches a switchback at 1.7 mi. It then slabs left and will remain northwest of the ridge until reaching Jenkins Meadow at 3.1 mi. The trail passes a flat lichen-covered rock and large boulders and outcroppings at about 1.9 mi. There is a spring at 2.2 mi. on the left, 40 paces below the trail; pass through a cut-section in a dead chestnut tree near two stumps.

At 2.4 mi. there is a small spring branch which is usually dry in late summer and fall. After passing by some large oaks, the climbing becomes steep. Yellow birch is now common along the trail. At 2.9 mi. the trail reaches the top of Haoe Lead. Following the crest of the lead to the west, it reaches Jenkins Meadow at 3.1 mi., climbs steeply and then moderates to descend slightly at 3.5 mi. Passing through a massive rhododendron bed, it starts its final steep climb. A trail junction is reached at 3.8 mi. The trail to the left is a short by-pass to the Naked Ground Trail. The Haoe Trail goes right and ends at the Haoe summit at 3.9 mi. The remains of an old cabin and fire tower can be seen. There are good views in several directions.

You can see better views from Hangover Mtn., 0.4 mi. to the north via a short connector to the Hangover Lead Trail. The connector begins at the trail junction on top of Haoe and runs north along the crest of a ridge. The trail descends sharply on switchbacks. At 0.1 mi. the Deep Creek Trail terminates on the right. According to trail signs, down that trail it is 2.5 mi. to Rock Cove Branch, 6.5 mi. to Deep Creek Hunters' Shelter and 8.5 mi. to U.S. 129. The connector ends at 0.3 mi. at a gap in a grassy beech forest and a trail junction. There the Hangover Lead Trail (see p. 347) enters from the left from Big Fat Gap. Straight ahead (N) the Hangover Lead Trail runs along the ridge for 0.1 mi. more to end at a heath bald on the top of Hangover Mtn. (5,170 ft.). At this spot there is a rock promontory which drops sharply to the green valley below. The summit affords excellent views in all directions.

---

(116) **NAKED GROUND** 1.5 mi.

Foot trail / Max. elev. gain 455
Start: Haoe Mtn., 5,250 ft.
End: Stratton Bald, 5,300 ft.
USGS quads: Tapoco, N.C.
Trail connections: Hangover Lead, Deep Creek, Haoe,
    Little Santeetlah Creek, Stratton Bald

This is a perimeter trail which travels along the ridge line common to both Joyce Kilmer and Slickrock Creek basins. It is the proposed general route for the Robbinsville-Tellico highway, which has been temporarily halted because of potential damage to the area's wilderness values. This trail links together the three major trails of the Kilmer basin. It also provides an easy route between two outstanding highland features—Haoe-Hangover and Stratton Bald.

You can camp at Naked Ground. Wild boars are fairly common along this short trail; evidence of their rooting can usually be seen. If you meet one, it will usually flee, leaving you free to continue on.

Trailhead: The trail starts at the summit of Haoe Mtn., which is reached via a connector from the Hangover Lead Trail (see p. 347), the Deep Creek Trail or the Haoe Trail.

Trail Details: The trail goes west along the top of Haoe Mtn. and soon begins to descend. At 0.1 mi. a side trail enters from the left; it is a by-pass from the Haoe Trail. The Naked Ground Trail continues to descend and at 0.2 mi. goes by a view into the Slickrock basin. It passes through a stunted beech forest and then levels out after 0.3 mi. for an easy walk. Again running downhill, at 1.0 mi. it reaches Naked Ground (4,845 ft.) and a trail junction. There on the left the Little Santeetlah Creek Trail has climbed 4.6 mi. from the Joyce Kilmer parking lot (see p. 331).

Naked Ground is no longer an open area but adequate camping space is available in the young forest. You may find water by walking 0.3 mi. down the Little Santeetlah Creek Trail to a sharp left bend where you will hear a small trickle. There is also a spring about 300 ft. to the north of the trail signpost, but boars may have fouled it.

The Naked Ground Trail continues along the ridge top, heading southwest. It begins a moderately steep climb and at 1.5 mi. arrives at a sign which says "Stratton Bald .25 mi." Just beyond, the Stratton Bald Trail enters from the left, having climbed 5.7 mi. from the Kilmer parking area, and continues straight ahead (SW) 0.2 mi. to the summit of the bald. The bald is a pleasant grassy area with an excellent display of flame azalea in June.

> (117) **STRATTON BALD** 5.9 mi.
>
> Foot trail / Max. elev. gain 3,140
> Start: Joyce Kilmer parking lot, 2,200 ft.
> End: Stratton Bald, 5,300 ft
> USGS quads: Santeetlah Creek, N.C.
> Trail connections: Haoe, Little Santeetlah Creek,
>   Wolf Laurel Basin, Naked Ground, Bob Bald,
>   Unicoi Mtn.

Stratton Bald has one of the better shows of flame azalea in the Appalachians. It is infrequently visited and should suit you if you seek solitude and beauty. A long, strenuous loop for a single day would go to the bald via the Stratton Bald Trail and return to the Kilmer parking lot by way of the Naked Ground and Little Santeetlah Creek trails. You can camp at Bob Bald or Naked Ground. Of the three major trails in Joyce Kilmer, this one is probably used the least and therefore may be slightly overgrown at times.

Trailhead: The trail starts at the Joyce Kilmer parking lot, where there is ample parking, and toilet facilities. The Haoe and Little Santeetlah Creek trails also begin there (see p. 335 and 331). The Stratton Bald Trail begins beside a small shelter and goes toward the left.

Trail Details: Almost immediately the trail crosses Little Santeetlah Creek on a foot log. A trail junction is soon reached. The Plaque Loop Trail leads right 0.4 mi. to the Memorial Plaque (see p. 333).

Bearing left, the Stratton Bald Trail passes through a beautiful stand of hemlocks and rhododendron. Ascending steeply, it crosses a stream at 0.4 mi. which is the source of water for the fountains at the parking lot. At 0.5 mi. a sign placed there for the benefit of downhill hikers indicates the parking lot is 660 yds. away. The trail passes a small spring branch and then at 0.7 mi. a large red oak. There is a concentration of hemlocks at 1.1 mi. The trail winds steeply upward through thick rhododendron and crosses to the south side of the ridge at 1.8 mi. It climbs on the south side of the ridge to pass Obadiah Gap at 2.4 mi. Continuing on the south side, it enters a larger gap at 3.0 mi.

The trail then follows the ridge at a more moderate grade. Goldie Deaden is reached at 3.5 mi. and the Wolf Laurel Basin Trail junction at 4.5 mi. in a small gap. That trail leads about 0.5 mi. southwest to the end of the Wolf Laurel Basin Road, which is open for travel from the Big Santeetlah Creek Road. The Stratton Bald Trail continues, undulating up and down over small prominences, until 5.4 mi. where it begins to climb steeply. At 5.7 mi. there is a trail junction: the Naked Ground Trail terminates on the right, having come 1.5 mi. from Haoe Mtn.

The Stratton Bald Trail turns left and runs along the ridge to end at Stratton Bald at 5.9 mi. From there a 0.6-mi. connector leads west along a narrow ridge with up-tilted slabs of rock to Bob Bald. Bob Bald is the trailhead of the Unicoi Mtn. Trail (see p. 342), the terminus of the Bob Bald Trail and a good place to camp.

---

(118) BOB BALD (Stratton Bald) 1.6 mi.

Foot trail / Max. elev. gain 880
Start: Cold Springs Gap, 4,400 ft.
End: Bob Bald, 5,280 ft.
USGS quads: Big Junction, Tenn.; Santeetlah Creek, N.C.
Trail connections: Unicoi Mtn., Stratton Bald

This trail provides the shortest and easiest access to the

beautiful Bob and Stratton balds, where there is an excellent display of flame azalea in the middle of June each year. No water is available on the way, but some may be found near Bob Bald. A good camping site is located there on the summit. This trail also gives access to the Unicoi Mtn. Trail, which runs along the western rim of Slickrock Creek basin.

Trailhead: Drive to Santeetlah Gap on County Road 1127 (2.3 mi. southeast of Horse Cove Campground, or 10.5 mi. from Robbinsville). From there go west on a Forest Service gravel road which winds down to Santeetlah Creek. Follow it 12 mi. to Stratton Meadows on the state line. There turn sharp right and go 2 mi. to Beech Gap. You can park there or turn right onto the new gravel Beech Gap Road along the ridge top. This road slabs right and curves sharply after 1.2 mi. A second sharp curve and descent is made at 1.5 mi. Cold Springs Gap and the trailhead are reached at 1.7 mi. From there the gravel road slabs left and runs downhill, while an old road enters from the right. The trail begins straight ahead, climbing the bank between these two roads. There is no trail sign.

Trail Details: The open, maintained trail goes up the nose of the ridge. At 0.2 mi. in a flat grassy place, an old wagon road enters from the right. Steep climbing is then encountered for the next 0.2 mi. The trail traverses a knife-edge ridge at 0.8 mi. and soon afterwards enters a rhododendron tunnel. At 1.2 mi. a trail junction is reached; there the Unicoi Mtn. Trail leads left to Cherry Log Gap and the Crowder Place.

Turn right and continue, still through rhododendron. At 1.4 mi. an old trail enters from the left through a small bald, and immediately after that the Bob Bald Trail enters the meadows of Bob Bald. It ends at 1.6 mi. on the summit of Bob Bald.

To reach Stratton Bald, walk through the upper end of the meadow (there is a sign) and follow a 0.6-mi. connector along a narrow ridge, with up-tilted slabs of rock, to a bench mark on top of Stratton Bald. There the Stratton Bald Trail terminates, having climbed 5.9 mi. from the Joyce Kilmer parking lot.

Bob Bald is a good place to camp. Water is available in wet weather at a spring 200 ft. down a draw in the woods south of the widest point of the meadow. In dry weather, bear right at the widest point in the meadow and look for an old wagon road. On the road descend to the south 0.3 mi., turn left and drop over the ridge about 500 ft. to a spring branch.

---

(119) UNICOI MOUNTAIN (Fodderstack) 8.8 mi.

Foot and gated jeep trail / Max. elev. loss 2,360
Start: State line and west end of Bob Bald, 5,160 ft.
End: Farr Gap, 2,800 ft.
USGS quads: Big Junction, Whiteoak Flats, Tenn.
Trail connections: Stratton Bald, Bob Bald, Cherry
    Log Gap, Pine Ridge, Mill Branch, Big Stack Gap
    Branch, Crowder Branch, Little Slickrock Creek

This trail is a major portion of the perimeter trail around the Slickrock area. It runs north along the crest of the Unicoi Mtn. Range, which forms the western boundary of the Slickrock Creek watershed, passing near the peaks of Rockstack, Big Fodderstack and Little Fodderstack. The Tenn.-N.C. state line coincides with the trail for about half its distance. At the trailhead, Bob Bald and nearby Stratton Bald are outstanding examples of grassy balds with excellent flame azaleas.

There is no source of water along this entire trail, although a spring branch may be found near the trailhead, 0.3 mi. south of Bob Bald. The first half of the trail receives only light use, so a moderate growth of vegetation may crowd the path. Along the way several access trails climb the ridge from the west from the Citico River Valley and join the Unicoi Mtn. Trail. (These were not accurately measured.) Camping is possible at several places along the trail.

Trailhead: The trail starts at the western end of Bob Bald where there is an intersection with the state line. The Bob Bald Trail ends nearby, having climbed 1.2 mi. from the Beech Gap Road in Cold Springs Gap. Bob Bald may also be reached via a 0.6-mi. connector from Stratton Bald, the terminus of the Stratton Bald Trail (see p. 339).

Trail Details: An unmaintained but obviously used trail descends north steadily on a moderate grade through upland oak and hickory forest. At 0.8 mi. the trail passes through Cherry Log Gap. There a maintained trail enters from the left, coming 1.5 mi. from the end of the Beech Gap Road. A small camping spot is located in the gap.

The Unicoi Mtn. Trail continues north through a rich forest along the ridge crest, passing through Glenn Gap, and a nice camping spot, at about 1.8 mi. The trail climbs moderately, slabbing around the left (W) side of Rockstack Mtn. Then it passes to the right of a recording rain gauge. After descending to a low gap at 3.2 mi., it starts a moderate but steady climb up the south and west sides of Big Fodderstack Mtn. A short bushwhack to the right will lead to the mountaintop (4,200 ft.) where there are some worthwhile views to the east into Slickrock. The best overlook is on the east end of the mountain where the forest is somewhat sparse, and there are some exposures of pebble conglomerate. From the east end of Big Fodderstack, the state line goes east and descends into the valley.

The Unicoi Mtn. Trail descends the north side of Big Fodderstack on steep grades. In the early part of the descent at about 4.0 mi., the Pine Ridge Trail enters from the left, coming about 5.0 mi. from the Citico Valley. The main trail goes right at the trail intersection and descends steeply northwest to Big Stack Gap (3,400 ft.) at 4.7 mi. Near there an obscure side trail enters from the left, having come 3.2 mi. up Mill Branch from Doublecamp Creek in Citico Valley.

The Unicoi Mtn. Trail continues northwest, ascending and descending moderately. At 5.7 mi. the Big Stack Gap Branch Trail begins on the right (E) and descends steeply 1.8 mi. to Slickrock Creek. At 5.8 mi. the Unicoi Mtn. Trail reaches the Crowder Place, a beautiful area suitable for camping. It is a former homesite, and water should be available nearby. The most likely source would be down the Crowder Branch Trail (jeep road), which goes west from the Crowder Place 2.4 mi. to the Doublecamp Creek road in the Citico Valley.

North from the Crowder Place, the Unicoi Mtn. Trail runs on a jeep trail, following white painted blazes along the ridge crest. At first there is a steep climb to the top of a knoll, but then the grade becomes rather moderate. At 6.5 mi. in an area recently cleared there is an excellent view to the west.

The trail slabs left around Little Fodderstack Mtn. at 7.4 mi. and then descends moderately and levels out. At about 8.2 mi. there is an excellent view to the east of the Slickrock watershed, and on a clear day, of Cold Spring Knob and impressive Hangover Mtn. to the southeast. A few stands of white pine grow along this stretch of trail. After passing a cleared view to the west, the trail descends steeply to end at Farr Gap. About 40 yds. before the gap, the Little Slickrock Creek Trail begins and goes right (E) 3.4 mi. to Slickrock Creek (see p. 346). Farr Gap is accessible by car from the Doublecamp Creek gravel road in the Tellico Wildlife Management Area, Tenn.

BIG STACK GAP BRANCH 1.8 mi.

Foot trail / Max. elev. loss 1,500
Start: Crowder Place, 3,400 ft.
End: Slickrock Creek, 1,900 ft.
USGS quads: Whiteoak Flats, Tenn. (trail not on
    map)
Trail connections: Unicoi Mtn., Crowder Branch,
    Slickrock Creek

The Big Stack Gap Branch Trail is the only present connection between the Unicoi Mtn. Range and the middle and
upper sections of Slickrock Creek. The trail seems to be
fairly well used but is not known to be regularly maintained. It descends steeply to follow Big Stack Gap Branch.

Trailhead: The trail starts 0.1 mi. south of the Crowder
Place on the east side of the Unicoi Mtn. Trail, or about 1.0
mi. north of Big Stack Gap. The trailhead can also be
reached from the west via the Crowder Branch Trail which
comes 2.4 mi. from the Doublecamp Creek (Farr Gap)
gravel road in the Citico Valley.

Trail Details: The trail descends moderately to steeply to
reach a small creek at 0.1 mi. which it soon crosses. There is
a switchback at a small open rocky area on the spine of the
lead at 0.6 mi.; it is easy to lose the trail at this point. It
makes a sharp right turn and descends moderately to steeply with major switchbacks at 0.8, 1.0 and 1.4 mi. At 1.5 mi.
it reaches Big Stack Gap Branch and the grade becomes
moderate. The trail crosses Big Stack Gap Branch at 1.7
mi., then the N.C.-Tenn. state line at 1.8 mi. The trail ends
shortly thereafter at Slickrock Creek and a trail junction. A
bridge directly ahead leads across Slickrock Creek. Downstream the Slickrock Creek Trail leads 0.3 mi. to Wildcat

Falls and 5.6 mi. to Lake Calderwood (see p. 353). Upstream it leads 0.7 mi. to the terminus of the Big Fat Branch Trail (see p. 350).

---

(121) **LITTLE SLICKROCK CREEK** 3.4 mi.

Foot trail / Max. elev. loss 1,400
Start: Farr Gap, 2,800 ft.
End: Slickrock Creek, 1,400 ft.
USGS quads: Whiteoak Flats, Tenn.; Tapoco, N.C.
   (trail not on Tapoco map)
Trail connections: Unicoi Mtn., Slickrock Creek,
   Nichols Cove

This trail connects the Unicoi Mtn. Range with the lower part of Slickrock Creek. Along the way it fords Little Slickrock Creek many times. Unfortunately, the trail is being abused by people riding trail bikes. Please report any damage you may see to the Forest Service office at Tellico Plains, Tenn.

Trailhead: Drive 10 mi. east of Tellico Plains, Tenn., and go left on F.S. 35, which leads 3.0 mi. to Citico River. Downstream 1.5 mi., at the Doublecamp Campsite, the Doublecamp Creek gravel road leads right about 5.0 mi. to Farr Gap. (The road continues to the Cold Spring Lookout Tower.) The trail begins 40 yds. above (SE of) Farr Gap on the Unicoi Mtn. Trail, 8.8 mi. from its trailhead on Bob Bald (see p. 342).

Trail Details: The trail follows double white blazes consisting of a large rectangle with a small rectangle above it. There is a gradual descent to a stream at 0.2 mi., then the trail slabs left around a ridge on moderate grades until making a very steep descent to a gap at Stiffknee Top at 0.8 mi. The trail leaves the ridge at the gap, turns right (E), descends at a moderately steep grade and leaves the hemlock zone behind at 1.0 mi. The trail is moderate to easy the rest of the way to Slickrock Creek. It crosses several tributaries and at 1.3 mi. arrives at a logging camp area where old building foundations and remains of a chimney can be seen. The trail then proceeds to cross Little Slickrock Creek at 2.4, 2.8, 2.9, 3.1 and 3.2 mi. All the crossings are fords but the stream is shallow and narrow and can be negotiated without your getting wet. The trail ends at 3.4 mi. at the confluence of Little Slickrock and Slickrock creeks and a trail junction. There Slickrock Creek Trail (see p. 353) goes left, downstream, on the west side of the river—0.6 mi. to the Yellowhammer Gap Trail, (see p. 352) and 2.6 mi. to Lake Calderwood. To the right it goes upstream 0.2 mi. to pass the trailhead of the Nichols Cove Trail (see p. 357).

 HANGOVER LEAD 2.1 mi.

Foot trail / Max. elev. gain 2,120
Start: Big Fat Gap, 3,060 ft.
End: Hangover Mtn., 5,180 ft.
USGS quads: Tapoco, N.C. (trail not on map)
Trail connections: Big Fat Branch, Cold Spring Knob,
    Deep Creek, Haoe, Naked Ground

This very steep trail is part of the trail system extending around the perimeter of the Slickrock Creek basin. It runs south along Hangover Lead, the basin's eastern boundary, to Hangover Mtn., which is an outstanding feature and offers the best views in the entire area. On the way the trail passes through a grove of uncut trees, one of the few within Slickrock accessible by trail. There is no water along this trail except for a variable spring near the end.

Trailhead: The trail begins at Big Fat Gap on the Slickrock Creek Road, 7.2 mi. from U.S. 129. There is plenty of parking space. The trailhead is located beside a sign on the south side of the gap. This spot is also the trailhead of the Big Fat Branch Trail (see p. 350) and the Cold Spring Knob Trail.

Trail Details: The trail climbs steeply at first. After that the ascent is moderate to steep, but continuous, along the crest of Hangover Lead. At 0.2 mi. the trail slabs right of a small knob; at 0.3 mi. it slabs left of another. Then it regains the ridge crest at a level area where the unmaintained Buckeye Branch Trail leads right into the Slickrock Creek drainage. After passing a short depression, the trail reaches another level area at 0.7 mi. At 0.9 mi. it begins to climb steeply again and passes large rocks on the right. It slabs right at 1.1 mi., giving a good view of Hangover Mtn. The trail then enters a large level grassy area where rhododendron and hemlocks grow—a good spot for a picnic lunch.

Slabbing right at 1.3 mi., the trail climbs steeply and then goes downhill. This general area is essentially a virgin forest. The trail soon begins a very steep climb through a rhododendron slick. The trail is rough there, being in a deeply eroded cut. At 1.7 mi. it reaches a knob north of Hangover Mtn., from which there are excellent views. After descending from the knob, the trail slabs right and climbs steeply. At 1.9 mi. it passes a spring. At 2.0 mi. in a grassy beech forest, the trail reaches a junction. The trail to the right is a connector which leads south 0.3 mi. to the summit of Haoe Mtn., where the Haoe Trail terminates (see p. 335) and the Naked Ground Trail begins (see p. 337). At 0.2 mi. along the connector, the Deep Creek Trail runs in on the left.

The Hangover Lead Trail goes left and ends at 2.1 mi. at the summit of Hangover at some rocks at the top of a cliff.

Looking northeast, you can see the Cheoah River Valley below and, in the distance, the western Great Smokies.

---

(123) **COLD SPRING KNOB** 2.4 mi.

Foot trail / Max. elev. gain 420
Start: Big Fat Gap, 3,060 ft.
End: Yellowhammer Gap, 1,800 ft.
USGS quads: Tapoco, N.C.
Trail connections: Ike Branch-Yellowhammer Gap,
    Big Fat Branch, Hangover Lead

The Cold Spring Knob Trail is not recommended for the general hiker. There are few views in the summer; there is no water, and the trail is not adequately marked or maintained. The trail descends 1,680 ft. to reach the terminus.

The trail runs north along the crest of Hangover Lead on the eastern boundary of the Slickrock Basin. It is part of the perimeter trail system.

Trailhead: The trail begins at Big Fat Gap on the Slickrock Road, 7.2 mi. from U.S. 129. This is also the trailhead of the Big Fat Branch Trail and the Hangover Lead Trail. There is plenty of parking space. The trailhead is located behind the signpost on the north side of the gap.

Trail Details: The trail climbs steeply to reach the summit of Cold Spring Knob (3,480 ft.) at 0.4 mi. A trail to the left marked "Slickrock Creek" leads 0.5 mi. back to the terminus of the Slickrock Road, which is 0.7 mi. past (and north of) Big Fat Gap. The Cold Spring Knob Trail continues straight north and downhill. A jeep road joins the trail at 0.6 mi. At 1.5 mi. the trail reaches the summit of Caney Ridge. Caution: the trail then slabs left of the summit of

Caney Ridge, still heading north, while the jeep road turns right (E) and descends to Tapoco. This trail separation is not marked and the tendency is to follow the jeep road. Use your compass. (If you have erred, you will see signs on the left saying "Watershed No Trespassing.")

The Cold Spring Knob Trail, now primitive, descends steeply to end at a trail intersection at Yellowhammer Gap at 2.4 mi. From there the Ike Branch Trail runs straight 1.8 mi. to the U.S. 129 bridge at the Cheoah Dam, and the Yellowhammer Gap Trail descends left 0.4 mi. to Slickrock Creek (see p. 352). Avoid the trail to the right (E) because it runs through a closed watershed which supplies clean water to the resort at Tapoco.

---

(124) BIG FAT BRANCH 1.6 mi.

Gated jeep and foot trail / Max. elev. loss 1,060
Start: Big Fat Gap, 3,060 ft.
End: Slickrock Creek, 2,000 ft.
USGS quads: Tapoco, N.C. (trail not on map)
Trail connections: Hangover Lead, Cold Spring Knob,
    Nichols Cove, Slickrock Creek

This trail provides the major access to the Slickrock basin, which it enters about halfway up Slickrock Creek. For most of its length, the trail runs downhill rather steeply. There is camping at Big Fat Branch campsite near the end of the trail.

Trailhead: The trail begins at Big Fat Gap on the Slickrock Creek Road, 7.2 mi. from U.S. 129. There is ample parking space and some fair views. The trailhead is located beside a sign to the left of the road at the top of the gap. This spot is also the trailhead of the Hangover Lead Trail (see p. 347) and the Cold Spring Knob Trail.

Trail Details: The trail immediately begins a steep, zigzag descent going generally westward. It reaches a tributary at 0.4 mi. and crosses Big Fat Branch at 0.6 mi. Still running steeply downhill, it reaches a primitive camping area at 0.7 mi. A sign calls this Big Fat Campground. At 0.8 mi. you reach an obscure trail junction, which may not be visible during the winter. There the trail splits. Although both paths join together later, the path that goes left and crosses the brook is the better one.

The trail crosses the brook on a log bridge and begins following an old railroad grade. It soon crosses small streams. The grade switchbacks to the right at 1.2 mi., descending sharply. At 1.3 mi. it switchbacks left beside Big Fat Branch. The alternative path runs in at this point. From there to Slickrock Creek, the grade is easy. At 1.5 mi. the Big Fat Branch campsite (also called Slickrock campsite) is located on the right as the trail leaves the stream. The Nichols Cove Trail (see p. 357) terminates by a sign near the campsite, having come 2.9 mi. from Slickrock Creek and Trail in the lower portion of the basin.

At 1.6 mi. in a large flat, the Big Fat Branch Trail terminates at the Slickrock Creek Trail (see p. 353). To the right the Slickrock Creek Trail leads 1.0 mi. to Wildcat Falls and 6.3 mi. to Lake Calderwood. To the left it leads 1.0 mi. to Hangover Creek and 1.3 mi. to its trailhead at Glen Gap Branch.

(125) **IKE BRANCH-YELLOWHAMMER GAP** 2.2 mi.

Foot trail / Max. elev. gain 800
Start: U.S. 129 at Cheoah bridge, 1,120 ft.
End: Slickrock Creek, 1,360 ft.
USGS quads: Tapoco, N.C. (most of trail omitted)
Trail connections: Cold Spring Knob, Slickrock Creek

This is the only trail that provides quick and easy access to the lower portion of Slickrock Creek. It borders Lake Calderwood and then climbs through the ravine of Ike Branch. After topping the ridge, it descends to Yellowhammer Gap. (This circuitous route avoids the more direct trail along Yellowhammer Branch to the gap, which passes through the water supply area for the Tapoco resort and is closed to hikers.) From Yellowhammer Gap, Slickrock Creek is less than 0.5 mi. away.

Trailhead: The trail begins on a jeep road at the south (Tapoco) end of the U.S. 129 bridge over Lake Calderwood at the Cheoah Dam. There is little parking space at the trailhead, but adequate parking is available at the north end of the bridge, only a short distance away. Unload at the trailhead and then park. The highway is narrow; use caution.

Trail Details: The Ike Branch Trail follows the lake until the jeep road ends at 0.6 mi. After continuing along the lake a little farther, the trail begins to climb steeply above Ike Branch. The steep climbing continues until moderate to easy grades are reached at 0.9 mi. The trail continues to climb moderately until it reaches the crest of the ridge at 1.7 mi. It slabs right around a knoll (1,920 ft.) and then descends to Yellowhammer Gap and a trail intersection at 1.8 mi.

There the Cold Spring Knob Trail terminates straight ahead, having come 2.4 mi. from Big Fat Gap (see p. 349). The trail to the left (the watershed trail) is closed.

Turn right (W) on the Yellowhammer Gap Trail and descend, sometimes steeply, to Slickrock Creek. The trail follows a branch at 2.0 mi., crosses the branch at 2.1 mi. and ends at Slickrock Creek at 2.2 mi. The Slickrock Creek Trail goes right, downstream, 2.0 mi. to Lake Calderwood, and left to the middle and upper sections of the basin.

---

(126) SLICKROCK CREEK 7.6 mi.

Foot trail / Max. elev. loss 1,400
Start: Glenn Gap Branch, 2,500 ft.
End: Lake Calderwood, 1,100 ft.
USGS quads: Tapoco, N.C. (trail not on map)
Trail connections: Big Fat Branch, Nichols Cove, Big Stack Gap Branch, Little Slickrock Creek, Yellowhammer Gap

---

The trail along Slickrock Creek is the major trail passing through the center of the valley. Numerous side trails connect it with the perimeter trail except at the upper end of the basin. There the terrain is steep and the vegetation is extremely dense, so off-trail hiking is *very* difficult.

At present, both ends of this trail are dead ends. Plans for the future might include an extension of the upper section to connect with the perimeter trail somewhere near Glenn Gap or Cherry Log Gap; check with the Forest Service for recent developments. Trail's end at Lake Calderwood is accessible by boat from a landing at Magazine Branch on the north shore of the lake. To reach the landing, drive to the north end of the U.S. 129 bridge which crosses the lake and go west 0.5 mi. on an old road along the lakeshore. At the road end there is good access to the lake, and camping is allowed.

Outstanding features of the Slickrock Creek Trail include Wildcat Falls and good fishing for native trout in the
creek. The trail follows an old railroad grade which used to
cross the creek in many places on trestles, which have now
rotted and washed away. Until recently hikers and fishermen had to negotiate frequent fords, but now the Forest
Service has installed foot logs at most crossings. The trail
may be somewhat obscure in a few places but it is
definitely passable.

Many primitive campsites are located along this trail and
water is abundant. But you should boil any water you take
from the creek because the stream is a popular place and
there are no privies anywhere along it.

Trailhead: Although most hikers will probably enter this
trail from Big Fat Gap or Ike Branch, the guidebook description begins at the upper (southern) end because in the
future the Slickrock Creek Trail may be connected there
with the perimeter trail.

Trail Details: At Glenn Gap Branch a definite trail can be
seen. (South of this stream the trail quickly fades out and is
impassable.) To the east of the trailhead there is a good
camping area. The trail runs north on a wide railroad grade
and crosses diagonally through a clearing to reach Hangover
Creek at 0.3 mi. This area is part of an abandoned homesite
known as Deputy Field. The trail makes an easy, dry
crossing of Hangover Creek. Many primitive hunting trails
may be found roundabout, but they are not maintained.
The trail continues northward, downstream, and passes a
small camping area by a small stream at 0.4 mi. Two larger
camping areas are located at 0.7 and 1.0 mi. The former is a
flat about 20 ft. to the left below the trail; the latter is large
enough for about 20 people and is situated just before the
trail crosses Buckeye Branch at 1.1 mi. At 1.3 mi. in a large

flat area the Big Fat Branch Trail terminates on the right, having run 1.6 mi. from Big Fat Gap on the Slickrock Creek Road (see p. 350). From the Big Fat Branch (or Slickrock) campsite, located 0.1 mi. from this junction, the Nichols Cove Trail runs north and connects at 2.9 mi. with the Slickrock Creek Trail. (Along the way there is a possible connection with Yellowhammer Gap.)

The Slickrock Creek Trail continues straight north and immediately crosses Slickrock Creek on a log bridge. This is the most exciting bridge along the trail, since its three wobbly legs make crossing in an erect position somewhat hazardous. On the other side, the trail turns right and proceeds down the railroad grade. Primitive campsites abound in this area. The trail crosses a tributary on a log at 1.8 mi. and the main stream at 2.0 mi., where the N.C.-Tenn. state line joins the creek. There the Big Stack Gap Branch Trail enters from the left by a bridge, having come 1.8 mi. from the Crowder Place (see p. 345).

Continuing downstream, at 2.3 mi. the Slickrock Creek Trail crosses a bridge near the top of Wildcat Falls—a beautiful series of falls, well worth the hike from Big Fat Gap. Orange paint-marks that you will now start to see on rocks indicate the state line which follows the creek bed to Lake Calderwood. That is, Tenn. is on your left as you walk downstream. The fish and game laws are strictly enforced by both Tenn. and N.C. There is no reciprocity along this creek.

The trail reaches a big camping area at 2.5 mi. At 2.6 mi. it seems to continue along an elevated railroad grade with a 5-foot-deep cut across it. Don't continue there; backtrack from the cut and look for a new trail on the west side of the railroad grade. (The railroad grade then crosses Slickrock Creek, but the new trail avoids the crossing.) On the new trail, a long log crosses a steep tributary 50 ft. above the main creek. On the other side the trail deteriorates almost completely for 100 yds. Then it reaches the main creek at 2.8 mi. and fords it to N.C. You might be able to make a dry crossing in the vicinity if the water is low enough. At 3.0 mi. the trail crosses to Tenn. on a bridge and reaches a small campsite with a stone table at 3.3 mi. It enters a small gorge at 3.8 mi. and the trail becomes rocky. It crosses to N.C. on a bridge at 4.5 mi. It crosses Nichols Cove Branch at 4.7 mi. At 4.8 mi. the Nichols Cove Branch Trail begins on the right where a sign is posted.

The Slickrock Creek Trail crosses Slickrock Creek via a bridge to Tenn. at 4.9 mi. At 5.0 mi. it makes a dry ford of Little Slickrock Creek at its mouth. This spot is the terminus of the Little Slickrock Creek Trail, which has followed that creek downstream 3.4 mi. from Farr Gap (see p. 346).

The Slickrock Creek Trail continues straight ahead across a large flat area suitable for camping. At 5.1 mi. there are several large islands in the river. The trail runs along the edge of Slickrock Creek. At 5.4 mi. it crosses the creek on a bridge to N.C. At 5.6 mi. the Ike Branch Trail goes right to Yellowhammer Gap and then descends to reach U.S. 129 Cheoah Bridge after 2.2 mi.

The Slickrock Creek Trail crosses to Tenn. and continues downstream. At 6.2 mi. it passes the Lower Falls; at 6.5 mi. it crosses the last bridge. Near 6.9 mi. it runs on a narrow ledge about six ft. above the creek. The trail ends at the slack water of Lake Calderwood at 7.6 mi. To continue farther, you must have a boat meet you at the mouth of Slickrock Creek or retrace your steps to the Ike Branch Trail.

NICHOLS COVE 2.9 mi.

Foot trail / Max. elev. gain 2,380
Start: Slickrock Creek Trail just below Nichols Cove
  Branch, 1,440 ft.
End: Big Fat Branch campsite, 1,880 ft.
USGS quads: Tapoco, N.C. (trail not on map)
Trail connections: Slickrock Creek, Little Slickrock
  Creek, Big Fat Branch

This trail connects the lower portion of Slickrock Creek to
the middle area, passing through a hanging valley which lies
to the east of the Slickrock gorge. It could be used to create
a 6.5-mi. loop around the middle of the Slickrock drainage
basin. The trail is not frequently hiked, so the instructions
here should be followed carefully.

Trailhead: The trail begins at 4.8 mi. on the Slickrock
Creek Trail, 0.1 mi. north of (downstream from) the mouth
of Nichols Cove Branch and 0.2 mi. south of the end of the
Little Slickrock Creek Trail (see p. 346). There is a sign
there which reads "Nichols Cove Branch."

Trail Details: The trail begins on an old railroad grade
which initially runs upstream and gradually departs from
the Slickrock Creek Trail, rising gently above Slickrock
Creek. At 0.2 mi. it passes a waterfall on the right. At this
point there are several more waterfalls and a long cascade as
Nichols Cove Branch falls out of a hanging valley. The trail
enters a cut at the top of the cascades and then fords the
stream. After about 100 yds., it fords left to an island and
continues to the upstream end of it, where it fords to the
left bank. The trail runs, at first very wet, alongside the
branch. It fords again at 0.4 mi. just below a 5-foot ledge.
At 0.5 mi. it fords again, then crosses a tributary at 0.6 mi.

It fords again at 0.7 mi. and then gradually ascends above the branch as the valley opens out and flattens. At 1.2 mi. an unmarked trail enters at a sharp angle from the left, down a bank. This trail leads about 200 ft. to a low gap where there is a semi-circular rockpile campsite, and seems to end there but may continue to Yellowhammer Gap, as an old map shows.

About 100 ft. past this trail junction, the railroad grade appears to end. The Nichols Cove Trail is now about five ft. in elevation above the branch, and a worn path leads down to the water. Turn left, ford Nichols Cove Branch for the last time and angle across open woods and old fields at approximately a right angle to the railroad grade and branch. There are one or two blazes but no definite trail. Pass rock piles and rock terraces to reach a trail on a terrace at 1.3 mi. A sign there nailed to a tree reads "Big Fat Branch." About five ft. behind it is a grave with tombstones. About 100 yds. to the left of the sign is an open half-acre field, with ruins of a cabin beyond. The Nichols Cove Trail goes to the right, at first running parallel with the branch and the railroad grade. It is well blazed with an axe and sometimes a chain saw, but is not painted.

At 1.7 mi. the trail crosses an open space, then a small tributary, and soon begins a moderate ascent. At 1.8 mi. it begins to climb steeply to reach the nose of a ridge at 2.0 mi. There it makes a 90° turn to the left up the ridge crest. To the right at this turn, about 100 ft. down the ridge, you will see a good view of Hangover and Haoe Lead. Note: this turn is not marked and can be easily missed when hiking the trail in the opposite direction.

The trail continues to climb on or near the crest of the ridge to its end against the side of the mountain. At 2.2 mi. a blazed trail (now blocked) leads left (E). The Nichols Cove Trail continues straight ahead (S), slabbing along the right side of the mountain. There are good views of Slick-

rock Valley to the right. The trail crosses ridges at 2.3 and
2.4 mi. and then begins to descend. At 2.5 mi. the descent
becomes steep, following what remains of an old cattle
trail. The steepness ends at 2.8 mi. as the trail crosses a
spring branch. It leads on the level to Big Fat Branch
campsite (also called Slickrock campsite) at 2.9 mi. and
then crosses Big Fat Branch (sign) and ends 100 ft. farther
at the Big Fat Branch Trail (see p. 350). On the left the Big
Fat Branch Trail has come 1.5 mi. from Big Fat Gap; on the
right it leads 0.1 mi. more to the Slickrock Creek Trail.

Appendices

Acknowledgments

This guidebook has been a cooperative effort from start to finish and represents the hard work of many volunteers who really love the Smokies in a way which I hope all the readers of this book can someday share. The Smokies are something special—a piece of a vanishing heritage meaning much to many. To the contributors belongs the credit for this guide, for without them there could have been no book. Many, many thanks to major contributors:

Doris B. Hammett, M.D. of Waynesville, North Carolina, who traveled with her horse over most of the trails in the Cataloochee and Big Creek sections.

Theodore Snyder, Jr., of Greenville, South Carolina, who organized the Joseph Le Conte Chapter of the Sierra Club to hike and measure all the trails in Deep Creek, Forney Creek and Noland Creek.

W.E. Phillips, National Park Service Ranger at Twenty-mile Creek, North Carolina, who found time in his busy schedule to gather the information on Hazel Creek.

C.T. Coffey, D.D.S., of Knoxville, Tennessee, who re-hiked the trails in the Cosby section.

Leroy G. Fox of Knoxville, former president of the Smoky Mountains Hiking Club, who once again hiked many of the trails in the Greenbrier section and on Mount Le Conte, and also wrote the section on off-trail hiking.

Sam Tillet of Knoxville, who contributed the information on the trails in Elkmont.

Dr. Randolph Shields, chairman of biology, Maryville College, Tennessee, who is himself a part of the tradition of Cades Cove and Tremont, and shared his knowledge of these areas.

Dr. Michael Pelton of the Department of Forestry, University of Tennessee, Knoxville, who is a great friend and knows his bears.

Dr. Gordon E. Howard of the Department of Recreation, Clemson College, South Carolina, who organized the hiking of the Slickrock and Joyce Kilmer trails.

Dr. Robert L. Hatcher of the Department of Geology, Clemson College, who wrote the geology section.

Many other individuals and organizations deserve our thanks as well. Joe Armstrong, sales representative for Charles Scribner's Sons, gave the Sierra Club the idea for the book. John B. Gilstrap of Liberty, South Carolina, contributed information on the history of Joyce Kilmer and Slickrock. Bill Rolen helped with history and place names in the Deep Creek and Noland and Forney creeks sections. Southern Bell Telephone and Telegraph Company of Greenville and Anderson, South Carolina, loaned us their measuring wheels. The Potomac Appalachian Trail Club, Inc., furnished back copies of its bulletin. We wish to acknowledge also the assistance of Raymond Caldwell, Carl Leathers, Mrs. Rolland Swain, Raymond Paine, Wayne Shepard, Joe McFee, Lionel Edney, the Cherokee Historical Association and the Smoky Mountains Hiking Club.

We are indebted to the staff of Great Smoky Mountains National Park for providing time, information and other assistance in the preparation of this guidebook. Assistant Superintendent Merrill D. Beal was particularly helpful in acting as general liaison with the rest of the staff. But special thanks must go to rangers B.B. Cantrell, Jr., Coy J. Hanson, Richard W. Hougham, Beauford C. Messer, Robert S. Miller, Clarence W. Rice, Rolland R. Swain and Edward

J. Widmer for their personal assistance. Frank Hyatt, chief of maintenance, South District, provided useful information. Raymond Dehart, trail foreman, South District, knows almost all of the North Carolina trails and was extremely cooperative. Edward Menning, park naturalist, provided aid when my car ran out of gas. Retired ranger Mark Hannah and seasonal ranger James Waldrop helped prepare the Cataloochee material.

Grateful thanks must go to the following people who measured the trails in Joyce Kilmer Memorial Forest and Slickrock Creek: Bruce Byers, Harrison Burns, Dana A. Carver, F.T. Terry Darby, Harold Harkins, Jack L. Holeman, Gordon E. Howard, Robert C. Hoyle, Melinda McWilliams, D. Miller Putnam, Karen Talley, Sam Thomas, Dillard Thompson, Michael Thompson and J. Steve Waldrop, Jr.

Finally, I thank my wife, Joyce, for typing the manuscript, for her helpful comments, and for having the patience to work with me through the preparation of this book; and my boys Keith and Dougie for being willing to postpone our outings so that others might enjoy theirs a little more.

                                              —*Dick Murlless*
                                           Savannah, Georgia
                                              August, 1972

Recommended Reading

Adams, Paul J. *Mt. Le Conte*. Holston Printing Co., Knoxville, Tenn. 1966. 63 pp.

    The personal account of Paul Adams as he hiked and lived on Mount Le Conte during prepark days in 1925.

Appalachian Trail Conference. *Guide to the Appalachian Trail in Tennessee and North Carolina: Cherokee, Pisgah, and Great Smokies*. Washington, D.C. 1971. 353 pp.

    This is the standard reference for hiking the Appalachian Trail in the Smokies. Much of the material concerning that trail in this Sierra Club guidebook comes from this Trail Conference guide.

Brewer, Carson. *Hiking in the Great Smokies*. Holston Printing Co., Knoxville, Tenn. 1966. 58 pp.

    For many years this has been the only guide to the trails in the Smokies. It is designed for day hiking and contains many interesting stories and observations about the park flora, fauna and people.

Brooks, Maurice. *The Appalachians*. Houghton Mifflin Co., Boston. 1965. 346 pp.

    Any naturalist will enjoy reading this excellent general account of the Appalachian region from Newfoundland to Georgia.

Campbell, Carlos C. *Birth of a National Park*. Univ. of Tenn. Press, Knoxville. 1960.

    The history of all the trials and tribulations of creating a national park in the Great Smokies is presented here.

Fink, Paul M. *That's Why They Call It . . .: The Names and Lore of the Great Smokies*. Watson Lithographing Co., Kingsport, Tenn. 1964. 20 pp.

　　The foremost expert on local names in the Smokies has put this pamphlet together for enjoyable reading. Many of the place-name descriptions in this guide are from Fink's material.

Frome, Michael. *Strangers in High Places: The Story of the Great Smoky Mountains*. Doubleday and Co., Inc., Garden City, N.Y. 1966. 394 pp.

　　This publication is a truly incredible compilation of the history of the Smokies region from the distant past to the present. It is highly recommended to all.

Henry, B.L., et al. *Climatological Summary of Gatlinburg, Tenn.* U.S. Dept. of Commerce, Washington, D.C. 1962.

　　This is the source of the Gatlinburg data presented in the weather section.

Huheey, James E. and Arthur Stupka. *Amphibians and Reptiles of Great Smoky Mountains National Park*. Univ. of Tenn. Press, Knoxville. 1967. 98 pp.

　　This is a guide to the herptiles of the Smokies, which should be useful to both the amateur and professional naturalist.

Hutchins, Ross E. *Hidden Valley of the Smokies*. Dodd, Mead & Co., N.Y. 1971. 214 pp.

　　The natural history of the Little River Valley near Elkmont is delightfully described for the general park visitor.

Kephart, Horace. *The Cherokees of the Smoky Mountains*. The Atkinson Press, Ithaca, N.Y. 1936. (Westland Printing Co., Silver Spring, Md., Fourth Printing, 1971.) 36 pp.

　　A short history of the Cherokee Indians is presented with great sensitivity.

Kephart, Horace. *Our Southern Highlanders*. The Macmillan Co., N.Y. 1963. 469 pp.

Kephart is the most outstanding narrator of the life and times of the prepark mountaineers.

King, Philip B., Robert B. Neuman, and Jarvis B. Hadley. *Geology of the Great Smoky Mountains National Park, Tennessee and North Carolina.* Geological Survey Professional Paper 587. U.S. Government Printing Office, Washington, D.C. 1968. 23 pp.

A technical account of the general geology of the Smokies is presented here.

Shanks, R.E. Climates of the Great Smoky Mountains. *Ecology* 35(3): 354. 1954.

A technical account of the climate is presented, which was used when writing the weather section.

Stevenson, George B. *Ferns of the Great Smoky Mountains National Park.* Buckhorn Press, Gatlinburg, Tenn. 1969. 16 pp.

This layman's guide to the ferns is very useful for field identification.

Stevenson, George B. *Trees of the Great Smoky Mountains National Park.* Published in cooperation with The Great Smoky Mountains Natural History Association. 1967. 32 pp.

The layman will enjoy using this guide for identifying trees in the park.

Stupka, Arthur. *Great Smoky Mountains National Park Natural History Handbook, Series No. 5.* U.S. Government Printing Office, Washington, D.C. 1960. 75 pp.

This is the best general description of the natural history of the Smokies and is highly recommended. A portion of this publication is quoted in the Flora and Fauna chapter of this guidebook.

Stupka, Arthur. *Trees, Shrubs, and Woody Vines of Great Smoky Mountains National Park.* Univ. of Tenn. Press, Knoxville. 1964. 186 pp.

This is a complete guide to the natural history of the macro vegetation in the park. It provides useful information on the distribution, general habitat, flowering dates and record size of these plants.

Stupka, Arthur. *Wildflowers in Color*. Harper & Row Publishers, N.Y. 1965. 144 pp.
An excellent picture guide describes the southern Appalachian wildflowers to the layman.

Index of Trail Descriptions

Field Notes

Field Notes

Field Notes

Field Notes

Field Notes

Field Notes

Field Notes

Field Notes